LIFECYCLE OF A
TECHNOLOGY COMPANY

LIFECYCLE OF A TECHNOLOGY COMPANY

STEP-BY-STEP LEGAL BACKGROUND AND PRACTICAL GUIDE FROM START-UP TO SALE

EDWIN L. MILLER JR.

JOHN WILEY & SONS, INC.

Copyright © 2008 by John Wiley & Sons, Inc. All rights reserved.

Published by John Wiley & Sons, Inc., Hoboken, New Jersey.

Wiley Bicentennial Logo: Richard J. Pacifico

Published simultaneously in Canada.

For general information on our other products and services, or technical support, please contact our Customer Care Department within the United States at 800-762-2974, outside the United States at 317-572-3993 or fax 317-572-4002.

Wiley also publishes its books in a variety of electronic formats. Some content that appears in print may not be available in electronic books.

For more information about Wiley products, visit our Web site at http://www.wiley.com.

Library of Congress Cataloging-in-Publication Data:

Miller, Edwin L.
    Lifecycle of a technology company : step-by-step legal background
and practical guide from startup to sale / Edwin L. Miller, Jr.
        p. cm.
    Includes index.
    ISBN 978-0-470-22392-5 (cloth : alk. paper)
    1.   High technology industries–Law and legislation–United States. 2.
High technology industries–Finance–Law and legislation–United States.
3.   Intellectual property–United States. 4.   Consolidation and merger
of corporations–United States.   I. Title.
    KF1890.H53M55 2008
    346.73'065–dc22

2007028030

Printed in the United States of America.

10 9 8 7 6 5 4 3 2 1

This book is dedicated to my extraordinarily tolerant and supportive family—my wife, Barbara, and my children, Russ and Lindsay.

CONTENTS

PREFACE

This book attempts to convey a working knowledge of the principal business terms, customary contractual provisions, legal background, and how-tos applicable to each stage in the life of a technology, emerging growth, or other start-up company—from formation, through angel and venture financing, intellectual property protection, private placements, initial public offerings/public company regulation, and acquisitions. It is not a book about how to start and run a business, and it is not a book primarily about law or legal theory.

In any business situation or transaction, there is a constant interplay among legal and business concepts, structures, and terms. In a sense, there is no distinction. One of the roles a business lawyer plays is to protect the client from being taken advantage of by prospective business partners and their lawyers. It is critical for both the businessperson and the lawyer to be able to differentiate between what is customary and fair and what is unfairly slanted to the benefit of the other party. This book attempts to point out these distinctions. In addition, an astute businessperson or lawyer also needs to be familiar with the whole picture of the lifecycle of a business enterprise to make sound judgments regarding any one stage. Decisions and actions (or failures to act) at one stage can have significant consequences later, both positive and negative.

I hope that reading this volume will benefit entrepreneurs and executives who want to understand more deeply the legal milieu in which they operate; venture capitalists and other investment professionals who want to understand better the legal rationale behind their deals with portfolio companies and their portfolio companies' business deals with others; lawyers who would like to know, or need a refresher on, what they should be discussing with clients seeking advice on critical transactions; law students who want to get a jump on real-world business law practice; and entrepreneural business school students who want to level the playing field for their first encounters with business lawyers.

Each chapter consists of commentary on what's really going on in typical situations in each stage and an in-depth discussion on the particular subject. The appendices include model or sample documents for a number of common transactions as well as additional materials.

This book is for educational purposes only and is not intended to be legal advice. The views expressed in these materials do not necessarily reflect the views held by members of the author's law firm.

Comments and questions are welcome. Contact me at *edwinl miller@gmail.com.*

Boston, Massachusetts
December 2007

ACKNOWLEDGMENTS

Colleagues from Sullivan & Worcester, including Howard Berkenblit, Aaron Fiske, Kim Herman, Carl Smith, and Paul Oakley, were kind enough to review various parts of this book.

This book also incorporates the work of some of my former colleagues at Morse, Barnes-Brown & Pendleton in Waltham, Massachusetts: the first section in Chapter 1 is based on materials originally written by Jon Gworek and Jeff Steele; the second section in Chapter 1 is based on materials originally written by Chip Wry; the first section in Chapter 2 was co-authored with me by Peter Barnes-Brown and Lea Pendleton; and Chapter 3 was originally written by Mike Cavaretta and Howard Zaharoff.

I, nevertheless, remain responsible for the entire contents of this book.

ABOUT THE WEB SITE

As a purchaser of this book, you have access to the supporting Web site:

www.wiley.com/go/lifecycle

The Web site contains files for the appendices that are mentioned in this book:

Appendix 1A: Start-Up Suite of Incorporation Documents:
  Certificate of Incorporation (Delaware)
  Bylaws (Delaware) Corporation
  Action of Sole Incorporator (Delaware)
  Initial Written Consent of the Board of Directors (Delaware)
  Shareholders' Agreement
  Employee Confidentiality, Inventions, and Noncompetition Agreement
  IRS Section 83(b) Election
Appendix 1B: Stock Option and Incentive Plan
Appendix 1C: Stock Option Agreement (Companion to Stock Option and Incentive Plan)
Appendix 1D: Employment Agreement
Appendix 2A: Term Sheet for a First-Round Venture Capital Financing (Annotated)
Appendix 2B: Legal Due Diligence Request List
Appendix 2C: Closing Agenda for a Convertible Preferred Stock Financing
Appendix 2D: Subordination Provisions—Senior Creditor Draft/ Subordinated Creditor Comments
Appendix 2E: Summary of Terms for an Investment (Buyout) Fund
Appendix 3A: Software License Agreement: Licensor Draft/ Licensee Comments
Appendix 3B: Uniform Biological Materials Transfer Agreement
Appendix 4A: Private Placement Memorandum
Appendix 4B: Subscription Agreement for a Private Placement
Appendix 4C: Investor Questionnaire for a Private Placement (Including Unaccredited Investors)

Appendix 4D: Summary SEC Compliance Checklist

Appendix 4E: Memorandum on Insider Reporting and Liability for Short-Swing Profits

Appendix 4F: Memorandum on Implementing Procedures Designed to Prevent Insider Trading

Appendix 5A: Confidentiality Agreement

Appendix 5B: Letter of Intent

Appendix 5C: Investment Bank Engagement Letter with Seller's Comments

The password to enter the site is: Miller.

CHAPTER 1

START-UP PHASE

FOUNDERS' CONTRACTUAL ARRANGEMENTS
AND MECHANICS OF THE INCORPORATION PROCESS

Entrepreneurs who want to start a business are extremely diverse. They range from college dropouts (e.g., Bill Gates) to so-called serial entrepreneurs or those who have started multiple businesses in the past and always seem to want to do so again (e.g., Steve Jobs), even though many are wealthy beyond imagination. The issues surrounding the organization of start-ups differ little in these cases and do not really depend very much on the type of technology or business.

Lawyers are sometimes asked by those intending to start a business when to hire a lawyer. I like to compare the situation to when you should see a doctor. Many people dread the idea and want to put it off (particularly as they get older). But the conventional wisdom in both cases is that going early may be a bit painful, but going too late can be deadly. If the entrepreneurial idea is just coming together and the founders are short of funds, it is probably not necessary to hire a lawyer at that point. If the founders are beginning to get serious about starting the business and are beginning to devote substantial time to their idea, then going to a lawyer is essential. Believe it or not, it is not unprecedented for five founders to come in for a first interview with a lawyer thinking each is getting 50 percent of the equity.

The fundamental deal among the founders of a business is that the business entity itself owns the business idea and the associated intellectual property (IP)—trade secrets, patents, copyrights, and the like. This point is crucial. The overriding concept here is that the company is like a hub, and the spokes are all of the contributors of time, talent, energy, IP, and capital by the founders, investors, employees, and others. Those constituencies benefit from the increasing value of the hub, which is dependent on it's ownership of all relevant assets.

Notwithstanding the hub-and-spoke concept, all of the IP need not necessarily be transferred irrevocably to the business at the outset. The scientific genius among the founders may want to defer transferring ownership of the brilliant idea until the company becomes real (i.e., gets funded) or some other milestone is achieved. In that case, it is always advisable to avoid a future change of heart to put an IP license and transfer agreement in place at the outset where the transfer irrevocably becomes effective on the occurrence of one or more specified events.

What is the role of the company's lawyer? Once the entity is formed, all parties should understand that their lawyer's real role and duty at that stage is to the entity, not to the individuals. The lawyer customarily counsels the founders as to the business and legal decisions they must make and what is typical in the situation, but he or she should not decide these issues for the client. To a certain extent, the goals of each founder are adverse to those of the other founders and to those of the business. If, however, every founder of every business hired his or her own lawyer at the outset of the business, the start-up industry would be in serious trouble.

It is ultimately in each founder's interest to make decisions that are the best for the enterprise as a whole. The money to be made by each founder is as much dependent on the ultimate success of the enterprise as it is on the individual founder's deal. For example, one or more of the founders may well be fired from the business or quit before an initial public offering (IPO) or other liquidity event. A mechanism must be put in place, if possible, to permit termination of a founder by the other founders. This mechanism is a voting agreement that specifies a board of directors composition consisting of multiple founders. Under this mechanism, a majority of the board can terminate one founder. The ability to terminate a non-performing founder is crucial to the success of the enterprise. Conversely, not permitting an unproductive founder to be fired is not in the interest of the business. Each founder should be willing to put this voting mechanism in place not knowing which end of the stick he or she is ultimately going to get: He or she may be among the board members firing another founder or may be the founder who is being fired by the board. Without an effective power structure, the business may fail simply because the founders' time and energies are focused on dispute resolution and not on the business.

In an initial meeting between the prospective founders and their lawyer, what are the most important issues? There are several fundamental questions to be answered:

- Who gets what percentage of the equity (founders' stock) of the business?
- What are the vesting terms of the stock—what do you need to do going forward to earn the right to keep all of your stock? Surely, it is not fair if one founder quits the business the day after it is founded and keeps all of his or her stock, and the other founders have to sweat it out for years with long hours and low pay in order to **earn** their equity (hence the term "sweat equity").
- When are the business idea and the related IP to be transferred to the enterprise: at the outset, upon funding, or upon funding from outsiders? In other words, the business has to own its IP in order to get funded and in order for the founders or others to risk working for the company. However, if the business fails before it gets funded, it is not inappropriate for a mechanism to be set up for the IP to be transferred to the founder who created it. This arrangement can be accomplished by an irrevocable license for the start-up exclusively to use the IP for some period of time and that provides for automatic transfer of the IP to the start-up on the occurrence of specified favorable events.
- Who is to hold what office; who is to perform what function; and when should some or all of the founders be required to quit their jobs and join the new business full time? What happens if the business gets funded and a founder decides not to join the new company: Does that founder lose a portion of his or her founders' stock?
- How do the founders legally extract themselves from their current employment without being sued by their current employers? What are the danger areas? How do you minimize the risk of a suit by current employers for theft of trade secrets or a breach of a noncompetition covenant? What is an employee of one business permitted to do to get a new business going while he or she is employed by another company? Does a founder's business idea really belong to his or her (former) employer?

- What is the budget for the initial phase of the business, and where is the money to come from?

These issues are discussed in more detail later in this chapter.

INTRODUCTION.   This section provides an overview of the main corporate and business considerations in organizing an emerging business entity. The discussion begins chronologically by addressing the question of when to incorporate. Following this is an overview of the basics regarding initial capitalization and equity allocation among founders. Next is a focused discussion of the most prevalent form of legal entity, the corporation, beginning with a discussion of choice of state and then moving on to cover the mechanics of the organization process, the corporation's key governing documents (charter and bylaws), and other typical agreements. This section then explores the basics of corporate stock splits, dividends, and redemptions and finishes with an overview of fundamental fiduciary duty laws as they apply to officers and directors. This section assumes that the corporation has been formed under Delaware law.

WHEN TO ORGANIZE THE BUSINESS.   Entrepreneurs often ask their lawyers for guidance on the timing of corporate formation and may be hesitant to form a company for any number of reasons, including the costs associated with formation, uncertainties regarding the identity of the founders, the equity split among the founders, or conflicts of interest with existing employment obligations. Although these are all legitimate concerns, there are several good reasons to form the company as early as possible. These reasons are discussed next.

Holding Periods.   The earlier the company is formed, the sooner the founders' stock can be issued and the sooner the capital gains holding period (for income tax purposes) begins to run. Upon a liquidity event in which the stock is sold, stock that has been held for one year or more will be taxed at the long-term capital gains rate, which is significantly lower than the tax rate for ordinary income. Conversely, gains on stock sold that has been held for less than one year at the time of sale are taxable at an individual's ordinary income tax rate, which is significantly higher than the capital gains tax rate. This is not a critical factor, however, because a sale within one year of start-up is extremely rare (other than during the Internet bubble).

Cheap Stock Issues.   Founders of companies often make the mistake of waiting until they have received a strong indication of interest from an investor before they decide that it is time to incorporate. Forming a company on the eve of raising capital may create a tax liability for the founders. The difference between what the founders pay for their stock and the fair market value of the stock at the time of purchase (as determined by reference to what outside investors are willing to pay) may be characterized as income, possibly resulting in significant tax liability to the founders. For example, if stock is issued to the founders at the time of formation for $.01 per share and, within a short period of time thereafter, outside investors pay $1 or more per share, the Internal Revenue Service (IRS) may take the position in connection with an audit of a founder that the founders issued themselves stock at significantly below the fair market value per share.

This risk is significantly mitigated by the issuance of preferred stock to the investors in the company. This capital structure is discussed in detail in Chapter 2, but in sum, investors will invest in a start-up only if their investment receives the protection of a preferred stock/common stock structure. To take an extreme example, imagine that the company sells 50 percent of the outstanding common stock to investors for $1 million and then liquidates the next day; in that case, the founders and the investors will split the investors' $1 million equally. If, instead of common stock, the investors received preferred stock with a liquidation preference, upon dissolution and liquidation in that situation, the investors would get all of their money back, with nothing left for the founders. That is as it should be. Given that the founders would not realize any increase in value of their common stock in that situation, in a very early stage company, common stock typically is viewed as being worth in the range of 10 to 25 percent of the price of preferred stock. The price differential should narrow as the company matures, so that the common stock and preferred stock are priced the same at the point at which the liquidation preference of the preferred stock ceases to be of any real value.

Ability to Contract.   The founders may want to establish relationships with third parties that require entering into contracts. For example, an independent contractor may be developing software code. For the company to own this code, it needs to enter into a work-for-hire agreement with the contractor. This cannot be done until the company is formed.

Nondisclosure agreements (NDAs) raise a similar issue. Founders are often in contact with potential strategic partners, advisors, employees, and others at the very earliest stages of a company's formation. Although the individual founders may, and often do, enter into these types of agreements with third parties before the formation of the company, this arrangement is not ideal; in some instances, it may raise issues regarding enforceability of the contracts by the company once it has been formed and may create potential personal liability under such contracts for the founders.

At minimum, contracts entered into by founders in their role as promoters prior to incorporation should be transferable to the corporation once formed and should then result in protection by the company of the founder from any related personal liability.

Limited Liability.   The most fundamental benefit of incorporating is the protection of the corporate shield. Individual stockholders generally are not liable for the liabilities of a corporation (or limited liability company) in which they hold an equity interest. Until a corporate entity is formed, the individuals are acting in their personal capacity, and thus they may be held personally liable for their actions or omissions in conducting their business. Once a corporate entity has been formed, to enjoy the benefit of the corporate shield, certain corporate formalities must be adhered to, including the maintenance of separate corporate records and accounts, the holding of annual meetings of the stockholders and directors, and the execution of contracts and other documents in the name of the company.

CHOICE OF JURISDICTION.   Once it has been decided that a corporation is the preferred form of organization for a new entity, the question of the state of incorporation remains to be answered. As a practical matter, lawyers have two choices: incorporation in the state in which they practice, or incorporation in Delaware.

Sophisticated practitioners usually incorporate in Delaware. First, Delaware corporation law is generally considered to be the most sophisticated, comprehensive, and well defined. It is extremely flexible and is updated frequently to adapt to emerging practices. It is also the most familiar to the widest range of people, including lawyers, investors, and executives. For this reason, venture capital investors, investment bankers, and others tend to be more comfortable with Delaware corporations.

Second, an emerging business often must move quickly to obtain stockholder approval. An example of this is stockholder approval of a charter amendment that may be necessary in order to close a round of financing. All major corporation statutes permit stockholder votes to be taken at a meeting or by written consent in lieu of a meeting. In contrast to many state corporation law statutes that require unanimous stockholder written consents or impose other limits, Delaware law permits such consents to be effective if signed by holders of the number of shares that would be sufficient to approve the matters at a stockholders' meeting. Although the requirement of a unanimous written stockholder consent may be valuable protection for minority stockholders in the context of a closely held corporation (and may otherwise be seen as valuable protection for founders or other groups who are or may become minority stockholders), most companies that plan to grow quickly and obtain venture financing find this requirement of unanimity in connection with any written stockholder consent to be more of a burden than a benefit.

INITIAL CAPITALIZATION AND ALLOCATION OF EQUITY OWNERSHIP AMONG FOUNDERS.   Determining how to divide the founders' equity is one of the earliest and most difficult decisions that founders confront. Unfortunately, the discussions among founders regarding how the founders' stock is to be divided may sometimes expose divisions among the founding team due to different motivations, concerns, risk profiles, and the like. Although such divisions present challenges to the business lawyer who is, after all, engaged to represent the corporation and not the founders, it is often in the best interests of the founders and the company to have such divisions play themselves out at the start and not remain dormant until a later date. This section offers some guidance on how to think about this sensitive and often pivotal decision in a company's formative days.

BASIC DEFINITIONS.   To better understand the discussion that follows, the meaning of certain terms that are often used in the context of equity capitalization are set forth here

- **Authorized stock.** The total number of shares of capital stock, whether common or preferred, that a company may issue at any given time pursuant to its charter. This number can be easily changed later and is not that important.

- **Issued and outstanding stock.** The total number of shares of capital stock that is actually issued, whether founders' stock, stock issued pursuant to financings, the exercise of stock options or otherwise.
- **Issued and outstanding common stock on an "as-converted" basis.** The total number of shares of common stock that are issued and outstanding at any time, plus the total number of shares of common stock that the issued and outstanding convertible preferred stock (and other outstanding convertible securities) would convert into at such point in time.
- **Issued and outstanding common stock on an as-converted, fully diluted basis.** The total number of shares of issued and outstanding common stock on an as-converted basis, plus the total additional number of shares of common stock that would be issued and outstanding if all holders of outstanding options, warrants, and other similar rights to purchase stock were to exercise such rights in full.

Selecting the Number of Authorized Shares and the Number of Shares to Be Issued to Founders.   In forming a company, decisions must be made as to the total number of authorized shares of capital stock the company will have, what classes of stock will be authorized, and how many shares will be issued to the founders. The total number of authorized shares, and the total number of issued and outstanding shares at the time of formation of the company, is largely arbitrary, and in the end may be modified based on external circumstances, such as the preferences of a venture capital investor. What really matters initially is the relative percentage allocation of the outstanding equity among the founders. It does not matter if you own 1 out of 10 shares issued and outstanding, or if you own 1 million out of 10 million shares issued and outstanding. In either case, it is completely irrelevant how many shares are authorized and unissued. More shares always can be authorized down the road when needed. Issued and outstanding shares can be, and often are, adjusted upward through stock splits, where each share outstanding is converted into a higher number of shares. Issued and outstanding shares can also be reduced by a reverse stock split, where a specified number of outstanding shares are converted into a specified number of fewer shares. For example, there could be a 10-for-1 stock split, where each outstanding share is converted into 10 shares, or a 1-for-10 reverse split, where each 10 shares outstanding are converted into 1 share. Nevertheless, a couple of guiding considerations exist.

The number of shares issued to the founders should be large enough so that an option pool can be created that allows the company to grant restricted stock or stock options for a large number of shares. Fair or not, prospective hires often focus more on the total number of shares awarded to them (either outright in the form of a restricted stock grant or by the granting of options to purchase the shares) than the percentage of the company's outstanding shares that such shares represent. As a result, the company should consider putting in place an equity incentive plan that has a significant number of shares, often between 1 million and 2 million shares. This will allow the company to make awards in the range expected by prospective hires. For a company that has just been formed, an equity incentive pool might have a number of shares equal to 15 to 25 percent of the number of committed shares (i.e., the total number of founders shares plus the number of shares in the incentive pool). For example, to establish an equity incentive pool that has 1 million shares in it and that represents 20 percent of the committed shares, the founders would need to own 4 million shares in the aggregate.

Who Are the Founders; What Does the Title Mean? Differences of opinion exist regarding the significance, if any, the title "founder" carries, and no one "correct" answer exists. The word "founder" is really nothing more than a designation that the original promoters of an idea to start a company bestow on one another to identify to the outside world the people credited with getting the company off the ground. The founders usually are the people who are present at the time the company is formed and participate in the original allocation of equity. However, it is not unusual for a key hire who joins the company well after its formation to be described as a founder.

Although the founder title is primarily honorary and has no legal significance per se, situations exist in which being a founder can make a difference. Sometimes this difference is beneficial to the founder; sometimes it is burdensome. For example, venture capital firms often distinguish founders from other employees for certain reasons. In the first round of financing, venture capitalists often require founders to make certain representations and warranties about the company and their ability to work for it individually. Making such representations and warranties subjects the founders to potential personal liability if any such representation or warranty were later determined to be false. Founders are also often asked to subject their stock to first refusal rights of the company or the investors and to co-sale rights of the investors. (These concepts are explained in Chapter 2.) Being a founder may have its advantages in the context of a financing transaction, however. For example, founders may be able to negotiate for certain rights to have their shares registered with the Securities and Exchange Commission (SEC) for sale in an IPO (these are called registration rights). They may also get the benefit of a more favorable stock vesting schedule than later employees, including, for example, a portion of their stock considered to be vested on issuence and acceleration of vesting upon a change of control.

Considerations in Dividing Up Equity.   The issuance of stock among the founding group is a determination to be made among the founders and typically is based on relative contributions to the formation of the company, including the conception of the idea, leadership in promoting the idea, assumption of risk to launch the company, expenses incurred preorganization, role in writing the business plan, assembling the team, approaching prospective investors and customers, and the development of any underlying technology. In addition to preformation contributions, the potential for future impact on the growth and development of the company may also be a factor, including the background, experience, and reputation that each person brings with him or her, and the relative value of each to the company, and differing levels of commitment to working for the company following formation.

If three people jointly conceive of an idea that is based on a business model rather than a technology, they may split the founders' equity evenly at formation. However, if one person conceived of the idea, wrote the business plan, and assembled the team, a 50, 25, and 25 percent split might be more appropriate. In addition, when the business plan is based on a proprietary technology, the developer of the technology usually receives a significantly higher percentage of the company. However, if the technologist is fortunate enough to attract as a cofounder a chief executive officer (CEO) with established industry credentials and connections, the business experience of this other person might level the playing field and argue in favor of a more equal split of the founders' equity.

Often, if one person is primarily responsible for pulling the founding team together, he or she may initiate the discussion by making offers of equity to the other prospective founders. These offers typically result in discussions and negotiations before the final equity split is determined. Anyone in the position of being the lead promoter of an idea and faced with making the initial proposal regarding the division of equity should keep in mind that nibbling around the edges of a prospective cofounder's equity position may be penny wise and pound foolish. Such an approach will not engender the level of trust and cohesiveness that is essential among the members of a founding team. The objective is to reach an allocation that is perceived to be fair and that provides all of the founders with the incentive to do what is necessary to make the business a success.

Intellectual Property Ownership Issues.   Before a corporation is formed, the founders often have developed intellectual property that will be a central asset of the corporation once it is formed. At the time of incorporation, it is important to make sure that all of this IP is properly contributed to the corporation. Failure to properly make and document these transfers can have serious later consequences to the corporation, especially if one of the founders leaves the corporation. For example, investors will be interested in evaluating the ownership of any IP of the company in connection with their due diligence and will likely find any defects in this initial transfer process to be an impediment to the deal. This transfer generally is accomplished by means of a transfer and assumption agreement pursuant to which the contribution is made, often as consideration for the equity issued to the founders. Often this IP is transferred to the company in exchange for all or part of the founder's initial stock allocation. As mentioned, where the funding of the company is uncertain, a founder may irrevocably license the technology to the company, with the license to terminate if specified milestones are not achieved in specified time frames; in addition, an irrevocable transfer of the IP to the company can be built in if the milestones are achieved on the specified timetable.

If a founder has any IP that might be construed as related to the business of the company but that is not intended to be transferred to the company, this fact should be made explicitly clear in the instrument of transfer, usually by specifically listing the IP of the founder that is not being transferred. Finally, to properly transfer certain types of IP to the corporation, filings may be necessary with the U.S. Patent and Trademark Office (and, if Internet domain names are being transferred, compliance with any filing or other process requirements of a domain name registration authority). To minimize the risk that the contribution of appreciated property will result in taxable gain, a tax attorney should be consulted to ensure that the contribution is tax-free under Internal Revenue Code (IRC) Section 351.

Stock Restriction (or Vesting) Agreements.   If a company has more than one founder, it is a good idea to have the founders enter into stock restriction agreements pursuant to which each founder is required to "earn" his or her shares by continued service to the company. Such a stock restriction agreement is important not only to the company, but to any founders who may find themselves in the position of continuing with the company after one or more of the founders has left. Because such a situation would result in a significant portion of the outstanding stock of the company being held by a then "nonproductive" person, the ability of the company to retrieve the unearned portion of a prematurely departing founder's stock is important. Even if the founders decide not to enter into stock restriction agreements at the time of formation, they should be advised of the high degree of likelihood that sophisticated investors will require such agreements from them at the time of financing. For this reason alone, it may be preferable to enter into such agreements at formation. If the terms of such agreements are reasonable, investors may be willing to allow such agreements to remain in place instead of requiring new agreements on less favorable terms. Any stock restriction agreement entered into at founding that deviates too significantly from what sophisticated investors will require likely will not survive the investment process without significant changes.

Other types of agreements typically entered into between the company and its founders, or among the founders, at the time of formation frequently are incorporated into a single agreement called a stockholders' agreement. For example, one agreement might govern a right of first refusal to either the company or the other founders (or both) to purchase the shares of a founder who may wish to sell the shares before they can be transferred to a third party. Founders frequently ask if they should enter into buy/sell agreements whereby the parties agree that upon the death of one of the founders, the other founder(s) or the company (or both) will have the right to purchase the stock of the deceased, often with the proceeds of a life insurance policy that was purchased for that specific purpose. For technology companies, these agreements are completely inappropriate because it is essentially impossible to arrive at a fair valuation of the company or even a fair process for determining such a valuation, particularly in the early stages.

Because this book focuses on technology and other emerging businesses, this discussion concentrates on the types of agreements most common among founders of companies that expect to grow quickly by raising capital through the private sale of equity.

The way stock restriction agreements work is to give the company the right to buy at original cost a declining percentage of the shares held by a founder in the event that the founder leaves the company prematurely for any reason. This purchase option applies only to shares that are unvested (i.e., subject to such forfeiture) at the time of the founder's departure from the company, with shares becoming vested over a predetermined, usually time-based, schedule. Sometimes a stock restriction agreement allows the remaining founders to purchase the stock of the departing founder instead of, or along with, the company. Although this move can be advantageous for the remaining founders, it will be resisted by investors, who want all shareholders, including themselves, to benefit from the forfeiture by having all shareholders' percentage interest in the company increase proportionately.

Founders who enter into stock restriction agreements should be aware that the lapse of the repurchase restrictions can have significant tax consequences unless the founder makes an election under IRC Section 83(b) within 30 days after the purchase of shares subject to such restrictions, and possibly the later imposition of such restrictions if part of a plan when issuing the shares. Without the election, as the shares vest, the founder is subject to income tax on the amount by which the value of the vested shares at the time they vest exceeds the amount he or she paid for such vested shares. If the founder makes a Section 83(b) election upon the imposition of such restrictions, he or she is taxed only on the amount by which the value of the shares at the time of receipt exceeds the amount paid for the shares, which usually is considered to be zero. Therefore, if the founder's shares are likely to appreciate significantly in value, a Section 83(b) election is essential. In preparing a stock restriction agreement, these issues should be addressed:

- The amount of stock that will be considered vested at the time the agreement is entered into, if any. (If some of the stock is to be fully vested on day 1, this is referred to as up-front vesting.)
- The time period over which the unvested shares will vest and the increments in which the shares will vest (monthly, quarterly, yearly, etc.).
- Whether a certain minimum period of time must elapse before any unvested stock vests, for example, a year. (If this is the case, the stock is subject to cliff vesting.)
- Whether any acceleration of vesting will occur upon termination of employment by the company without cause.
- Whether any acceleration of vesting will occur upon a sale of the company.

Some general guidelines with respect to these questions follow. These guidelines are subject to change from time to time because of the venture investment climate and other external factors, and can vary by industry and by region of the country.

Founders' stock generally vests over a period of three or four years. Usually founders have some percentage of their stock vested up front as an acknowledgment of the efforts, assumption of risks, and the like already taken with forming the company. The range of up-front vesting typically falls between 10 and 25 percent. Six- and 12-month cliff vesting is also fairly common, with 12 months being the most common. The rate of vesting (subject to the use of a front-end cliff vest) is usually in equal monthly or quarterly installments. Equal annual installments are seen occasionally. In determining the installments to be used, careful consideration should be given to the consequences of the installment periods, including the impact on possible later termination of the founder's relationship. The less frequent the vesting installments, the more likely the timing of the vesting installments will have an impact on such things as the timing of a termination of an employment relationship. A strong argument can be made not to encourage keep an unproductive employee to stay for a long period until the next vesting date. Also termination by the company at the end of a long vesting period exposes the company to a claim that the employee was fired in bad faith.

Some arrangements provide that a portion of the founder's shares vest on termination ("accelerate") depending on the circumstances surrounding the termination. The termination of a founder's employment with the company may occur for four basic reasons:

1. Resignation (for no reason or for good reason)
2. Termination (for cause or without cause)
3. Death
4. Disability

If the founder resigns voluntarily or is terminated for cause, typically no additional stock vests on the theory that he or she has forfeited the right to vest further by either quitting or engaging in conduct that is sufficiently egregious and detrimental to the company that a "for cause" termination is justified. If the founder resigns for good reason (in other words, is forced out) or is terminated without cause, the vesting schedule may provide for partial acceleration so the founder gets to keep more stock than he or she otherwise would have been entitled to keep based on the duration of employment. Although such acceleration is not universal, when it is in effect, the vesting will accelerate for anywhere from an additional six months up to full vesting. This type of provision (especially if the accelerated vesting is in the range of six additional months) seems to strike a reasonable balance between the underlying premise that stockholders need to earn their stock and the fairness principle, which suggests that a company should not be able to unreasonably deprive a stockholder of the ability to earn the stock subject to vesting. Harsh as it may seem, in the event of a founder's death or disability, acceleration of vesting is not common; death and disability benefits are more properly provided by insurance. Many sophisticated investors do not like to see a distinction drawn between the treatment of different types of termination of the employment relationship because of the potential for litigation over whether there is cause for termination or whether the individual's employment has been terminated for good reason. In this view, the effect of an early departure by a founder is the same whatever the reason for departure. This effect is that a significant stockholder, if allowed to continue to hold his or her entire stock position after such an early departure, will continue to benefit from the efforts of others (whether those efforts are actual day-to-day work at the company or investment of money in the company) without any further effort on the stockholder's part. In the process, this will likely create difficulties for the company in its efforts to strike a proper balancing of the stock positions of the remaining founders/management/employees with those of the outside investors. Investors also want to mitigate the dilutive effect of hiring a replacement and issuing new stock to him or her.

Definitions of "cause" and "good reason" vary considerably. They are discussed in the last section of this chapter.

Founders often are entitled to some acceleration of vesting upon a sale of the company. There is a discussion of this issue in the section "Stock Option Plans and Other Equity Compensation Arrangements."

CONTROL AND DECISION-MAKING ISSUES: OFFICERS, DIRECTORS, AND STOCKHOLDERS.   A company is managed on a daily basis by its officers, who in turn are overseen by the board of directors, who owe duties of loyalty and care to the stockholders.

Election of Board of Directors; Role of Directors in Corporate Governance.   The business and affairs of every corporation are managed by or under the direction of the board of directors. Certain major decisions, such as a merger of the company, require stockholder approval by law, under the company's charter (certificate of incorporation), or under agreements with investors. The business and affairs of a company may encompass a wide range of activities, including the election of officers, the development of the business plan and strategy for the company, the issuance of equity and grant of stock options, and the payment of bonuses and dividends. The board of directors meets periodically at meetings called in accordance with the company's bylaws to review the state of the company's affairs and to take certain actions reserved for the board of directors.

A company's board of directors is elected by the stockholders of the company. Directors hold office until their successors are elected and qualified, or until their earlier resignation, removal, or death.

Election of directors is generally done by plurality vote of the stockholders at the stockholders' annual meeting or at a special meeting in lieu of an annual meeting. Plurality voting provides for election to the board of directors of the top vote receivers until the number of seats established for the board is filled (thus, if the board is to have four members, the top four candidates based on votes received are elected), irrespective of whether any particular candidate receives a majority of the votes cast. Delaware law provides, with certain exceptions, that any director, or the entire board of directors, may be removed, with or without cause, by the holders of a majority of the outstanding stock then entitled to vote at an election of directors. These provisions are largely academic in a technology company because the shareholders' agreement or other similar agreement among the founders or among the founders and the investors will require the signatories to vote in a specified way for the election of directors.

A majority of the total number of directors constitutes a quorum for the transaction of business at a board meeting, unless the certificate of incorporation or the bylaws provide otherwise. The board of directors may designate one or more committees to exercise the powers and authority of the board of directors in the management of the business and affairs of the corporation (subject to a few statutory exceptions and to such exceptions as may be set forth in a company's charter or bylaws).

Issuance of Stock; Role of Stockholders in Corporate Governance.
In Delaware, the authority to issue stock resides in the board of directors of a corporation. Stock issued to the founders usually is authorized by the board of directors in its initial meeting. Generally speaking, stock may be issued in exchange for cash, services rendered or to be rendered, tangible or intangible property, debt or promissory notes, or a combination thereof. In Delaware, a subscriber of stock paying for such stock in the form of a promissory note (or for services to be rendered in the future) must pay at least the aggregate par value of the stock being issued in cash. The typical par value for a start-up company is either $.01 or $.001 per share.

Unless the charter provides otherwise, each stockholder is entitled to one vote for each share of stock owned. Although the charter may provide for different voting rights between classes or series of stock, in the absence of any such distinction in the charter, all shares of stock are, subject to certain exceptions, such as the right of a class to vote as a separate class if the class is adversely affected by the action that is the subject of the stockholder vote, treated the same for voting purposes.

The composition of the board of directors is largely a function of the company's stage of development. For a newly formed company in which the only stock outstanding is held by the founders and the founders therefore control the composition of the board of directors, the board typically would be comprised of some or all of the founders. A majority vote would allow the company to take adverse action against a founder. The board's composition will likely change as the company grows. Outside investors and, in particular, venture capitalists usually require one or more seats on the board of directors. The balance of power in these situations is extremely important and closely negotiated. This balance of power is discussed in Chapter 2.

With respect to size, emerging companies tend to work better with smaller boards. A board comprised of five members seems to work well for many emerging companies; seven may be seen as an outside limit before the size of the board begins to get unwieldy. The board of an emerging company often may be called on to act quickly and with little notice. Coordination among a smaller group is easier than with a larger one. Boards of emerging companies tend to meet frequently as well—as often as once a month for a company with venture capital or other sophisticated investor backing. Again, attempting to coordinate the schedules of five members on a monthly basis is often substantially easier than coordinating the schedules of a larger group. When possible, choose an odd number of directors to avoid the problems associated with deadlocks.

As mentioned, a number of actions cannot be taken without the consent of the stockholders. These actions include amendments to the charter; approval of a plan of merger or consolidation (subject to certain limited exceptions); reorganizations and recapitalizations; the sale, lease, or exchange of all or substantially all of its property or assets; and the liquidation or dissolution of the corporation.

Election of Officers; Role of Officers in Corporate Governance.   The officers of a corporation are responsible for managing the daily operations and affairs of the corporation and for taking actions within their authority to allow the corporation to pursue its business objectives, in each case under the direction and supervision of the board of directors. Officers typically include a president, treasurer, secretary, and such vice presidents and other positions as the board of directors deems appropriate.

Under Delaware law, every corporation must have such officers as are stated in the bylaws of the corporation or in a resolution of the board of directors. Assuming the company wants to issue shares of stock, these officers must include such officers as are necessary to sign the corporation's stock certificates: the chairperson or vice chairperson of the board of directors, or the president or vice president and the treasurer or assistant treasurer, or the secretary or an assistant secretary. Officers are elected in such a manner and hold office for the terms that are prescribed in the bylaws or that have been established by the board of directors, and each officer holds such position until such officer's successor is elected or until such officer's resignation or removal. The bylaws of a Delaware corporation typically provide for the board of directors to elect and remove officers with or without cause. One of the officers should be responsible for keeping records of the meetings of the stockholders and directors; this is usually the secretary or assistant secretary.

MECHANICS OF ORGANIZING THE CORPORATION (FOR LAWYERS ONLY)

Certificate of Incorporation. The first action to be taken is for a person called the incorporator to file the certificate of incorporation with the Delaware secretary of state. The incorporator is typically the lawyer who represents the company or one of the founders. Companies called service companies handle the actual filing. These companies also act as statutory agents in Delaware to accept service or process and the like. It is a statutory requirement to have such an agent. One initial mistake that is often made is to have an individual employee of the service company act as the incorporator. This may cause problems later if the incorporator does not take certain essential actions (to be discussed). It may be impossible to fix the mistake later since the individual at the service company may be long gone.

For Delaware corporations, the charter is known as the certificate of incorporation. Later amendments are referred to as certificates of amendment. The charter is, in effect, a contract between the corporation and its stockholders as well as a contract among the stockholders.

The charter includes certain items that are required by statute and other items that may be added at the incorporator's discretion so long as such terms do not violate law. The name of the corporation is required to be set forth, and the name must include either "corporation" or "incorporated" (or Corp. or Inc.) or some other indication of the limited liability nature of the entity, as allowed by statute for purposes of putting the public on notice of such limited liability. Also, the name chosen may not be confusingly similar to the name of a then existing corporation either incorporated in the state or registered to do business as a foreign corporation in the state. The determination of whether a name is confusingly similar is made by state authorities. It is prudent to check in advance of incorporation to make sure the preferred name is available and, if it is, to reserve it. Names of Delaware corporations are published on the Delaware secretary of state's Web site. Such an advance reservation is allowable but may be maintained for only a limited period of time (with limited rights to renew the reservation). Keep in mind, however, that simply because a name is available for use as a corporation's name in a particular state does not mean that the use of the name does not violate the trademark or trade name rights of others. Another corporation may have incorporated in another state (or may be doing business under a name other than its corporate name) and may have developed trademark or trade name rights in such name. Therefore, an appropriate search, and possible registration, of trademarks and trade names should also be undertaken.

Also required is a statement regarding the purpose or purposes of the corporation. Delaware law requires only a simple statement that the corporation is being formed for the purpose of "engaging in any lawful act or activity for which corporations may be organized under Delaware law." Limiting the statement of purpose to this simple statement is all that is normally done in order to avoid any issues later as to the proper authority of the corporation to take a particular action.

The authorized capital stock of the corporation is required to be set forth in the charter. In deciding on the authorized capital structure, it will be necessary at the least to include common stock. It is not, however, immediately necessary to include preferred stock. Even in the case of corporations that intend to raise venture capital or other sources of sophisticated investor financing and therefore will need to authorize and sell preferred stock, because the actual terms of the preferred stock are determined by negotiation with investors, such preferred stock cannot be set up in detail ahead of time. However, it is possible to establish "blank check" preferred stock. Blank check preferred stock allows the board of directors of a corporation to establish one or more series of preferred stock from shares of undesignated but authorized blank check preferred stock without the consent of the stockholders that is normally required for a charter amendment. In effect, the stockholders have authorized the board of directors to designate and issue these shares in advance.

Although blank check preferred stock can be very useful, for example, to quickly and easily establish a series of preferred stock for sale to venture capital investors following a simple initial round of financing without going back to any of the corporation's stockholders for approval, its convenience has become diluted by the increasing prevalence of veto and other approval rights that prevent later rounds of financing without the approval of existing investors, irrespective of the existence of blank check preferred stock. Although these veto and other rights have long been standard in institutional venture capital deals, they have increasingly worked their way into seed and first-round angel deals as angel investors become more sophisticated in structuring their deals. Nonetheless, blank check preferred stock may be useful in allowing a company to have to go only to its preferred stock investor group, and not back to its common stockholders as well, to approve subsequent rounds of financing. Clearly, however, the value of blank check preferred stock is at its lowest in a true start-up situation, in which the only stockholders are the founders of the company.

Because the number of shares of stock that is authorized always may be changed by a charter amendment, the number of shares to authorize initially is largely a matter of personal style. Differences in filing fees must be considered.

The par value of the authorized stock is required to be stated. It is advantageous to set the par value at a low number (e.g., $.001 per share) so founders may purchase their shares for the minimum amount of consideration they wish to put into the company without creating problems with respect to the fully paid nature of their stock.

Delaware law requires that there be a registered office in Delaware and that the name and address of the corporation's registered office in Delaware be listed in the charter. As discussed, the registered office will be the office of a service company located in Delaware that provides the registered office for an annual fee, as well as other useful services, such as the filing of charter amendments, obtaining good standing certificates, and answering inquiries regarding Delaware procedure.

The name and address of the incorporator of the corporation are required to be listed in the charter. The incorporator will be required to sign the initial charter too. Later charter amendments, as well as restatements, will be signed by an authorized officer. Often the attorney for the company acts as the incorporator. This can simplify the mechanics of the process.

Although often useful in public companies, staggered board provisions, supermajority voting provisions, poison pills, and other anti-takeover provisions are not used in the charters of emerging companies because such companies are not susceptible to hostile takeovers. Hostile takeovers effectively require that there be a public market for the stock. Also, first refusal and other restrictions set up at the outset effectively preclude a private tender offer for the outstanding stock of a private company.

Initial Consent of the Incorporator.   Under Delaware law, the incorporator is required to hold an organizational meeting after the filing of the certificate of incorporation at which the incorporator adopts the initial bylaws of the corporation, elects the initial board of directors, and accomplishes other organizational actions. Since there is usually only one incorporator, this is done by written consent. It is also possible under Delaware law to substitute an initial directors' meeting for such organizational meeting (or a unanimous written consent) if the certificate of incorporation lists the initial directors. Such initial directors' action would involve the same tasks as the incorporators' organizational meeting except that instead of electing the initial directors, the officers of the corporation would be appointed. As a general rule, the incorporator will merely perform the ministerial tasks relating to incorporation and will thereafter hand over the running of the corporation to its initial board of directors. This said, it is possible in Delaware for the incorporator to continue to run the corporation following incorporation by putting off the date of election of the initial directors. Better practice is to immediately elect a board of directors to take over the business of running the corporation from the incorporator.

Minutes of Board of Directors' First Meeting.   The initial meeting of the board of directors, as appointed by the incorporator(s), or written consent should occur as soon as reasonably practicable after the directors are elected (which will occur when elected by the incorporator(s) in Delaware). The purpose of this initial meeting or action is for the board of directors to, among other things:

- Elect officers
- Adopt the seal of the corporation
- Specify the fiscal year of the corporation
- Adopt banking resolutions
- Accept the subscriptions for and approve the initial issuance of stock to the founders and approve any related stock restriction agreements
- Adopt a form of stock certificate for use with the company's common stock
- Make, subject to appropriate stockholder approval, a Subchapter S election (if applicable)
- Authorize employment agreements (as applicable)
- Authorize the company to qualify to do business in other jurisdictions
- Authorize the lease of business premises
- Approve other material transactions, agreements, and documents as may then be necessary (such as any agreements or documents relating to the transfer of the intellectual property being transferred to the company by the founders)

Specimen Stock Certificate.   The form of stock certificate for the company's common stock is generally adopted at the initial meeting of the board of directors. Forms of stock certificates for various series of preferred stock are adopted at the time such series of preferred stock is established.

Subscription Agreement.   In conjunction with the issuance of capital stock of the corporation to the initial stockholders of the corporation, the corporation should use an appropriate subscription agreement or incorporate those provisions in the shareholders' agreement.

In its most basic form, the subscription agreement addresses, among other things, these issues:

- Identity of the purchaser
- Amount and class of the capital stock being purchased
- Consideration paid or to be paid for the stock purchased
- Appropriate representations of the purchaser for securities law compliance by the company (purchase for investment only, knowledge or sophistication of the purchaser, acknowledgment of the risks associated with an early-stage company, and the like)
- Issues relating to the possible later registration under applicable securities laws of the capital stock being acquired
- Restrictions on transfer of the capital stock, if any

Bylaws.   Bylaws set forth certain rules and procedures regarding the governance of a corporation's internal affairs. The bylaws supplement the applicable corporate law and the corporation's charter. When a conflict or inconsistency exists among these three sources, the applicable corporate law controls first, followed in most cases by the charter and then the bylaws. To the extent a corporation enters into any agreement that is contradictory to any of these three, it is likely to be unenforceable.

HOUSEKEEPING

Periodic Filings.   Once a corporation has been formed, it has an obligation to maintain current information with the state in which the entity is incorporated. The primary periodic filing for a Delaware corporation is the annual franchise tax report. The State of Delaware sends a standard form and franchise tax invoice directly to each Delaware company at the beginning of each year. Companies are required to file franchise tax reports "annually on or before the first day in March."

In practice, while the failure to make either of these filings when due usually can be corrected quickly and easily, until it has done so, the company will be out of good standing with the state. This may make it difficult for the company to close a round of financing or effect any other significant transaction.

In addition to filings required by the state of organization, practitioners should be aware that similar filing requirements may exist in any state in which the company is qualified to do business.

Stock Issuance, Legends, and Transfer.   Maintaining complete and clear stock records is an absolute necessity for any corporation. The company's lawyer typically maintains a stock record book containing copies of issued stock certificates. Good practice is for the lawyer to keep the signed stock certificates in the stock record book and furnish a copy of each issued stock certificate to its owner. This practice rarely is objected to and saves time and effort later if the stock certificates must be produced in connection with stock transfers and various corporate purposes, such as mergers. In addition, the lawyer's firm or the company should keep an Excel spreadsheet that shows outstanding stock options and warrants as well as outstanding stock. This spreadsheet always must be produced in connection with later financings. Copies of all stock option agreements and warrants should also be kept on file.

Securities law compliance should be addressed from the outset. Because emerging companies are private companies, compliance with securities laws will hinge on qualifying for an exemption from registration under federal and state securities laws. Certain federal regulations and many state laws address not only the issuance of stock but also the offer of stock. Accordingly, the practitioner should review the anticipated securities law exemptions before any offering of stock occurs. During an offering, corporations should keep complete records of the offering process, including a list of all recipients of any offering memoranda or disclosure materials and addresses and residencies of offerers and purchasers, because this information may be necessary to complete federal and state securities law exemption filings. Additionally, prior to the issuance of any stock, the corporation must have authorized the securities to be issued in the company's charter.

Evidence of payment for shares (either a copy of a check or wire receipts) and executed subscription agreements should also be kept on record.

Legends must be placed on the back of the certificates stating the existence of any restrictions. For private companies, the most basic restriction comes in the form of a '33 Act Legend, which is a statement that the shares have not been registered under the Securities Act of 1933 and, as such, any transfer of such shares must fall within an exemption from registration. Other common legends disclose the existence of more than one class of stock (a statutory requirement) and the existence of certain contractual agreements pertaining to the shares, such as agreements that impose restrictions on transfer or that impose voting obligations on the holder of the shares (also a statutory requirement).

Once stock is issued and outstanding, the stockholder may wish to transfer the shares to a third party. Documenting a stock transfer requires, at the very least, a stock power from the current holder that authorizes the transfer of the certificate to a new buyer. Transfers of stock in an emerging company also typically require navigating the restrictions that apply to a stockholder's securities. These include any contractual restrictions, such as the company's right of first refusal on the purchase of any shares transferred, the right of first refusal of other stockholders to purchase any shares in the event the company turns down its opportunity, and broad restrictions on transfers to outside third parties. In addition, any resale of securities needs to be done in compliance with the securities laws. Investors who sell immediately after receiving shares in an exempted transaction may be deemed to be involved in the unlawful resale or distribution of securities. Under certain circumstances, such an immediate subsequent transfer may destroy the exemption that the issuer was relying on in the initial offering.

Stockholders' Actions.   Stockholders own companies, but they do not run companies in their capacity as such. Stockholders elect a board of directors and charge the board with managing the company. Directors, in turn, elect officers and charge the officers with the day-to-day operations of a company. The officers report to the board of directors, and the board answers to the stockholders. Stockholders have the power to elect, remove, and replace the board of directors. This broad and general power is very typical of stockholder activity in an ongoing company. Stockholders have the final word on election of the board and authorization or approval of any event that significantly changes a company's legal structure, such as a charter amendment, the authorization of a new class of stock (other than blank check preferred stock), the sale of all or substantially all of the company's assets, or the merger of a company with another entity.

Directors' Actions.   Directors, being charged with managing a company, tend to meet much more often than stockholders, and must authorize and approve significant transactions and often other routine matters.

Electronic Communication.   Delaware law permits the conduct of certain corporate affairs, including certain matters pertaining to the taking of stockholder and board action, through electronic communications.

Foreign Corporations.   Once a company is incorporated, the company still may have filing obligations in states in which it does business. Most states require the registration of companies doing business in their state, even if those companies are incorporated elsewhere. The analysis of what level of activities rise to the level of doing business is different for each state. Most states have codified certain activities that they deem to be doing business, and such activities usually involve some sort of presence in the state, such as leasing a local office. Case law regarding "doing business" fills out the discussion for areas in which the statutes are vague or unclear. Failure to register as a foreign corporation where required in a state usually can be fixed easily later as a mechanical matter, but may also involve the payment of troublesome back sales and other taxes.

In significant transactions, parties generally will request good standing certificates not only from a company's state of incorporation, but also from each state in which the company is registered to do business.

STOCK SPLITS, DIVIDENDS, REPURCHASES, AND REDEMPTIONS

Stock Splits.   A corporation may subdivide each share of its outstanding capital stock into a greater number of shares (a stock split) or combine any number of its outstanding shares into a smaller number of shares (a reverse stock split). The primary reason for effecting such a transaction in a private company context is to adjust the company's capital structure so as to fall within certain established norms.

Stock splits and reverse splits will require an amendment to the corporation's charter and, thus, will require shareholder approval.

Stock Dividends.   A corporation can achieve the same result as a stock split via a stock dividend declared by the board of directors. Unless otherwise provided in the charter or bylaws, or by contract, a stock dividend does not, unlike a stock split, require shareholder approval. In Delaware, no dividends may be distributed other than out of capital surplus or profits in the year of distribution. These terms are described in the statute. In the case of a stock dividend, the corporation must transfer from its surplus to its capital account an amount necessary to cover the post dividend aggregate par value of its outstanding stock.

Stock Redemptions and Repurchases.   Redemptions and repurchases both involve the repurchase by the corporation of outstanding stock from one or more of its shareholders. A corporation may be required by its charter, bylaws, or other contract to redeem stock (usually preferred stock) under certain circumstances. Alternatively, a corporation may voluntarily elect to repurchase outstanding stock. If a corporation voluntarily elects to repurchase stock from one or more shareholders, careful consideration should be given to the rights of minority stockholders to participate in the transaction. It may be appropriate, depending on the particular situation, to obtain waivers from nonparticipating stockholders. Under Delaware law, stock may not be repurchased if the corporation's capital is impaired or would be impaired as a result of the redemption.

Before effecting a stock split, stock dividend, repurchase or redemption, a corporation should evaluate what, if any, approvals are required beyond the statutory approvals just described. A corporate charter or bylaws or a material contract may require the prior approval of a particular class or series of stock or the prior consent of a third party. Moreover, as with all material corporate transactions, consideration should be given to the accounting and tax implications of the transaction.

FIDUCIARY DUTIES OF DIRECTORS AND OFFICERS.   Directors and officers of corporations owe a fiduciary duty of care and loyalty to the corporation and its stockholders. The duty of care applies to all actions a director or officer takes on behalf of the corporation. The duty of loyalty arises primarily in situations in which directors or officers act on a matter in which they have a personal interest. The duty of care requires that directors and officers perform their duties in the best interest of the corporation, and with reasonable care under the circumstances. Under Delaware common law, the business judgment rule essentially establishes a presumption that in making a business decision, the directors of a corporation are disinterested and informed, and are acting in good faith for the best interests of the corporation. Generally speaking, provided that the directors have acted in the honest belief that their actions are in the best interest of the corporation and have exercised due care in making the decision, the decisions the board makes will not be subject to reexamination by the courts, and the directors will benefit from a presumption that they discharged their fiduciary duties to the corporation and its stockholders. If it can be demonstrated that the directors either failed to act based solely on what was in the best interest of the corporation and its stockholders (by, e.g., putting their own interests or that of an affiliate ahead of the corporation), or failed to exercise reasonable care under the circumstances (by, e.g., not taking adequate steps to make an informed decision under the circumstances), then the presumption of the business judgment rule will not be available. The deference accorded directors through the business judgment rule is intended to recognize that directors need to be given the benefit of the doubt in discharging the mandate that they safeguard the interests of the stockholders, without which directors might be discouraged from making difficult and potentially controversial decisions or even serving as directors in the first instance.

The duty of loyalty is related to the duty of care. Generally speaking, the duty of loyalty requires that a director not engage in self-dealing. The Delaware General Corporation Law directly addresses the issue of transactions that involve interested directors. It defines what types of transactions raise interested party issues and establishes a safe harbor of sorts by providing that no transaction involving an interested director or officer shall be void solely for this reason, provided that the nature of the interested party's interest is fully disclosed and a majority of the disinterested directors or stockholders approve the transaction. The Delaware code prohibits any limitation of the liability of a director for a breach of the duty of loyalty.

Notwithstanding this statutory provision, there is Delaware case law that insider transactions are subject to a higher standard, called the entire fairness standard, to the effect that both the substance and the procedure involving an insider transaction must be fair to the corporation and its noninterested stockholders. This standard is usually applied in the mergers and acquisitions context, but the principles of the cases establishing this standard apply in other contexts as well, such as down-round venture capital financings. Many Delaware cases deal in detail with a board's fiduciary duties in connection with a sale of the corporation or a change of control. A discussion of the landmark cases in this area, such as *Revlon* and the like, are beyond our scope.

MECHANICS OF ORGANIZATION: OTHER ENTITIES

Subchapter S Corporations.   A Subchapter S corporation is established the same way a C corporation is established except, unlike a C corporation, an S corporation and its stockholders make an election with the IRS to be taxed as an S corporation.

To elect S status, a corporation and its stockholders must timely file a properly completed S election form with the IRS within a prescribed time period. Once effective, an S election remains in effect until it is revoked by the corporation or terminated by the corporation's failure to satisfy the Subchapter S corporation eligibility requirements. An S election must include the consents of all of the persons who are shareholders on the date the election is made. In addition, if the election is to apply retroactively back to the first day of a taxable year, all persons who held stock at any time during the year but before the election is made must consent to the election. The S election must be signed by an officer with authority to sign the corporation's tax returns. Special consent requirements apply to spouses who hold shares jointly and to trusts.

Delaware Limited Liability Companies.   A Delaware limited liability company (LLC) is formed by filing a certificate of formation with the Delaware secretary of state.

The Delaware LLC statute permits a Delaware LLC to have only a single member. A single-member LLC is disregarded as an entity separate from its owner for tax purposes unless it elects to be classified as a corporation. A single-member LLC, therefore, has the unique advantage of not existing for tax purposes but existing for purposes of serving as a liability shield.

Next we discuss the factors relevant to deciding whether an S corporation or an LLC is a better vehicle to conduct the business of the new entity.

CHOICE OF ENTITY

One issue that needs to be addressed in the organization of a business is the legal form that the entity will take. There are several choices: C corporation, S corporation, general or limited partnership, and LLC. The parameters for the choice include tax efficiency, impact on future financing sources, simplicity and cost, and familiarity for the various stakeholders, including employees, financial backers, lenders, strategic partners, and others. The choice in the vast majority of cases is a C corporation, but it is always advisable to consider the feasibility and desirability of another form when organizing a start-up entity.

The three most common entity types for a new company are the C corporation, the S corporation, and the LLC. While all three entity types insulate the founders from personal liability, the differences among the three types for tax purposes are substantial. A C corporation reports and pays tax on its income separately from its owners. The income or loss of an S corporation or LLC generally is reported by the owners on their personal returns. The choice, therefore, is often tax-driven and requires an analysis of how the founders expect to profit from the business.

C CORPORATION.   A C corporation reports and pays taxes on its income. Because any income (including gain from an asset sale) that a C corporation distributes to its shareholders is taxable again in the hands of the shareholders (double-taxed), distributed income of a C corporation can be subject to tax at higher effective rates than those applicable to the distributed income of an S corporation or LLC. The losses of a C corporation are also reported by the corporation rather than by its shareholders. With limited exceptions, owners report any losses of their investments as capital losses only when they dispose of their shares. Individuals may use capital losses to offset only capital gains and small amounts of ordinary income (and may carry unused capital losses forward but not back).

Factors Favoring the C Corporation.   While the potential for double taxation is a serious concern, a number of factors may favor the C corporation. Those factors include:

- Venture capital funds prefer to invest in C corporations. The funds may not make equity investments in S corporations because the funds are partnerships and partnerships are not S corporation eligible shareholders. Equity investments in LLCs can cause tax problems for the funds' tax-exempt and foreign partners. In addition, the funds usually want to purchase preferred stock, which is not permissible in an S corporation.

- Equity-based compensation arrangements are simplest with C corporations. C corporations (and S corporations, but not LLCs) may grant tax-favored incentive stock options (ISOs). In practice, it can be difficult to provide corporate equity incentives that permit the participants to avoid tax (or an obligation to pay the then fair market value) upon receiving their stock and report the benefits of their arrangements at long-term capital gain rates. Through the use of profits interests, LLCs are able to structure arrangements with service providers in ways that achieve the service providers' tax objectives without requiring that the service providers pay a purchase price or tax upon receiving their interests. But these arrangements are somewhat complicated, and many are not willing to use this approach.

- Only shares of stock in C corporations may be qualified small business stock. The disposition of such stock at a loss can be treated as an ordinary loss within certain limits.

- If certain requirements are satisfied, the shareholders of a C corporation (or an S corporation, but not an LLC) may exchange their stock for stock of a corporate acquiror without tax in a tax-free reorganization (other than on any cash or other non-stock property they receive). Instead, the shareholders defer the reporting of their gains until they dispose of their stock in the acquiror.

- Depending on the amount and nature of a C corporation's income and the tax brackets of its shareholders, reinvested income of a C corporation can under certain circumstances be taxed at a lower effective rate than reinvested income of an S corporation or LLC.

- The use of a C corporation prevents the owners from having to file personal tax returns in all the states and other jurisdictions in which the business has a tax presence.

When a C Corporation Makes Sense.   Founders should consider the C corporation if they intend to grow their business for a public offering or sale by obtaining venture capital financing and motivating employees and consultants with equity. The primary risk to forming the business as a C corporation is the potential for double taxation if the business becomes a cash cow or if an acquiror wants to buy the assets of the business in a taxable transaction. Sometimes founders of a business with this type of plan want to take a wait-and-see approach to preserve their ability to sell assets without double tax and at individual capital gain rates and to report early-stage losses (subject to applicable passive activity loss, at risk, and other limitations) on their personal returns. The wait-and-see approach is generally better served by using an LLC as the interim entity. Conversion from an LLC to a C corporation usually can be accomplished without triggering tax. Converting from an S corporation somewhat is more complicated.

S CORPORATION.   The income and, subject to certain limitations, losses of an S corporation are reported by the corporation's shareholders in proportion to their shareholdings. Thus, the use of an S corporation usually avoids the double taxation of distributed earnings characteristic of the C corporation. Special rules apply to an S corporation that has assets acquired, or earnings and profits accumulated, while it or any corporation it acquired in a tax-free exchange was a C corporation. Since the focus of this book is on structuring a new business venture, those special rules are not discussed. Distributions of "tax-paid" S corporation income are not subject to further taxation in the hands of the shareholders. Unfortunately, due to qualification requirements, the S corporation is not always available as an option. Among the more onerous qualification requirements are that the corporation have only a single class of stock (differences solely in voting rights are permissible) and have 100 or fewer shareholders (all of whom must be U.S. citizens or resident individuals, estates or certain types of trusts, qualified retirement plan trusts or charitable organizations); certain family members count as a single shareholder.

It should also be noted that S corporations may have different state tax consequences.

Factors Favoring the S Corporation.   Often founders must first decide between a C corporation and an S corporation or an LLC (i.e., between a taxable entity and a nontaxable, or pass-through, entity). Once the founders have ruled out the C corporation (usually because

they suspect that their returns may take the form of periodic distributions of operating income or a distribution of the proceeds of a sale of
the assets of the business), they must decide between the S corporation
and the LLC. Among the factors that may favor the S corporation over
the LLC are:

- S corporations may be more versatile than LLCs in terms of exit
  strategy. Like shareholders of a C corporation (but not the owners of an LLC), shareholders of an S corporation may exchange
  their stock for stock of a corporate acquiror without tax (other
  than on any cash or other nonstock property they receive) if
  the exchange is part of a transaction that qualifies as a reorganization for tax purposes. In addition, it may be easier for
  the owners of an S corporation than for the owners of an LLC
  to report their exit gains as capital gains rather than ordinary
  income by structuring their exit as a stock (as opposed to asset)
  sale.
- Although equity incentive arrangements are more complicated
  with S corporations than with C corporations, they are simpler
  with S corporations than with LLCs. Like C corporations, S
  corporations may grant incentive stock options (ISOs).
- If a participating owner of an S corporation receives reasonable
  wage payments from the S corporation as well as S corporation
  distributions, only the wage payments are subject to employment tax. A participating owner of an LLC, however, may
  be subject to self-employment tax on his or her entire share
  of the LLC's business income. While the amount of income
  subject to the social security component of the employment or
  self-employment tax is subject to a cap, the cap does not apply
  to a Medicare component.
- S corporations may be eligible for local property tax exemptions
  that are not available to LLCs. These exemptions can be particularly important if the business will have significant amounts
  of inventory, machinery, or other personal property.

When an S Corporation Makes Sense.   Founders should consider
the S corporation if they want a simple arrangement that will avoid
double taxation while preserving their ability to sell the business for
stock of an acquiror on a nontaxable basis, maintaining their ability to

motivate employees and consultants by granting ISOs, and minimizing employment tax issues.

LIMITED LIABILITY COMPANY.   Unless an LLC elects to be treated as a C corporation, it is treated as a partnership (or, if it has only a single owner, as a sole proprietorship) for federal tax purposes. Because the income and, subject to certain limitations, losses of an LLC are reported by the LLC's owners (referred to as members) in accordance with their agreement, the LLC also avoids the double-taxation issues presented by a C corporation. While an LLC is far more flexible than an S corporation in many respects, the added flexibility often comes at the price of added complexity. There may, though, be situations where the LLC is simpler than the S corporation. For example, an LLC with a single owner generally need not even file separate tax returns.

Factors Favoring the LLC.   Among the factors that may favor the LLC over the S corporation are:

- An LLC is not subject to the S corporation qualification requirements. In particular, an LLC may have multiple classes of owners (with different economic rights and preferences), and may include entities and foreigners among its owners. (Note that foreigners may be reluctant to invest in an LLC because of other tax complications.)
- With certain exceptions, an LLC may distribute appreciated assets without triggering gain. Assets may therefore pass in and out of an LLC more freely than with an S corporation. For this reason, the LLC is the type of entity that is most easily converted to another type if circumstances change. (Note that conversion as part of a transaction intended to qualify as a tax-free reorganization may cause the transaction to be taxable.) The conversion of a C corporation or S corporation to an LLC generally triggers tax on any appreciation in the value of the corporation's assets.
- To avoid tax on a contribution of appreciated property to an S corporation (or C corporation) for stock, the person making the contribution must, among other things, own (either individually or together with other persons making contemporaneous contributions of cash or property) at least 80 percent of the outstanding stock of the corporation as of the time immediately

after the contribution is made. No such control requirement applies to contributions of appreciated property to LLCs. As a result, adding new owners for property contributions can be simpler for LLCs than for S corporations.

- If the owners of an LLC exchange their LLC interests for shares of stock in a conversion of the LLC to a C corporation, the shares of stock issued to the owners are not precluded from being qualified small business stock by reason of the prior existence of the LLC. If all the other requirements for qualified small business stock treatment are satisfied, the owners have merely postponed the beginning of their holding periods until they receive their shares of stock.

- Unlike an S corporation, the owners of an LLC may include their shares of the LLC's borrowings in their tax bases in their interests in the LLC, even if they are not personally liable for the borrowings. The inclusion of borrowings in basis enables the owners to withdraw borrowing proceeds from the LLC on a tax-free basis and (subject to applicable passive activity loss, at risk, and other limitations) report greater amounts of loss.

- If an LLC makes a special tax election, people who acquire an interest in the LLC by purchase or inheritance may write up their share of the LLC's basis in its assets to their initial basis in their interest in the LLC (thereby enabling them to report less income or greater deductions with respect to the assets). The same election permits the LLC to write up its tax basis in its assets when an owner's interest is redeemed by the LLC at a gain. Once made, the election applies to all transactions and could result in a write-down if values fall.

When an LLC Makes Sense.   Founders should consider the LLC if they want to avoid the double taxation of distributed corporate earnings (or any taxation on in-kind distributions) while preserving their ability to issue interests of multiple classes (providing holders with different economic rights and preferences) or to owners who could not qualify as S corporation shareholders. The LLC is also the best choice when the founders want to use a pass-through entity on an interim basis. The LLC may also be better suited than the C corporation or the S corporation to activities involving investments in assets such as real estate or securities.

CONCLUSION.   In conclusion, a C corporation may be the best choice if the founders intend to reap their profits by selling their shares after growing the business using venture capital financing with the expectation that the equity will be broadly distributed. If the founders anticipate reaping their profits in the form of distributions of income from the business (including gain from an exit structured as an asset sale), however, they should consider using an S corporation or an LLC.

STOCK OPTION PLANS AND OTHER EQUITY COMPENSATION ARRANGEMENTS

Equity compensation (restricted stock and stock options) is one of the principal factors that has driven the technology revolution in the United States. Technology entrepreneurs are willing to work for substantially less cash income at a start-up in exchange for equity compensation. Enormous fortunes have been made by thousands of technology entrepreneurs over the last two decades; the mechanism was equity compensation. Most already-public companies have stock option programs as well, but the potential appreciation is much greater at the start-up stage.

The equity compensation game is to get restricted stock in a start-up at a low purchase price per share or a stock option with a low exercise price. The hope is that the company will appreciate in value substantially over a relatively short period of time and then go public or be sold. The normal time period for such a liquidity event is 4 to 10 years. During the Internet bubble, frequently this time period was compressed to less than a year. Entrepreneurs with a hot new Internet or telecom technology would start a company and then sell it within a year, sometimes for many hundreds of millions of dollars. These get-rich-quick stories are mostly gone, but the prospect of accumulating great wealth in a relatively short time persists.

One important point to understand about equity compensation is that the percentage of a company's equity that the person owns is what counts, not the absolute number of shares. In order to understand why, it is important to understand some basics about the IPO process. When a company goes public, the price at which the stock is sold to the public is first approximated by the underwriters' so-called pre-money valuation of the company. A range of per share values is set forth in the preliminary prospectus for the offering that reflects the pre-money valuation per share. Underwriters arrive at pre-money valuations using a number of valuation methodologies, but the object is to set a price or range of prices at which they think they can sell the shares, given the current stock market environment and the reception that other similar companies have recently received. So, let us say the underwriters value the company at $100 million before the offering. The offering price to the public per share is simply that number divided by the number of shares outstanding and share equivalents (options, etc.) at the pre-IPO company. But, because the price per share for IPOs is customarily set at around $10 or $15 per share, the underwriters require the company to do a stock split or reverse stock split to arrive at the correct price per share. A forward split increases the number of outstanding shares, and a reverse stock split lowers the number of outstanding shares—with the objective being to arrive at a number of shares that, when divided into the pre-money valuation, results in a price per share of $10 to $15.

This process is often poorly understood by the engineers and others who work at technology start-ups. It is not uncommon for highly intelligent and well-educated employees to go through a mental exercise that says "If I get options on 10,000 shares and the typical price per share in the IPO is around $10, then I'll make around $100,000 less the small amount I have to pay to exercise the stock option." Big mistake. This analysis has no validity whatsoever because of the almost universal requirement to split or reverse split the stock. That is why private companies typically like to give out loads of options—to create an unjustifiable expectation of value. Again, the number of shares under an option is meaningless without knowing how many shares are outstanding. It is the *percentage* of outstanding stock that counts. That information is rarely given out as a matter of routine.

FORMS OF EQUITY COMPENSATION.   Several forms of equity compensation are common in private companies. The most common are restricted stock purchases and stock options—with the options being both in the form of ISOs and nonqualified stock options (NQSOs). A restricted stock purchase is simply the purchase of a company's stock in a private transaction, with the stock typically being subject to declining vesting (forfeiture) provisions and to sale restrictions. Upon termination of employment, the company can buy back the unvested stock at its original, and presumably low, purchase price. The other form of equity compensation is the stock option, where the employee is given the right to buy the stock at a fixed price for a specified period of time. The optionee is given the opportunity to exercise only a portion (or none) of the option at the outset, with that portion increasing (or vesting) over the period of employment. When employment ceases, vesting ceases. In effect, companies granting equity to employees or others rendering services to the company provide that the equity holder must earn this equity over time by continuing to remain in the employment/service relationship. This is what is known as sweat equity.

One disadvantage of options, other than tax disadvantages, is that employers frequently provide that the employee must exercise the vested portion of his or her option within a certain number of days after termination of employment. Doing this requires the employee to make a difficult investment decision and to pay the cash exercise price, which can be significant, particularly where the company is past the start-up stage. In the case of a NQSO, because the difference between the fair market value of the stock received on exercise over the exercise price is compensation income, the employee also incurs a tax liability on exercise that cannot be funded by a sale of the stock because of the legal and practical restrictions on selling stock in a private company.

Vesting schedules vary. Sometimes a portion of the equity is vested up front; this is usually the case for founders and often for senior executives; the rest vests over a period of three or four years. Sometimes the first vesting installment is after a year of service, with monthly or quarterly vesting thereafter. Another provision that is nego-tiated by senior management, but rarely by others, is to provide more favorable vesting if the employee is terminated without cause or if the employee terminates the employment relationship for good reason, meaning that he or she has been effectively forced out by a pay cut or otherwise.

Vesting tied solely to tenure with the company is by far the most common form. The reason for this is that historically, time vesting was the only form of vesting that was eligible for favorable account-ing treatment. Under the old accounting rules, options granted at fair market value with the vesting tied to tenure resulted in no accounting charge (expense). Under new rules, options are valued based on certain standard mathematical formulas (such as Black-Scholes) and that value is charged to (deducted from) earnings over the vesting period of the option, whether time-based or based on some performance measure. Because all options now result in an earnings charge, companies are more frequently structuring vesting to tie more closely to individual and company-wide performance goals. Achievement of performance goals is what the company really wants to incentivize, not just hanging around.

Other than stock issued upon incorporation, restricted stock and options typically are issued to employees pursuant to what is known as an omnibus stock plan—a plan that permits the issuance of restricted stock, stock options, and other forms of equity compensation. An example of such a plan can be found in the appendices to this chapter.

In order to avoid adverse tax consequences, restricted stock must be sold to the employee at its fair market value, and stock options must be granted with an exercise price equal to fair market value. In a private company, fair market value is largely in the eye of the beholder. In venture-backed start-ups, venture capitalists always buy convertible preferred stock that has a liquidation preference over the common stock. That means that upon a liquidation (defined to include a sale) of the company, the preferred stockholders get their money back (or more) before the common stockholders get anything. In a big success story, where the stock is sold for multiples of the liquidation preference of the preferred stock, the value of the common stock equals or approaches the value of the preferred stock.

Because of the inherently greater value of preferred stock, the common stock is usually sold, or the option exercise price is set, at a price that is a discount to the price per share of the preferred stock. In the early stages of the company, this is usually 10 to 25 percent of the preferred stock price. This practice became so frequent that many directors came to believe that the formula automatically was a fair reflection of the value of the common stock. Occasionally the company's accountants would challenge the price because the pricing of options has accounting consequences. In an IPO, the SEC often challenged the price of the common stock if it was set at a significant discount to the IPO price, particularly if the price was set within a year or maybe two before the IPO.

New tax and accounting rules, including IRC Section 409A, have resulted in more attention being paid to the price of restricted stock and the exercise price of employee stock options. These developments have effectively forced boards of directors to make a much more professional analysis of fair market value. In many cases, boards are involving outside valuation experts to support the company's equity pricing. In the very earliest stages of a start-up, however, the old rules of thumb continue to be used since valuing the company at that stage is as much guesswork as anything else.

There are also more exotic forms of equity compensation, including stock appreciation rights (SARs), phantom stock, and other forms of compensation tied to equity value. SARs are issued by some public companies and represent the right to have the company cash out the difference between the original value of the stock and the current fair market value (in other words, the stock appreciation). The employee never owns the stock itself. Phantom stock is sometimes issued by private companies. It is a contractual right to be treated *as if* the employee were the holder of a specified number of shares, so that the employee would be entitled to dividends and the proceeds of sale if the company were sold. Phantom stock is issued by private companies where the existing owners of the business do not want to have any new owners with the technical rights of stockholders: voting and so on. All of these alternative forms of equity compensation do not entitle the holder to capital gains treatment; the income from gains is treated as compensation income taxed at ordinary rates.

Companies sometimes provide, particularly for senior executives, that all or a portion of the options or restricted stock will vest on an acquisition of the company. Rarely, a portion may vest on an IPO. This provision has important employee morale implications and is a potential impediment to an acquisition.

Equity rarely accelerates in connection with an IPO. The reason is the perception that acceleration would impair the marketing of the stock in the IPO. The buyers of the stock in the public offering want the founders to continue to "sweat."

With respect to accelerated vesting on an acquisition, there are competing considerations.

- From the company's and a potential acquiror's point of view, no acceleration is best because what the acquiror is paying for in a technology acquisition is, in part, the expected continuing contribution of the company's employees, particularly the technologists. The acquiror wants them to have an incentive to continue working and do not want them to get so rich via accelerated vesting as to lose the incentive to continue to work.

• The competing viewpoint is that the employee has earned something from the venture capitalists (VCs) and other stockholders by delivering an acquisition and allowing the VCs to realize value. Why should the VCs cash out with the employee being required to continue to earn his or her equity through continued vesting?

The normal solution, at least for senior management, is a compromise between no vesting and complete accelerated vesting (i.e., partial acceleration on an acquisition). A portion of the options are accelerated on an acquisition, with the balance continuing to vest, perhaps at an accelerated rate or with a shortened full vesting date, provided the employee remains employed by the acquiror. A fixed number of options can vest; a percentage of the unvested options can vest; or a specified additional vesting period can be deemed to have elapsed; there are subtle differences among these alternatives. In addition, full vesting can be provided for after a transition period—say six months or one year. Frequently in that case, the employee is also relieved from the threat of loss of unvested equity if he or she is terminated without cause; in that event, there is full vesting. Some might argue that if the employee is never offered a job with the survivor/acquiror then there should be full accelerated vesting, either on general fairness principles or because the acquiror should not care; if the employee is not wanted, then incentives are not needed to keep the person on board. The problem with this approach is that employees who are not hired are treated better than those that are hired.

TAX ASPECTS OF STOCK OPTIONS AND RESTRICTED STOCK. Historically there has been a significant disparity under the federal income tax laws between the maximum ordinary income rate and the maximum long-term capital gains rate. This disparity results in the employer and the employee attempting to structure equity-based compensation arrangements in a manner that will produce capital gains.

A stock option generally allows for the taxation of pre-exercise appreciation in the value of the underlying stock at long-term capital gain rates only if the option is an ISO and the grantee satisfies a holding period requirement with respect to the option itself and with respect to the stock after exercising the option. Not all options, however, qualify for treatment as ISOs. In addition, while the exercise of an ISO is not a taxable event for the optionee under the regular tax regime, the exercise may subject the grantee to federal alternative minimum tax (AMT) liability. In practice, the ISO qualification rules, the holding period requirement, and the potential AMT liability often serve to render the capital gains advantages of ISOs unavailable or undesirable.

Nonqualified Stock Options.   The grantee of an option that is not an ISO (a NQSO) generally recognizes ordinary compensation income upon exercising the NQSO in an amount equal to the excess of the fair market value of the stock received upon exercising the NQSO (measured as of the time of exercise) over the exercise price of the NQSO (the excess is sometimes referred to as the spread). (Where the exercise price is so low as to be a sham, this treatment does not apply.) The grantee then receives the underlying stock with a fair market value basis and a capital gains holding period beginning on the date of exercise. If the stock received upon exercising the NQSO is restricted (i.e., non-transferable and subject to a substantial risk of forfeiture; see discussion under "Restricted Stock"), however, the grantee is deemed to exercise the NQSO when or as the restriction lapses unless he or she makes a Section 83(b) election with respect to the stock (in which case the restriction is disregarded and the exercise of the NQSO is the relevant tax event). Subject to any applicable deducibility limitations, the corporation granting the NQSO has a compensation deduction that mirrors the compensation income of the grantee in both amount and timing if it properly reports the grantee's compensation income on a Form W-2 or 1099, as the case may be. The corporation must also withhold and pay employment tax with respect to the grantee's compensation income if the grantee is an employee.

NQSOs may be attractive because they are not subject to the various requirements and limitations applicable to ISOs, they may be granted to nonemployees and they entitle the granting corporation to compensation deductions. In the absence of special circumstances that would preclude ISO treatment, however, an employee generally will prefer to receive an ISO so as to avoid taxation of pre-exercise appreciation in the value of the underlying stock at ordinary income rates at the time the option is exercised. If a NQSO is required to be exercised by the terms of the option agreement within a specified period after the employee's employment terminates (usually 90 days by analogy to ISO requirements), the grantee is put in an extremely difficult position—not only does the grantee have to come up with the cash to pay the exercise price, but he or she also is taxed on the appreciation in the stock at the time of exercise.

Many people are under the misimpression that an option agreement relating to an ISO must provide that the option must be exercised within 90 days after termination of employment. This is not the case. The ISO rules require that *in order to receive ISO treatment*, an option must in fact be exercised in the 90-day period. An option agreement for an ISO can provide, without violation of the ISO rules, that the option will not expire for a specified period of time whether employment has been terminated or not. In that case, the ISO is effectively converted into a NQSO if it is not exercised within 90 days of termination of employment.

Incentive Stock Options.   An option may qualify as an ISO only if:

- It is granted pursuant to a plan that specifies the aggregate number of shares that may be issued and the employees or class of employees eligible to receive grants and is approved by the stockholders of the granting corporation within 12 months before or after the date on which the plan is adopted.
- It is granted within 10 years after the earlier of the date of the adoption of the plan or the date of the approval of the plan by the granting corporation's stockholders.
- It is not exercisable more than 10 (or, if the grantee is a 10 percent stockholder, 5) years from its grant date.
- The exercise price of the option is not less than the fair market value (or, if the grantee is a 10 percent stockholder, 110 percent of the fair market value) of the underlying stock as of the grant date.
- The option is not transferable by the grantee other than by will or the laws of descent and distribution and is exercisable during the grantee's lifetime only by the grantee.

- The grantee is an employee of the granting corporation (or of a parent or subsidiary corporation) from the date of the grant of the option until the date three months (or one year in the case of the grantee's death or disability) before the exercise of the option.

In addition, an option will not qualify as an ISO to the extent that the underlying stock with respect to which the option is exercisable for the first time during any calendar year has a value exceeding $100,000 as of the grant date. For example, if an employee is granted an option to acquire stock worth $500,000 on the grant date and the option is immediately exercisable, only 20 percent of the option ($100,000/$500,000) may qualify as an ISO. If the option vests 20 percent per year over five years, the option may qualify as an ISO in its entirety.

The exercisability of an ISO may be made subject to conditions that are "not inconsistent" with the rules just described. Accordingly, ISOs (like NQSOs) may be granted subject to vesting provisions.

With two caveats, the grantee of an ISO is not taxed upon exercising the ISO, and the grantee reports long-term capital gain upon selling the underlying stock equal to the excess of their amount realized in the sale over the exercise price of the ISO. The corporation granting the ISO reports no compensation deduction with respect to the ISO.

The first caveat is that the grantee must hold the underlying stock until at least two years after the grant of the ISO and at least one year after the exercise of the ISO. A disposition of the underlying stock before the holding period has run (referred to as a disqualifying disposition) requires the grantee to recognize ordinary compensation income for the year of the disposition equal to the lesser of the spread on the option at the time of exercise or the gain realized by the grantee on the disposition. If the grantee fails to satisfy the holding period requirement, the corporation can deduct the compensation reported by the grantee subject to any applicable deductibility limitations and the compliance by the corporation with applicable reporting rules.

The second caveat is that the AMT rules accord no special treatment to ISOs. Thus, the grantee must include the spread on the ISO at the time of exercise in computing the alternative minimum taxable income for the year of exercise. Depending on the size of the spread and the grantee's other adjustments and preferences, the AMT rules can subject the grantee to tax for the year of exercise on some portion of the spread at the time of exercise.

RESTRICTED STOCK.   As an alternative to options, corporations sometimes offer restricted stock to employees, consultants, and other service
providers. The term "restricted stock" means stock that the corporation
issues to a service provider subject to a right of the corporation to repurchase the stock at the service provider's cost (or some other amount
that is less than fair market value at the time of repurchase) if specified
service-related vesting conditions are not met. Technically, the applicable tax regulations refer to stock that is both "nontransferable" and
"subject to a substantial risk of forfeiture," as defined therein, upon
its issuance to the recipient as "substantially nonvested" stock. The
restricted stock we have been discussing is stock that is "substantially
nonvested" within the meaning of those regulations. Restricted stock
can be made subject to the same time- or performance-based vesting
conditions as might apply to options. In the case of an option, vesting
permits the grantee to exercise the option and thereby purchase the
underlying stock at a price fixed on the grant date. If the corporation
retains any right to repurchase stock purchased by the grantee by exercising a vested option, the repurchase price is typically the fair market
value of the stock at the time of the repurchase (or some formula price
intended to approximate fair market value). In the case of restricted
stock, vesting generally terminates the obligation of the recipient to sell
the stock back to the corporation upon termination of the employment
or consulting relationship at a price that is less than fair market value.
Thus, vesting in each case establishes the right of the service provider
to receive any value of the stock in excess of the price established at
the outset. The difference between restricted stock and stock options
approaches is that, under a restricted stock arrangement, the stock is
actually issued to the service provider up front subject to a right of
the corporation to repurchase unvested stock at the service provider's
cost if he or she fails to vest. Because of the additional complexity,
corporations often hesitate to make restricted stock available to a broad
pool of employees and other service providers. Also, the corporation
wants to avoid the bookkeeping and procedural complexities of keeping track of a large number of shareholders, each of whom is entitled
to participate in corporate governance.

   Occasionally, a company will want to maximise the tax planning
opportunities for the grantee of an option. The company allows the
optionee to exercise the unvested portion of the option, with the stock

received upon the exercise of that portion being unvested restricted stock.

A recipient of restricted stock generally has two choices for tax purposes. He or she may, within 30 days, make a Section 83(b) election with respect to the stock. In that case, the receipt of the stock is the relevant tax event, and the grantee is taxed at ordinary income rates on any excess of the value of the stock at the time it is received (without regard to the service-related restrictions) over the amount paid for the stock. The grantee takes a fair market value basis in the stock, and the capital gain holding period begins. The grantee then suffers no tax consequences upon vesting. Instead, the grantee reports capital gain upon the later sale of the stock equal to the amount received in the sale over the basis in the stock. If the stock is forfeited by failing to vest, however, the ability to take any loss is limited; the grantee is not entitled to recoup any income reported upon receiving the stock by taking a corresponding deduction upon forfeiture. The forfeiture rule may be even more harsh if the corporation is an S corporation and the recipient has had to report a share of the corporation's income without receiving a corresponding tax distribution. Subject to any applicable limitations and the compliance with applicable reporting rules, the corporation's compensation deductions mirror the recipient's compensation income in both amount and timing.

However, the recipient may forgo making a Section 83(b) election. In that case, the grantee is taxed at ordinary income rates when (or as) the stock vests (i.e., ceases to be "nontransferable" and "subject to a substantial risk of forfeiture") on the excess of the value of the stock at the time of vesting over the amount he or she paid for the stock. The postreceipt appreciation in the value of the stock is taxed at ordinary income rates (and at the time of vesting). The basis in the stock becomes the fair market value of the stock, and the capital gains holding period begins at the time of vesting. Again, subject to any applicable limitations and compliance with the applicable reporting rules, the corporation's compensation deductions mirror the recipient's compensation income in both amount and timing.

In practice, Section 83(b) elections are *always* made with respect to stock received in a technology or other emerging growth company. In practice, the board of directors purports to grant the restricted stock at fair market value, and the grantee purports to buy it at fair market value. The grantee fills out the Section 83(b) election form to show that the purchase price and the fair market value are the same. Voilá—no tax. Because the actual fair market value of a start-up technology company is almost impossible to determine fairly, it is extremely unlikely that price set by the board and used by the grantee will be challenged as not being fair market value. The recipient must file the Section 83(b) election with the IRS within 30 days after receipt of the stock. The grantee must also provide the corporation (and others in certain instances) with a copy of the election and attach another copy to the grantee's tax return for the year of receipt of the stock.

If the Section 83(b) election is not made, the grantee must pay tax equal to the fair market value spread of the stock on each vesting date over the purchase price. This creates an impossible situation for the grantee; the spread may be significant, and the grantee is unable to sell the stock to pay for the tax because of legal and practical restrictions on transfer of the stock of a private company.

The use of restricted stock raises a number of practical issues, including:

- Typically, the recipient must pay for the stock upon receiving it. If the recipient borrows the purchase price from the corporation, the IRS may attempt to treat the recipient as having only a NQSO if the recipient is not personally liable for a substantial portion of the debt. Arrangements that obligate the corporation to repurchase the stock can undermine the tax objectives sought in using restricted stock. In addition, under SEC rules under the Sarbanes-Oxley Act, loans from the corporation to officers must be repaid before the *filing* of the IPO registration statement, even though the IPO may never get to a closing.
- Often restricted stock is issued to a service provider solely to accommodate the service provider's tax objectives. If not for the tax laws, the corporation would have granted options to the service provider to condition his or her right to hold shares on the satisfaction of vesting requirements. For state law purposes, however, the recipient is a shareholder despite the fact that he or she might not yet have fully earned the shares. Issues may arise as to the extent to which the recipient is to be accorded rights of a shareholder under a shareholders' agreement.

- If the recipient does not make a Section 83(b) election, the recipient is not deemed to own the stock for tax purposes until vesting. Any distributions made to the recipient with respect to the stock before vesting are treated as compensation payments and not a dividend. If the corporation is an S corporation, the recipient does not report any of the corporation's undistributed income, even though he or she might be entitled to receive a share of the income if later distributed. It is not unusual, therefore, for S corporations to require recipients of restricted stock to make Section 83(b) elections.

EMPLOYMENT AGREEMENTS

Employment agreements, at least long, fancy, real ones, are relatively rare in start-up technology companies. Almost all employees, other than senior employees, are usually given a simple offer letter that describes their compensation and other employment basics. These offer letters always provide (or should provide) that the prospective employee will be an employee "at-will" (i.e., that the employee may be fired at any time with or without cause). In addition, all employees and consultants (and anyone who may come into contact with any of the company's trade secrets) also must be required to sign a confidentiality/invention assignment/noncompetition agreement. A sample "real" employment agreement and an employee confidentiality/inventions/ noncompetition agreement are included in the appendices to this chapter.

Most provisions of employment agreements are relatively non-controversial. The agreement specifies a salary and benefits, and may specify a formula for a bonus. If not already the subject of a separate agreement, the agreement will also contain relatively customary confidentiality, assignment of inventions, and noncompetition agreements.

There are, however, several critical areas of negotiation. The most important point to remember with respect to employment agreements is that they should never guarantee the employee the right to remain as an employee or in a specified position for a fixed or minimum period of time. Guaranteeing employment or a specified position is highly imprudent from the company's point of view. If the board decides that the employee must be fired, then the company must be able to do so for the well-being of the company. The company always needs to be protected from incompetent or nonperforming employees. There really is not (or should not be) such a thing as a "two-year employment contract."

What is properly understood by a two-year employment contract is that if an employee is fired, then he or she has to leave immediately, but the employee is entitled to some amount of severance. When and under what circumstances severance is paid is a critical element of negotiation. What many people mean by a "two-year employment contract," for example, is that if the employee is fired within the first two years of employment, he or she continues to receive a salary for the remainder of the term, in a lump sum or paid in the usual increments, even though no longer employed by the company—or he or she is entitled to receive the greater of a specified lump sum (or a specified number of months' installments). The employee's viewpoint is that he or she is entitled to the greater of the lump sum or specified installments, or the balance of the two years' salary. This is the key negotiating point.

The other key negotiating points are whether there is a difference in the employee's treatment if the employee is fired with cause, fired without cause, quits for good reason, or quits without good reason. Generally speaking, the employee is entitled to nothing other than accrued salary if fired with cause or if he or she quits without good reason. The employee typically gets severance only if fired without cause or if he or she quits for good reason. Thus the definitions of "cause" and "good reason" become critical in the employment agreement.

Astute lawyers for employees will ensure that the definition of "cause" does not include failure to perform according to expectations as long as the employee is making a reasonable effort. Such lawyers take care to limit the definition of "cause" to egregious acts where the malfeasance is clear and is not the subject of reasonable differing interpretations. Here are six increasingly onerous (to the employee) definitions of "cause." The real dividing line is between 5 and 6; the ones before the dividing line are within the reasonable control of the employee, but the one after the line may well not be. This is a huge distinction.

Examples of Cause Definitions

1. The employee's indictment for or the pleading of the employee of nolo contendere to a felony.

2. The commission by the employee of an act of fraud, embezzlement, or any other illegal conduct in connection with the employee's performance of his or her duties.

3. Disregard of the material rules or material policies of the company that has not been cured within 15 days after notice thereof from the company.

4. Gross negligence in the performance of the employee's duties, willful misfeasance in connection with the employee's work, or a breach of fiduciary duty by the employee.

5. Willful failure to perform the employee's employment duties, or willful failure to follow instructions of the board of directors, if such failure is in any way significant, but only if such failure does not result from an ambiguity in such duties or instructions; provided, however, that such duties or instructions are specific in nature and not in the nature of performance goals or objectives.

6. Unsatisfactory performance by the employee as determined in the sole discretion of the company's board of directors [or failure to meet performance goals and the like].

Another issue is whether the employment agreement will contain provisions dealing with the situation where the employee quits for good reason. The argument for the employee is that, to take an extreme example, if the employee's salary is reduced to minimum wage, then the employee is forced to quit, which is not substantively different from being fired without cause. This is tough to argue against. The only issue is how broadly "good reason" is defined. Here is a sample of a definition of "good reason":

"Good Reason" shall mean any of the following: (i) a material diminution in the Employee's responsibilities, duties or authority to which the Employee has not consented and which remains unremedied for thirty (30) days after written notice from the Employee [*Question:* What does this phrase mean if the company is acquired by a substantially larger company—does the employee have the right to be an executive officer of the acquiror?]; (ii) the relocation of the Employee by the Company outside the Company's main office without the Employee's written consent [or a change in the location of the Employee's office by more than a specified number of miles]; or (iii) a material decrease in the Employee's compensation or aggregate benefits without the Employee's written consent (sometimes with an exception for across-the-board reductions among all senior executives).

It is generally accepted that, from the viewpoint of the employer, generally the shorter and simpler the agreement, the better. Generally, other than confidentiality, invention assignment, and noncompetition provisions, what is in an employment agreement is viewed as being for the employee's benefit.

From the viewpoint of the employee, in addition to the critical issues just discussed, there are a myriad of negotiating points for the employee and his or her lawyer to consider. A list of issues for prospective employees to consider in negotiating an employment arrangement with a new employer follows.

Term

- A stated term is not necessary. The key issue to consider is the amount of severance, when it is paid (up front or periodically), and how the circumstances of termination affect or do not affect the severance provisions.

Compensation

- Bonus opportunity—clear definitions of metrics and ability to earn pro rata assuming no for cause termination.
- Benefit arrangements.
- Vacation, expenses, and so on—state initial agreement relating to these items.
- State that the executive is entitled to participate in all benefit programs for which other executives of the same level are eligible.

Position/Responsibilities

- Scope.
- Clear definition of duty of loyalty (i.e., devote full time/best efforts/noncompetition, etc.), which defines what activities can be pursued without violating the duty (e.g., service on other boards, nonprofits, private investing, etc.).
- Location of office or duties that tie in to executive's voluntary termination for "good reason" if the location of office or duties is materially changed.
- Board seat or not.

- Reporting structure (i.e., to whom will executive report)/tie into a voluntary termination for "good reason" (which may include demotion).

Termination

- For cause definition:
  - Narrow and clearly defined.
  - Eliminate any provisions that are performance standards or disguised performance standards.
  - Notice and opportunity to cure as to the others.
  - Materiality qualifications.
  - Willfulness/knowing qualifications as to misconduct provisions.
  - Opportunity to be heard for any termination decision.
- Death/disability.
- Voluntary termination by executive for "good reason."
  - If the contract makes any distinction as to consequences of a cause/no-cause termination, then a good reason provision is usually regarded as a corollary.
  - *Components of good reason*. Diminution of title or duties; diminution of salary or benefits; relocation, change of control or sale of the company.

Severance Arrangements

- Triggers/entitlement/amounts:
  - Payable if voluntary termination for good reason. What if the employee quits without good reason?
  - Is severance payable for balance of a stated term or x months, if greater?
  - Is the severance payable up front as lump sum?
  - Does periodic severance cease or become reduced if other employment is obtained during the severance period?
  - Upon death or disability?
  - Does severance include provision of health benefits during severance period or payment of COBRA (Consolidated Omnibus Budget Reconciliation Act) premiums?
  - Will employer include payment for outplacement services of employee's choice?

○   Will arrangements be made for use of offices/technology voicemail upon termination?

○   Will employer agree to reasonable reference arrangements?

Equity Compensation

- Stock/restricted stock. Restricted stock is much better for the employee as a tax matter but does involve economic risk. If restricted stock is purchased and requires a substantial outlay of cash, consider using a note for all or part of the purchase price, and also maximize the nonrecourse portion of note. Is buyout at termination automatic or at option of the company? (Should be automatic if a real-money purchase price.)

- Options (ISO/NQSO)—both ISOs and NQSOs should provide for a fixed term to exercise and not terminate within a specific period after termination. As discussed, this is not an ISO requirement. This provision is particularly important for NQSOs because exercise is a taxable event.

- Vesting schedule—how much up front; vesting period and timing of balance; is there accelerated vesting if termination without cause?

- Acceleration upon change of control—if not full acceleration, try to obtain a specified amount of vesting on a change in control and a so-called double trigger clause which means that if executive is not offered employment, or if executive remains for a transition period, or if executive terminated without cause during the transition period, then full acceleration.

- Antidilution—examine (good luck) possibility of protection against dilution from extraordinary preferred stock terms and/or down round financings—so-called make-whole provisions. For example, the executive is entitled to a bonus equal to a fixed percentage share of the proceeds from the sale of the company, or a share calculated without regard to the liquidation preference of the preferred stock on an as-converted basis. Good luck with that one.

Restrictive Covenants

- Noncompete/nonsolicit/antipiracy:

  ○   Preferable to define precisely a competing business rather than just say that the employee will not compete with the business of the employer.

- ○ Does covenant terminate on substantial cessation of business?
- ○ Is period shorter (or nonexistent) if terminated without cause?
- ○ Make sure the definition of competing business does not generically include the business of a successor.
- ○ Can the employee go to work for a large company that competes but may not work in the competitive division?
- • Invention assignments
  - ○ Avoid invention assignments that cover posttermination inventions.

280G

- • Does the employee get protection from IRC Section 280G taxes? (This section is a tax code provision that imposes severe penalties for exces parachute payments.) Consider up-front shareholder approval of parachute provisions if a private company, or a tax "gross up" for parachute taxes.

Attorneys' Fees

- • Reimbursed by employer?

Merger Clauses

- • Ensure that employer is obligated to require assumption, in writing, of employment agreement in the event of a sale of the company.

Indemnification

- • Consider obtaining provisions requiring employer to indemnify the executive under the company's existing bylaws and provide that the executive is entitled to the fullest indemnification permitted by law if the bylaws are inadequate or are amended. Consider a requirement for insurance coverage under Directors and Officers (D&O) or other insurance policies.

APPENDICES

These appendices are located on the Web site that accompanies this book. For information on the Web site, see the "About the Web Site" section.

Appendix 1A: Start-Up Suite of Incorporation Documents:

Certificate of Incorporation (Delaware)
Bylaws (Delaware) corporation
Action of Sole Incorporator (Delaware)
Initial Written Consent of the Board of Directors (Delaware)
Shareholders' Agreement
Employee Confidentiality, Inventions, and Noncompetition Agreement
IRS Section 83(b) Election

Appendix 1B: Stock Option and Incentive Plan
Appendix 1 C: Stock Option Agreement (Companion to Stock Option and Incentive Plan)
Appendix 1D: Employment Agreement

CHAPTER 2

FINANCING THE VENTURE

In this chapter we explore the business and legal issues that commonly arise in connection with the first financing of a technology company by "angel" or venture capital investors. These financings are almost universally equity financings. These investors, however, often do interim bridge debt financings. Debt financings are also fundamental to companies that are acquired in a leveraged buyout (LBO). The chapter also discusses the fundamentals of debt financings and provides an introduction to the structure and operation of venture capital and buyout funds.

VENTURE CAPITAL FINANCINGS

The venture capital financing of a new technology company is a significant step in its corporate life. To put it simply, "It isn't just your company anymore."

There are, of course, a number of positives to venture capital financings. A very high proportion of successful technology companies achieved their success in no small part because of the availability of venture capital, which is, in the most commonly accepted definition, capital available for investment in early-stage ventures, which are, for that very reason, high-risk investments. While the consequences of the investment excesses of the late 1990s may have temporarily cast venture capitalists (VCs) in a less attractive light, venture capital funds, and the tax and legal infrastructures that have fostered their growth, have been a key engine for the growth in the economy of the United States over the last 30 years.

Not only do VCs provide necessary funding, but they often help their portfolio companies in a number of other ways. VCs typically have extensive experience with early-stage companies. Many have been successful entrepreneurs themselves. They contribute this expertise to the founding team and can provide access to a network of management talent, engineers, and service providers. They are attuned to the current market parameters for equipment lease and working capital debt financings, the local real estate market, and vendor relationships.

VCs are active, not passive, investors. In exchange for their funding and other support, VCs become actively involved in the management of the business. As discussed in detail later, the investors typically take one or more seats on the portfolio company's board of directors and impose a variety of affirmative and negative covenants on the company.

The real leverage that VCs exert over their portfolio companies, however, derives not from the legal documentation but from the company's need for their ongoing financing support, which as a practical matter must come at least in part from the existing VCs. If the company has fulfilled the VCs' performance expectations, then the need for additional financing is usually not problematic; the VCs will provide another round of financing themselves and help the company recruit new investors. If, however, the company has not lived up to the performance promises represented by its business plan, the VCs often deal with the company severely; they may provide additional funding, but at a price that results in significant dilution to the existing stockholders—a so-called down- round financing. Furthermore, there is no practical alternative for the company in this situation; outside VCs rarely, if ever, invest in companies where the existing VCs are not continuing to support the company. In difficult economic times, down-round financings may occur even though the company has met expectations because of general market or business cycle disruptions.

How can the emerging technology company protect itself from this scenario? The answer is at best imperfect, but the basic answer is to be sure to raise enough funding in the first round of VC financing to give the company a reasonable chance of achieving demonstrable progress in its business plan. The competing consideration is that companies should not raise more money than is needed in any round of financing because, if the company is performing well, the dilution to the founders is likely to decrease in successive financings at successively higher prices per share. But the bigger mistake is to not raise enough money. The potential consequences of that mistake are much more severe.

With respect to the terms of the initial financing itself, companies should attempt to solicit interest from a number of VCs in order to test the general availability of capital and the terms being offered. They should also be extremely protective of their existing cash resources. All leverage is lost if the company becomes desperate for funds. Conversely, there is no better leverage than to subtly let prospective investors know that they are not the only ones interested in investing in the company. However, this cat-and-mouse game can be played too vigorously with prospective investors. An alternative is for the company to obtain seed financing from so-called angel investors. These are wealthy individual investors, frequently successful entrepreneurs themselves (sometimes semiretired or between active positions), who invest in early-stage companies. There are also established networks of this category of investor. Terms from angels typically are more favorable to the company than the terms offered by VCs, and some angel investors intend to become actively involved in their portfolio companies, sometimes even at the operations level. VCs, however, add the imprimatur of their endorsement of the company and its technology in dealings with strategic investors, corporate partners, and service providers, and typically put more effort into shepherding their investments, but at the level of the board of directors. Participation in subsequent financing rounds by angels who invest in an early round should not be presumed. The larger capital needs addressed by follow-on rounds often are beyond the means of many angel investors; established VC firms have much deeper pockets and generally reserve funds for their portfolio companies' subsequent rounds.

APPROACHING PROSPECTIVE VC INVESTORS.   Before even considering the first approach to a VC, the founders need to have prepared a good business plan that addresses all of the important issues that will be of concern to a prospective VC investor.

It is beyond the scope of this chapter to explore the attributes of business plans that attract funding, but for entrepreneurs who have not done it before, good sources of advice on business plans include experienced legal counsel and accounting firms and a variety of consultants who specialize in the development of business plans and strategic planning. Many VCs will say, though, that it is often a mistake for a business to hire an outsider to write its business plan (as opposed to consulting on, refining and improving the company's efforts), because a business plan needs to be in the voice of the entrepreneur to adequately convey the message about the business opportunity and the market context in which the company must succeed.

While the entrepreneur should always develop a full business plan, the initial document sent to a VC will generally be a much shorter executive summary. The executive summary should be as brief as possible, but must summarize all important information from the full business plan in order to provide prospective investors with enough information to make an initial evaluation.

The first step in planning the approach to VCs is to identify appropriate potential investors. To do so, the entrepreneur needs to screen the now quite large universe of VCs for these factors:

- The firm's reputation and track record, including the experiences of other successful (and unsuccessful) entrepreneurs.
- Local offices, although there may be other factors with enough strength to justify looking at firms in other regions.
- An investing focus in the company's types of business.
- An investing focus in portfolio companies at the company's stage of development.
- An interest in deal sizes consistent with the company's capital needs.
- Ability to support the company in later financing rounds.

Although not a screening factor, the entrepreneur should also know whether the VC prefers to be, or insists on being, the lead investor or will allow another investor to lead.

The outcome of the screening will be a preliminary list of potential investors. This list should then be vetted by the company, its counsel, and its other advisors to determine the preferred firms for the initial approach. This determination is based on the screening factors as well as the likelihood of success at getting a meeting. The preliminary list should be pared down to between 5 and 10 VCs to be targeted initially. If any of the founders or the company's professional advisors have contacts with the firm, those contacts should be identified.

When the summary business plan has been completed, the most effective way to get a meeting with a VC is by an introduction (accompanied by delivery of the summary business plan) by someone known to and respected by him or her, particularly including successful entrepreneurs funded by the VC in the past and lawyers, bankers, accountants, or other professionals who have been a source of attractive opportunities previously. Once an expression of interest has been elicited, a meeting follows, typically with a single partner of the VC firm. If the partner's key concerns are addressed satisfactorily in that meeting, a meeting with the firm's other partners will follow.

The objective in these meetings is not to close the sale of the company's securities but to continue to help the potential investors understand the attractiveness of the opportunity and overcome their concerns. This tension between attraction and concern will always be present in discussions with prospective investors, and the entrepreneur's most important job is to continue patiently to answer the VCs' questions, which are designed to uncover reasons not to invest and to go on to the next opportunity.

At some point in this process, the VCs will conduct background due diligence on the founders and their technology. The due diligence investigation often includes reference checks on the founders, discussions with industry sources, and the assistance of outside technical experts in the industry.

Also at some point in this process, the VCs may begin to act and sound more like partners and consultants than inquisitors. This shift in tone can be a signal that an inclination to invest is strengthening.

TERM SHEET. Once a VC firm has made a preliminary decision to invest, the company will be presented with a term sheet that sets forth the terms of the investment deal being offered to the company and other matters involving the relationship between the company and the VC investors.

Term sheets are generally nonbinding, but sometimes they contain two provisions that are expressly made legally binding. Often there will be a requirement that the company not negotiate with other prospective investors for a period intended to afford a reasonable window of time to either complete the deal or conclude that it should be abandoned. In rare cases, VCs will also require that the company pay their expenses if the deal does not close. This provision usually can be resisted successfully.

Term sheets as well as the definitive agreements have become relatively standardized documents.[1] They use terms that are well understood in the venture capital community but are rarely understood by first-time entrepreneurs. For first-time entrepreneurs, unless company counsel have thought to offer a miniseminar in advance, the arrival of the initial proposed term sheet often necessitates a crash course in Venture Capital 101. Although most of the legal and business terms contained in the term sheet are standard, a number of key points are both important and negotiable. Bear in mind that there are no moral imperatives here; the economic terms of these investments are not inherently good or evil, or fair or unfair. It is a free market, and entrepreneurs are free to accept the terms offered by a prospective investor or reject them. Companies need to first identify from their legal advisors what terms may be negotiable and focus their energy on what is possible. The decision to take one VC proposal over another should be based on the valuation offered, the detailed technical terms, the likelihood of the particular investor being helpful to the company in nonmonetary ways, and personal fit (not necessarily in this order).

In general, the term sheet typically addresses these issues:

- The pre-money valuation proposed for the company, the amount the VC proposes to invest, and the percentage of the company they expect for their investment.
- The type of security that will be purchased by the VC (virtually always convertible preferred stock in investments by institutional venture capital firms, sometimes convertible notes in seed-stage investments by angels) and the terms of the security.
- Whether and to what extent vesting will be imposed on the founders' shares.
- The investors' rights to have their securities registered for public sale by the company.
- Whether the investors will have a right of first refusal for subsequent securities offerings by the company.
- Rules regarding the composition of the company's board of directors.

---

1.   In recent years, annotated documents published by the National Venture Capital Association (NVCA) have gained widespread acceptance. They are freely available at *www.nvca.org*. Beware, however, of the fox guarding the chicken coop.

- The proportion of the company's stock that must be allocated for employees (typically by means of an employee equity incentive plan providing for the award of stock options or the issuance of restricted stock).
- Any conditions that must be satisfied before funding will occur, including the somewhat gratuitous observation that the VC's counsel will conduct a due diligence investigation.
- The additional agreements that the VCs will expect to be entered into by the company and the founders.

The basic business and legal terms contained in term sheets are discussed in detail in the sections that follow, which also provide some guidance as to the normal give and take on terms and likely outcomes.

LEGAL DUE DILIGENCE AND CORPORATE CLEANUP.   Once the investors have done their preliminary due diligence and a term sheet has been agreed on, the lead investor will designate a law firm to serve as investors' counsel. The investors' counsel will usually draft the legal documentation for the transaction and perform legal due diligence, that is, investigate the company to determine whether it is on sound legal footing and has no identifiable legal risks.

The most important areas of legal concern for technology company investments include:

- Whether the company has full rights to the intellectual property that will be used in its contemplated business, including whether the founders have properly assigned any rights they may have to the company, whether all employees and consultants who have contributed to the company's technology have signed acceptable confidentiality and invention assignment agreements, and whether there have been any claims that its products infringe the intellectual property of others or any knowledge of infringement of its intellectual property by others.
- Whether the founders and key employees are legally free to work for the company and assign to the company their inventions related to the company's business. A related issue is whether there are any potential violations of prior agreements with past employers, such as noncompetition and nonsolicitation agreements and confidentiality or invention assignment agreements.

- Whether the company's corporate records are in good order. Critical issues here are whether the company has been duly organized, its outstanding equity securities have been validly issued, and all obligations to issue equity have been disclosed to the investors.
- Whether there is any litigation, actual or threatened, with respect to the company's products or operations.
- Whether the company is in breach of any material license or other agreement with vendors, customers, or creditors.

This process is frequently initiated by investors' counsel furnishing to the company and its counsel a legal due diligence request list outlining various legal and business documents that investors' counsel needs to review. However, a start-up technology company that is represented by counsel who are knowledgeable about the VC investment process can often manage its affairs in a manner that will facilitate the investors' legal due diligence. Appendix 2B presents a typical legal due diligence request list.

INITIAL VENTURE FINANCING: BASIC TERMS.   The security purchased by investors in virtually all venture capital financings is convertible preferred stock. The terms of this type of stock are discussed in detail later, but the essential elements of convertible preferred stock are:

- **Liquidation preference.** The investors have priority over the common stockholders upon a liquidation of the company, which is typically defined to include an acquisition of the company.
- **Redemption right.** At a certain point in time, if the company has not otherwise achieved liquidity for its investors by an initial public offering or sale, the investors may require the company to repurchase their shares.
- **Convertibility.** At the option of the investor, the convertible preferred stock will be converted into common stock at a ratio that is initially set at one common share for each preferred share, but which is subject to adjustment upon certain dilutive events, including a sale of stock at a price below that paid by the initial investors.
- **Voting rights on an as-converted basis.** The convertible preferred stock votes together with the common on must matters, but has a separate vote on selected matters.

Appendix 2A presents a sample annotated term sheet for a convertible preferred stock financing.

VALUATION: PRE-MONEY VALUATION AND THE EMPLOYEE POOL. The most important deal term in a venture capital investment is the valuation that investors put on the company, frequently referred to as the pre-money valuation. Essentially, this is the value that the investors place on the company before the financing. The value of the company will be higher immediately after the financing because it will have additional cash; this value is referred to as the post-money valuation.

One could logically assume that the price per share paid by the investors would be equal to this value per outstanding share. (If the value of the total enterprise is $x and there are y shares outstanding, then the value per share of the company would be $x divided by y shares.) Unfortunately, it is not that simple, and one important surprise for the uninitiated is the method by which the venture community calculates the value or price per share of the start-up company. The universal practice is for the total value of the company to be divided not by the currently outstanding shares but by the fully diluted number of shares outstanding, shares subject to issued stock options, and shares reserved for an employee stock option pool plus any increase to the size of this pool required by the VCs' term sheet.

This method, which has no foundation in the principles of corporate finance or accounting, includes in fully diluted shares outstanding not only stock options and warrants that have actually been issued (as is the case for accounting purposes), but also shares or options that are expected to be issued to future employees of the company in order to fill out its executive, administrative, and technical teams—the so-called employee pool. The employee pool is typically 15 to 20 percent (but can occasionally be even as high as 30 percent) of the post-money capitalization of the company. In this way, the dilution caused by the issuance of all of the shares reserved for the employee pool is borne by the founders and not by the VC investors.

As a simple example, assume that there are 1 million shares of common stock outstanding and held by the founders, no options have been granted to employees, the pre-money valuation of the company is $5 million, and the VCs' plan to invest $1 million. Exhibit 2.1 shows the results with and without an employee pool.

Deal Pricing Based on Outstanding Shares	Fully Diluted Deal Pricing With Employee Pool
$5 million divided by 1 million pre-deal shares equals $5 per share.	$5 million divided by 1.3 million pre-deal shares (1 million founders and 300,000 pool) equals $3.85 per share.
VCs' $1M buys 200,000 shares at $5/share.	VCs' $1 million buys 260,000 shares at $3.85/share.
Post-deal capitalization (stockholder/% of outstanding stock and number of shares) is:	Post-deal capitalization is:

Stockholder	%	No. Shares	Stockholder	%	No. Shares
Founders	83	1,000,000	Founders	79	1,000,000
Investors	17	200,000	Investors	21	260,000
	100	1,200,000		100	1,260,000

EXHIBIT 2.1   COMPARISON OF VC PERCENTAGE OWNERSHIP OF OUTSTANDING SHARES WITH AND WITHOUT EMPLOYEE POOL

A common instinct of founders is to be generous to the employees and make the pool as large as possible. Oddly, this may be against the founders' interests. At least in theory, it is in the interest of the stockholders that the board of directors grant stock options to employees as an incentive to attract and retain the best possible talent—but not one option more than is necessary. It is in everyone's interest—VCs and founders alike—to do so, and it is therefore likely, regardless of the pricing methodology of the deal, that the VCs will grant any waivers necessary to attract this talent. Thus, starting out with a smaller pool will result in less dilution to the founders, since post-deal expansions of the option pool will dilute the founders and the VCs proportionately.

Logical or not, the employee pool is a fixture of the venture financing. The actual size of the pool can depend on a number of things, including the industry that the company is in, but is related primarily to the number and types of hires that the company will need to make in the foreseeable future. Thus, a company that has a complete management team at the time of the initial convertible preferred round usually will have a smaller pool than a company that still needs to make one or more top management hires (each of whom may cost the company a significant amount of options or stock from the pool, depending on the current market for such talent).

In analyzing the best economic deal for the founders, the price per share (a function of valuation and the fully diluted capitalization) is the most critical issue. It will dictate the percentage of the company that the VCs acquire for a given amount of investment.

BOARD COMPOSITION POST-DEAL.   One of the critical negotiating points in a VC financing is the structure of the board of directors and the related issue of control of the company after the deal is concluded. This is often a very sensitive issue for all parties. Majority control of the board of directors effectively constitutes control of the company. The company and its officers legally must follow the board's direction, including the hiring and firing of personnel (founders included). This is, in part, what we meant at the outset in saying that "It isn't just your company anymore." Under certain circumstances, founders can and sometimes do find themselves fired by their "own" company.

Founders often are inclined to try to maintain majority control of the board, a situation that VCs tend to see as a red flag. The founders' typical position is that it is their company; they do not want outside investors to control it. The VC response (at least where they are purchasing a significant share of the company (e.g., 30 to 50 percent) is that they are unwilling to invest in a company that is controlled by the founders. In the large majority of cases, neither the founders nor the VCs wind up with a board majority. The solution is typically a compromise; the investors are entitled to nominate an equal number of directors with the founders, and those directors will jointly select one or more independent directors, ideally with relevant industry or entrepreneurial experience. In this manner, control is shared through a rough balance of power on the board. The founders are still at risk of being put out of their own company, but the independent board members will need to be convinced that such an action is in the best interest of the company. There is strong logic to the argument that, if they can be so convinced, it is a fair result for all of the stakeholders in the company. (The only consistent exception to this scenario is the relatively rare case in which the VCs are purchasing a small minority share of the company, for example, 10 to 15 percent; here they will normally be willing to accept one board seat out of three or five.)

Because the founders will be working extremely closely with the board members nominated by their venture backers, the founders should attempt to get an informal commitment from the VCs as to the identity of their board nominees. Typically, this is the senior venture investor who negotiated the deal, but that is not always the case. Junior staff sometimes are assigned to the board, particularly in busy times. The founders want to be sure that they are getting what they bargained for: the wisdom, experience, and assistance of a senior venture investors, not the know-it-all just out of business school. Most important, founders should not simply assume that the sponsor of the company at the VC fund will end up being the fund's designee on the board.

Under the corporate laws of Delaware and most other states, a majority-in-interest of the stockholders can elect the board of directors. Given the artificially arranged balance of board seats just described, this would not be a desirable outcome. The mechanism that is used to override these default provisions of the law is a voting agreement, in which the allocation of board seats is specified and all parties to the agreement (who must comprise, and continue to comprise, the holders of a majority of the voting stock) agree to vote their shares and take any other actions necessary to elect the nominees of the respective groups (i.e., both the founders and the investors). The same scheme applies to removals of directors and the filling of vacancies.

There is little to be negotiated in a voting agreement once the board composition is agreed on. However, care must be taken to ensure that the agreement expires on an initial public offering or an acquisition of the company.

An alternative technique that is sometimes employed to effect the desired board split is to amend the company's certificate of incorporation (while it is being amended to create the convertible preferred stock that is being issued in the deal) to specify that the preferred stockholders are entitled as a class to appoint the agreed-on number of directors. Some consider this approach legally necessary, but it has undesirable consequences. Voting agreements are enforceable, and the investment documents for the deal will always specify that the nominees of the VC investors will be elected to the board effective at the closing. Writing such provisions into the charter only makes the arrangement unduly rigid and inconvenient to change. The voting agreement/condition to closing approach is legally and practically sufficient to ensure the proper board split.

FOUNDER AND EMPLOYEE EQUITY COMPENSATION AND VESTING.   Another extremely important negotiable term in venture deals is whether, at what rate, and under what circumstances the common stock or stock options already issued to the founders will be subject to so-called vesting. It should be assumed that any stock or options held by employees, including founders, will be subject to a vesting schedule following the VC investment, whether the founders have imposed a vesting schedule on themselves or not.

All or a portion of the employees' shares will be subject to purchase (or "forfeiture") at original cost by the company upon termination of employment. "Vesting" is a shorthand term referring to the process by which the ownership interest of an employee stockholder or option holder in the stock or options gradually ceases to be subject to forfeiture over the course of his or her employment with the company. It is a generally accepted notion that, upon an employee's termination of employment, the company will have the right to buy back a percentage of the employee's shares at the price paid for them, or in the case of options, that the employee's right to exercise a percentage of the options will lapse. The percentage of shares that can be repurchased at cost or of options that lapse decreases over the employee's tenure with the company.

In a properly organized startup company, the founders will impose vesting on themselves. Even if they do not do so, vesting provisions are almost universally imposed on founders as part of an initial VC financing. This is the origin of the term "sweat equity." The rationale for vesting is that the founders must earn out their shares by their continued contributions to the company. If a founder's contributions cease, it is thought only fair that some portion of that founder's equity be forfeited and made available to the successor who must be hired to perform the terminated founder's function at the company. Implicit in this view is the assumption that the founders did not pay true fair value for their shares but effectively were allowed to buy cheap stock (typically at par or nominal value) because they will not be paid market-rate cash compensation for their services. (Where founders invest their own funds in a venture round, they are treated identically to the other investors with respect to the stock so purchased.)

As a side note, it is almost always advisable for the founders to impose vesting restrictions on themselves when they initially organize the company, and experienced counsel will advise them to do so. If the founders have already put in place a vesting scheme that is reasonable and within the normal range for the industry, the VCs may leave this scheme in place and not impose their own. The other reason to do so is that it is fair and makes business sense: The founders receive their founders' stock not only for their role in conceiving the ideas and business plan for the company, but, as stated, for their expected continuing efforts on the company's behalf. They view each other as making a commitment to continue their contributions during some period that is thought to be reasonably necessary to ensure the company's success. To illustrate the point another way, if each of three equal founders receives an equal number of shares upon the organization of the company, few would regard it as fair if one founder quits the next day and keeps all of his or her shares.

Whether there will be vesting is rarely negotiable. The precise terms and conditions of vesting are negotiable. Those terms and conditions are typically set forth in the proposed term sheet from the VCs and will be documented in an agreement between the founders and the company called a stock restriction agreement.

Conceptually, vesting provisions should be tied to the expected performance of the founder over a period of three or four years after the organization of the company. Looking at it this way, the founders should attempt to agree among themselves what these contributions are expected to be over the specified period of time. In the usual case, the founders will make a certain contribution to the company at the outset—it is their novel ideas that form the basis of the company. If the founders, for example, agree that these ideas fairly represent 20 percent of the anticipated aggregate contribution, then the founders should be 20 percent vested from the outset, or up front. The vesting would continue over the remaining period of their expected contribution. Where the founders have made significant progress in developing products or intellectual property or in achieving sales, a common range of vesting provisions would be 20 to 30 percent up front, with the balance vesting over three or four years. (The founders typically choose three years, and the VCs normally look for four-year vesting.) If all the founders have accomplished is writing the business plan, there may be no up-front vesting.

Vesting increments can occur annually, quarterly, monthly, or even daily. Generally, a relatively frequent vesting interval is considered preferable, both for the company and for the employee. From the company's perspective, it is undesirable to have an employee who has decided to leave hanging around for the next tranche of his or her vesting, and employees tend to assume the worst motives when a termination occurs shortly before a vesting date. Annual vesting periods magnify both concerns, while the amount at stake in a monthly vesting scheme is less significant and therefore less likely to control termination decisions. (A few companies even opt for daily vesting on the theory that they do not want employees treading water even for one day.) Perhaps the most common scheme for new hires is to have the first vesting installment occur after one year of continuous employment at the company, with the balance vesting monthly or quarterly over two or three additional years. This permits the company to evaluate and, if necessary, terminate new employees during the first year of employment, before they become entitled to any equity. Founders, however, should seek monthly or quarterly vesting from the beginning.

The percentage of up-front vesting and the vesting period are not the only issues that must be dealt with. Founders may be successful in negotiating for a partial or full acceleration of vesting upon an acquisition of the company (or, rarely, upon an initial public offering [IPO]). This provision has important employee morale implications and is a potential impediment to an acquisition. There are again competing considerations regarding acceleration clauses. With respect to acquisitions, from the point of view of the company and a potential acquiror, no acceleration is best because what the acquiror is paying for in a technology acquisition is, in part, the expected continuing contribution of the company's employees, particularly the technical employees. The acquiror wants them to have an incentive to continue working and does not want them to get so rich as to lose the incentive to continue to work. The competing viewpoint is that the employees have earned something for the VCs and other stockholders by delivering an acquisition and allowing the VCs to realize value. They question is why should the VCs be able to cash out while the employees are required to continue to earn out their equity. In any event, some amount of acceleration probably is representative of the market, at least for senior management and perhaps even deeper into larger businesses.

The most common solution, at least for senior management and other key personnel, is a compromise between no acceleration and full acceleration of vesting—that is, partial acceleration upon an acquisition. Some percentage of unvested equity is accelerated on an acquisition, with the balance continuing to vest, perhaps at an accelerated rate or with a shortened full vesting date, provided the employee remains employed by the acquiror. A fixed number of options can vest; a percentage of the unvested options can vest; or a specified additional vesting period can be deemed to have elapsed. There are subtle differences among these alternatives. If the first or the second approach is used, a reduced vesting rate would be specified for the balance so as to continue the existing vesting schedule. If a deemed time lapse is used, the agreement should expressly provide for clarity that all remaining vesting dates are similarly accelerated.

Frequently, the employee is also relieved from the threat of loss of unvested equity if terminated without cause following an acquisition; In that event there is full vesting. Some argue that if the employee is never offered a job with the survivor/acquiror, then there should be full acceleration of vesting, either on general fairness principles or because the acquiror should not care; if the employee is not wanted, then incentives are not needed to keep him/her on board. The problem with this approach is that employees who are not hired are treated better than those who are hired—an oddity with potential unwanted consequences. Further, some would argue that the employee not hired is in effect being terminated and that he or she is only entitled to the vesting that has occurred prior to the date of such termination, like any other employee who is terminated without cause. Another approach is to provide for full vesting after a transition period—say six months or one year following the acquisition, unless the employee quits or is fired for cause.

One further subtlety is that experienced VCs sometimes define an acquisition for acceleration purposes so that it includes only an acquisition where the consideration is cash or publicly traded stock or a combination. The thinking here is that the founders have not really delivered a liquidity event for the VCs if the company is acquired by another private company, particularly if both companies are troubled.

Considerations similar to those of acquisitions theoretically would apply to IPOs. The prevailing practice, however, is not to have acceleration clauses in this case. Presumably the controlling rationale is the possible loss of key employees that may result from the acceleration and investor concerns that would result from disclosure in the IPO prospectus.

Founders sometimes may be successful in negotiating more favorable treatment in the event they are terminated by the company without cause or quit for good reason, as opposed to voluntary departure (i.e., quitting without good reason) or termination by the company for cause. The advisability of this approach is subject to continuing debate among lawyers specializing in representing start-ups and in venture capital financings. However, it can be argued that a less harsh result is appropriate if a founder is terminated without cause or leaves because the company has failed to keep its obligations to him or her. The answering argument is that young companies do not want to be in the position of having to debate (or worse, litigate) whether a termination is with or without cause or for good reason, and because termination of a founder for failure in performance deprives the company of the benefit of its bargain in negotiating the founders' equity position in the first place—and a substitute must be found and compensated in any event—termination of a founder therefore should result in full forfeiture of unvested shares. Both points of view are legitimate, but the latter approach usually prevails in the negotiations.

Frequently the repurchase right for unvested shares is phrased as an option on the part of the company to repurchase the departing founder's shares for a specified period of time, typically 30 to 90 days. A better practice may be to make this a fixed obligation of both parties. The circumstances under which a company will not want to repurchase shares at par or nominal value are rare, and an automatic repurchase provision avoids a trap for the unwary that offers no offsetting advantages: the possibility of failure to timely exercise the repurchase option because of an administrative oversight.

Inexperienced counsel or entrepreneurs often impose an additional restriction on the vested shares, permitting them to be repurchased by the company at fair market value (usually as determined by the board of directors) upon termination of employment. Under this scheme, the odds of one side or the other being unfairly treated are about 100 percent, and the odds of litigation are needlessly multiplied. The reason is that early-stage technology companies are inherently difficult to value. There is really no adequate way to do so. The only real way to determine what a company is worth is to sell it or take it public. In a private technology company, repurchases at fair market value simply do not work well.

SECTION 83(B).   Whenever a company issues stock to employees that is subject to a repurchase option of the company, the employees should seek advice from their tax advisors regarding the relative benefits of filing or not filing an election under Internal Revenue Cod Section 83(b). Under IRC Section 83, an employee will recognize income in respect of property (including stock) received in connection with the performance of services; the amount of income is the difference between the value of the stock at the time he or she receives it and the amount he or she pays for it. However, where the stock is subject to restrictions that lapse over time, such as a repurchase option that lapses pursuant to a vesting schedule, the employee will recognize compensation (i.e., ordinary) income at the time or times the restrictions lapse, again in an amount equal to the difference between the value of the stock at the time the restrictions lapse and the amount paid. Thus, an employee who is issued stock during the start-up phase of a company that becomes successful, and whose stock is subject to vesting provisions over a period of years, will become taxable, at ordinary income rates, on the excess of the sometimes vastly appreciated value of the stock over what was paid for it as the company's repurchase rights lapse.

If the employee believes that the value of the stock is likely to appreciate (i.e., the company is likely to be successful) and that the shares are likely to vest, a Section 83(b) election can provide significant a tax benefit and is virtually always made. If the employee makes an 83(b) election, his or her receipt of the stock is the relevant tax event, and he or she is taxed at ordinary income rates on any excess of the value of the stock when received (without regard to the vesting provisions) over the amount paid for the stock. If the initial purchase price of the stock is equal to the fair market value, then the election results in no tax liability. More important, as a result of making the Section 83(b) election, the employee will recognize no income upon vesting, and if the employee vests, he or she will report capital gain (rather than ordinary income) upon selling the stock in an amount equal to the amount received in the sale over the amount paid for the stock.

Section 83 considerations may also apply in situations in which a founder or key employee purchases (or is granted) stock outright and then at a later date agrees to the imposition of vesting restrictions in connection with a venture capital financing, or in which stock acquired upon exercise of an option is itself subject to a repurchase option.

Section 83(b) elections must be filed within 30 days after the date on which the restricted stock is acquired. An inadvertent failure to file the election is a trap for the unwary with potentially very substantial tax consequences.

FORM OF SECURITY: UBIQUITOUS CONVERTIBLE PREFERRED STOCK. The virtually universal structure for a VC investment is convertible preferred stock. Because it is convertible into common stock at the option of the holder, convertible preferred stock entitles the VC investors to their full upside win if the company is successful, and it entitles the investors to the return of their investment before the founders if the company fails. Convertible preferred stock also permits various other protections for the investors that are discussed later: voting rights, antidilution provisions, various approval rights, and redemption provisions.

An exception to this structure sometimes is used for early-stage companies where it is too difficult for the investors, particularly angel investors, and the company to arrive at an agreed valuation; the investors have made a determination that the company is worth investing in, but they are unable to satisfy themselves (or cannot agree with the founders) at what price. A related exception is for the more seasoned company, where valuation is difficult because of turbulent private equity markets, or where a bridge loan is being extended to an existing portfolio company in anticipation of an impending next round, and a valuation decision is to be avoided because it will be independently set in negotiations with new VC investors in the upcoming round. In these cases, investors and the company may defer the valuation decision by structuring the investment in the form of a promissory note that is automatically converted into the next round of preferred stock financing either at the price of such round or at a discount thereto, or if such a round does not occur within a specified time frame at a specified (usually low) valuation. These transactions are relatively quick and inexpensive to implement.

LIQUIDATION PREFERENCE.   The first important economic aspect of convertible preferred stock is its liquidation preference. The common theme in various types of convertible preferred stock investments might be dubbed "heads I win, tails you lose." In so-called straight convertible preferred, upon a liquidation of the company, the investors are entitled to whichever of two options results in the greater return: (1) the amount they paid for the stock, usually with an accruing dividend of 5 to 10 percent on that amount, paid on redemption of their preferred shares; or (2) the amount distributable to the common stockholders, payable to the former preferred stockholders after conversion of their preferred shares to common stock. (It is important, when representing the VC, to phrase the clause as the investors being entitled to receive whichever of clause (1) or (2) ultimately turns out to be the greater, rather than requiring the investors to make an election up front. In some scenarios, particularly earn-out transactions, it is impossible to tell at the time of the liquidation whether the preferred holders are better off taking their liquidation preference or converting to common stock. Only later, when the amount of the earn-out has been determined, is it possible to make that assessment.)

In another variation of convertible preferred stock called participating preferred (or, more pejoratively, double-dip preferred), the investors are first entitled to receive their liquidation preference (price paid plus accrued dividends or in some cases a multiple thereof), and then, after they have received their liquidation preference, their preferred shares are deemed to have converted into common stock so that they share pro rata in the remaining proceeds with the common stockholders. This structure economically mirrors a note-and-warrant or note-and-common-stock structure, without the adverse credit consequences to the company of debt in the capital structure.

In difficult economic times, VC investors may also require that the liquidation preferences be tied to a multiple of the amount paid per share. With such a preference, the investors are entitled to be paid, for example, five times their original investment before the common stockholders get anything. Many commentators have questioned the wisdom of this practice, even from the investors' point of view, because of the severely negative effect on the chances of management and key employees realizing a return on their investment. The result may be that founders and employees will vote with their feet and leave for better opportunities elsewhere.

The choice of one type of liquidation preference over another is simply a matter of negotiation. Neither is inherently good or evil, fair or unfair. All things being equal, participating preferred stock effectively puts a lower valuation on the company. Obviously, the entrepreneur should try to negotiate for straight convertible preferred stock rather than participating preferred. If the founders receive offers with both structures, they simply need to compare the economics under various win scenarios to see which is more favorable. The higher the multiple of the price paid by the investors that is received in an acquisition of the company, the less significant is the participating preferred feature as an economic matter. Founders frequently can negotiate a cap on the participating preferred feature. With a cap, the formulation would be that the investors receive the greater of the liquidation preference plus their share of the remaining proceeds, but only up to a specified multiple of the original investment (typically three to five times), or the amount the investors would have received if they had converted to common stock immediately before the liquidation.

In either of these formulations, the term "liquidation" is defined to include an acquisition of the company. Until recently, there never were any real liquidations of VC-backed companies where proceeds were available to the equity holders. An acquisition typically is defined to include:

  (i)   Mergers, where the stockholders of the target in their capacity as such no longer own a majority of the equity securities and/or voting power of the surviving corporation or its parent.
 (ii)   A sale of substantially all of the outstanding capital stock of the company.
(iii)   A sale of all or substantially all assets of the company.

DIVIDENDS.   The convertible preferred stock terms in VC transactions do not affirmatively require payment of dividends on the preferred stock, except upon a liquidation of the company or a redemption of the preferred stock. Rather, they prohibit payment of dividends on the common stock, and they typically include a cumulative dividend on the preferred. This dividend accrues (or "cumulates") and is not payable unless declared by the board (which it never is because it would be hard to justify a dividend, given the growth company's need for cash and given that VCs typically do not control the board); there is a liquidation event (a sale of the company is considered a liquidation event, but an IPO usually is not); or the preferred stock is redeemed. The accruing dividend is a protective device intended to provide a minimum rate of return, but it is usually forfeited in the event of an IPO or upon conversion of the preferred stock to common stock. (The theory is that in such cases, the return on the investment will be more than the minimum that the accruing dividend provides; therefore, the protection is not needed and is forfeited.) There are various types of accruing dividends, including those that are payable in cash and those that are payable in additional shares of preferred stock. Also, although a basic accruing dividend involves the equivalent of a simple interest calculation, sometimes VCs require compound interest calculations.

ANTIDILUTION PROVISIONS.   Antidilution provisions are potentially the most threatening of all the aspects of convertible preferred stock to a start-up's founders. The ratio that is used to calculate the common stock issuable upon conversion is variable, with potentially severe adverse effects on the founders and other common stockholders.

Antidilution provisions are of two types and accomplish two basic objectives, one of which is noncontroversial and the other of which is potentially highly controversial.

The noncontroversial antidilution clauses are those that automatically adjust the conversion price in the event of stock splits, stock dividends, recapitalizations, and similar events. These are essentially corporate housekeeping provisions, but they nonetheless are necessary because of the risk of injudicious case law that may not protect the investors in such situations.

The other form of antidilution protection insisted on by VCs is price antidilution. To understand how antidilution provisions work, first one must understand that, when the preferred stock is initially issued, the conversion ratio of preferred into common is set at one for one. The formula to determine the ratio is the original issue price of the preferred divided by the conversion price, which originally is the price paid so as to achieve the one-to-one ratio. When a subsequent round of financing is done, it is to be hoped that the price for the securities issued will be higher, which it will be (market conditions and all other things being equal) if the company is succeeding. The price could also, however, be the same or lower. If the price is the same or higher, the antidilution provisions do not come into play. Only if the price in the subsequent financing is lower do the antidilution provisions operate to lower the original conversion price so as to give preferred stockholders a higher number of common shares upon conversion, on the rationale that this compensates them for the equity dilution they suffered when the later investors buy stock for a lower price per share.

There are two basic types of price anti-dilution protection, weighted average and full ratchet (or ratchet). Weighted average antidilution mitigates the impact of the antidilution adjustment. Put simply, weighted average antidilution protection accounts more accurately than does full ratchet antidilution for the actual dilutive effect that a particular issuance has on the investors' equity position in the company: a more significant adjustment in the conversion ratio of the preferred stock if a larger number of shares of stock is issued at a lower price, and a less significant adjustment if a smaller number of shares is issued at a lower price. With weighted average antidilution, upon a sale of stock at a price lower than the conversion price, the conversion price is lowered to a price that is an average of the price at which the company has sold all of its outstanding stock, valuing the common stock outstanding at the preadjusted conversion price. An issuance of warrants, stock options, or convertible securities is deemed to be a sale of the underlying stock. (There is a continuum of weighted average formulas, from broad-based to narrow-based; the difference is in which common stock equivalents are included in the fully diluted base over which the dilutive effect is spread.)

The harsher form, full-ratchet antidilution, however, treats all later stock issuances below the investor's purchase price as if they were the same, resulting in the same adjustment to the conversion ratio regardless of the number of shares issued. The conversion price is ratcheted down to the lowest price at which stock is sold after the initial issuance of the convertible preferred, even if only one share is sold at that price. Thus, if the next round of financing is for a price that is half of the first-round price, the conversion price of the original preferred will be cut in half. The original preferred investors will receive twice as many common shares upon conversion, all for no additional consideration, resulting in significant additional dilution to the founders and other common stockholders. In this way, the original preferred investors are effectively retroactively given the lowest price at which the company's stock is sold.

A representative weighted average antidilution clause reads in this way:

> In the event the Corporation shall at any time after the Series A Original Issue Date issue Additional Shares of Common Stock, without consideration or for a consideration per share less than the applicable Conversion Price in effect immediately prior to such issue, then and in such event, such applicable Conversion Price shall be reduced, concurrently with such issue, to a price (calculated to the nearest cent) determined by the following formula:
>
> $$p = p^1 q^1 + p^2 q^2 \div q^1 + q^2$$
>
> where:
>
> p = Applicable Conversion Price following new issuance
> p^1 = Applicable Conversion Price prior to new issuance
> q^1 = Number of shares of Common Stock outstanding prior to new issuance (or may be shares outstanding on a fully diluted basis—so-called broad-based formula antidilution)
> p^2 = Price per share of new issue
> q^2 = Number of Additional Shares of Common Stock issued in new issue

There are a number of customary exceptions to the operation of the ratchet or weighted average formula antidilution clauses. Sample exclusionary language listing issuances of stock or options where no antidilution adjustment is permitted follows.

> "Additional Shares of Common Stock" shall mean all shares of Common Stock issued by the Corporation after the Series A Original Issue Date, other than:
>
> (i) shares of Common Stock issued or issuable upon exercise of any Options outstanding on the Series A Original Issue Date or conversion or exchange of any Convertible Securities;

(ii)   shares of Common Stock issued or issuable as a dividend or distribution on Preferred Stock;

(iii) shares of Common Stock issued or issuable by reason of a dividend, stock split, split-up, or other distribution on shares of Common Stock that is covered by Section below;

(iv)   up to [ ] shares of Common Stock (or such greater number as is approved by a majority of the Board of Directors, including directors nominated by the holders of the Preferred Stock) (or Options with respect thereto) (subject in either case to appropriate adjustment in the event of any stock dividend, stock split, combination, or other similar recapitalization affecting such shares), previously issued or issuable in the future to employees or directors of, or consultants or advisors to, the Corporation or a subsidiary pursuant to a plan or arrangement approved by the Board of Directors of the Corporation (provided that any Options for such shares that expire or terminate unexercised, or shares issued thereunder that are repurchased at cost pursuant to the terms thereof, shall not be counted toward such maximum number); or

(v)   shares of capital stock, or options or warrants exercisable therefor, issued to banks, vendors, or equipment leasing organizations in connection with bank financing, vendor relationships, or equipment leasing arrangements to which the Corporation is a party, or shares of capital stock issued in connection with the acquisition of another business, in each case which has been approved by a majority of the members of the Board of Directors.

While it is beyond the scope of this chapter to discuss in detail the issues of down-round financings, any discussion of price antidilution protection, particularly in the post-Internet bubble venture capital climate, should mention a device sometimes proposed by companies to protect against earlier investors getting the benefits of full-ratchet antidilution without providing more capital to the company. So-called play-or-pay provisions provide a strong incentive for existing investors to participate in subsequent rounds. If a preferred investor subject to a play-or-pay provision does not participate (play) in a new round of financing, some or all of the privileges (e.g., the price antidilution protection, liquidation preferences, special voting rights, or redemption rights) attached to the investor's preferred stock are stripped, usually by automatic conversion into a series of preferred stock without those privileges or by outright conversion into common stock. Different investor groups often heatedly argue play-or-pay provisions.

MANDATORY CONVERSION INTO COMMON STOCK. Convertible preferred stock terms provide that upon the effectiveness of a registration statement under the Securities Act of 1933 covering a firm commitment underwritten public offering of common stock of the company by a nationally recognized underwriter, the preferred stock automatically converts into common stock immediately prior to the IPO closing. The reason for this automatic conversion into common stock is that the prospect of continued existence of the convertible preferred stock after the IPO would adversely affect the marketing and pricing of the IPO itself, and many of the terms and provisions of venture capital preferred stock are inconsistent with the operation of a public company.

In addition to the firm commitment underwriting requirement, the public offering price is usually required to be at least a specified multiple of the conversion price with specified aggregate gross proceeds received by the company from the IPO. These additional requirements are probably unnecessary as a practical matter and can be problematic in some circumstances. It is hard to imagine an IPO by a nationally recognized underwriter that venture investors would not welcome. Where the additional requirements are not quite met, the last-minute scurrying around to get the necessary waivers can be an impediment to getting the IPO priced and closed on time. Counsel who are experienced at doing IPOs will try to persuade the venture investors to eliminate these extra requirements from the outset.

COVENANTS AND SEPARATE VOTING RIGHTS OF THE PREFERRED STOCK. Because the investors do not have majority control of the board of directors, they believe it is necessary to have veto rights over certain major corporate actions. A typical list of the actions that the company will be prohibited from taking without the consent of a specified percentage of the preferred is set forth in the next sample language:

Without the consent of a [specified percentage] of the preferred, the Company will not:

(i) amend or repeal any provision of, or add any provision to, the Company's By-laws if such action would adversely affect the preferences, rights, privileges, or powers of or the restrictions provided for the benefit of the Preferred Stock;

(ii) pay or declare any dividend or distribution on any shares of its capital stock (except dividends payable solely in shares of Common Stock), or apply any of its assets to the redemption, retirement, purchase, or acquisition, directly or indirectly, through subsidiaries or otherwise, of any shares of its capital stock (other than repurchase of Common Stock at cost upon termination of employment or service);

(iii) reclassify any Common Stock into shares having any preference or priority as to assets superior to or on a parity with any such preference or priority of the Preferred Stock;

(iv) sell, lease, or otherwise dispose of all or substantially all of its assets, or properties;

(v) voluntarily liquidate or dissolve;

(vi) acquire all or substantially all of the properties, assets or capital stock of any other corporation or entity;

(vii) enter into any merger or consolidation, or permit any subsidiary to enter into any merger or consolidation; or

(viii) incur indebtedness for borrowed funds in excess of $[ ] in aggregate principal amount any time outstanding.

The choice of the requisite approval percentage requires care. Often the investors will be more concerned about being able to block a transaction that they do not like and will set the approval percentage quite high. Founders should try to convince the investors that this approach is not in their own interest; the risk of a group of investors not being able to do a deal they want to do because an unreasonable investor blocks it is greater than the risk of not being able to block a transaction that the group does not want to do.

REDEMPTION.   Convertible preferred stock issued in a venture capital financing typically has a redemption feature. In the event the company has not been acquired or gone public within a specified period of time, then a specified percentage of the preferred holders can require the company to redeem their preferred stock at the liquidation preference amount. The payout of the redemption price usually is spread out over several years. The purpose of this clause is to give the VCs control over a situation where the company no longer appears to be on a growth company track but is instead going sideways. Because venture capital funds have limited lives, there is some pressure on VCs to liquidate their investments within a fixed period of time; hence the redemption feature.

The actual use of the redemption feature is rare. It is the rare growth company that has the legally available capital to finance a buy-out. So the "threat" represented by these clauses is largely illusory. Unless the company has sufficient legal capital under the applicable business corporation statute, the company will be prohibited from redeeming the preferred stock. To put some teeth into this clause, investors may demand a clause providing that, if there is a default, the investors will get the right to control the board. Investors rarely take control of the board in any event because they are afraid of the liability that control imposes on them, particularly to creditors. Indeed, in the roaring 1990s, redemption clauses often were omitted from preferred stock terms.

Redemption features usually are phrased in terms of what is, in effect, a put right rather than an automatic redemption. The reason for this approach is that in a sideways-but-slightly-up scenario, where the company is worth more per preferred share than the redemption price, investors do not want to be limited to a redemption at a fixed price or, worse, an automatic redemption feature. An increasingly common feature is for investors to have a put right at the higher of the liquidation preference or fair market value as determined by an agreed valuation procedure.

In sum, redemption features probably are not worth the legal expense that it takes to create them, but nonetheless they are relatively standard features of VC financings.

ANCILLARY AGREEMENTS. In a typical venture capital closing (see the sample closing agenda for a convertible preferred stock VC financing in Appendix 2 C), a number of customary agreements are executed implementing a fairly standard suite of other business and legal terms.

Stock Purchase Agreement. The stock purchase agreement is the agreement pursuant to which the investors agree to make their investment in the company. It is much like any other purchase agreement. The purchase price of the preferred investment is specified, and there are conventional representations and warranties of the company, investment representations of the investors that are necessary to comply with securities law private placement requirements, affirmative and negative covenants, and conditions to closing. The most contentious issues with the stock purchase agreement are whether the founders are required to make separate representations and whether there will be a single funding or staged fundings based on the satisfaction of performance or other conditions.

As for personal representations by the founders, in a first-round financing, this practice is not unusual. In a sense, it is meaningless for the company alone to make the representations. If there later turns out to be a problem with a representation, it will be impossible to make the investors whole since the only cash invested in the company is theirs, some or all of which may already have been spent. The investors therefore would be entitled to get only a portion of their investment back if there were a misrepresentation. The approach to this problem by various VC firms and their counsel varies widely. At the extreme, the founders are asked to jointly make the same representations and warranties as the company, including such things as due organization of the company, valid issuance of its stock, and noncontravention of rights of, or agreements with, others. The founders and company counsel usually strongly resist doing this. A more balanced and fair approach is to ask the founders to represent only those things that they should know about—that there are no promises to issue equity other than as disclosed; that the founders themselves are not in violation of previous employment, inventions, confidentiality, and noncompetition agreements; and that they have no actual knowledge of any threats related to any of the foregoing or to intellectual property matters. In subsequent financing rounds, after the company has been up and running for a reasonable period, founder representations are relatively rare.

The number of fundings—one or multiple—significantly affects the economics of the deal. At times, investors require that the obligation to advance the committed funds be staged over several closings. Whether the availability of funds is immediate or over a period of time is not the important issue. The real issue is on what terms the investors will be excused from advancing the additional funds. Sometimes the condition to the second closing is only a reaffirmation of the representations and warranties, including that there has been no material adverse change in the business. If there is such a condition, particular care must be taken in the phrasing of the representations and warranties. For example, if the company has represented that a specific number of shares are outstanding, then that representation should need to remain correct only as of the date it was first made. Otherwise, the mere issuance of additional stock will constitute a breach of that representation and a failure of that condition to the subsequent closing. Usually there is also some variation of a "bring down" of the no-material-adverse-change representation. The investors argue that it is not possible to adequately cover all the events for which they need protection in the more specific representations and warranties. From the company's point of view, this representation is inherently vague and subject to dispute. The company would also argue that the risk of an adverse change is one that investors should be considered to have accepted in a high-risk technology company and should not be an excuse for them to abandon the company.

Similarly, at times, conditions to subsequent closings are imposed requiring the company to meet certain performance milestones. Investors argue that they are investing based on management's assurances as to the achievement of the specified milestones within a certain time frame. In effect, the investors are saying that they want to put their money where the company's mouth is. The company is in a difficult position to argue in some cases. The more nervous management appears about the milestones, the more it risks losing the investors. In any event, the company needs to be very careful that it receives enough funding at the first closing to achieve the milestones it is required to achieve before additional funds are advanced.

Right of First Refusal and Co-Sale Agreement.   In a private company, both the founders and the investors have a common interest in preserving the solidarity of the investor, employee, and founder group's ownership of the company's equity. The founders, and sometimes the investors, are prohibited from selling their shares to a new investor without giving first to the company and then to the investors (and sometimes the founders) a right of first refusal to purchase the securities available for sale at the price that has been offered. Typically a further requirement is imposed on the founders (but almost never on the investors) that if the first refusal rights are not exercised in full, then the selling founder must allow the investors to sell a pro rata portion of their securities to the new investor. These are called co-sale rights. The rationale for these provisions is that the investors are investing in the company based on the participation and equity incentives of the founders, and the founders are not supposed to be bailing out of the company before the investors. These provisions should be noncontroversial.

Sometimes an additional clause, called a drag-along right, is included in these agreements. With this clause, if a specified percentage of the investors want to sell the company, then the founders agree in advance to be dragged along in the sale—that is, to vote for that transaction and sign any agreements related to the transaction that the investors sign. These clauses are dangerous to the founders since there are many scenarios where the interests of the investors will differ from those of the founders. The investors may grow tired of a sideways investment and want to sell the company for the price they paid for their shares. Because they have a liquidation preference on such a sale (see "Liquidation Preference"), the investors would realize a return before other stockholders. The founders may have a different view of the desirability of the sale. One refinement on this type of clause is to impose certain economic and legal parameters for sales in which the founders can be compelled to participate.

Investors' Rights Agreement.   The investors' rights agreement is the vehicle for investors to impose various affirmative and negative covenants on the company. The affirmative covenants typically include access rights, preparation of monthly financial statements, preparation of annual budgets, and a contractual preemptive right of the investors to purchase new securities issued by the company in order to maintain their percentage interest (with exclusions typically similar or identical to those described above in the antidilution discussion). Negative covenants may include certain company-specific items that are either not covered in the voting section of the corporate charter or are considered more appropriate in this agreement.

Registration Rights Agreement.   The registration rights agreement specifies the criteria and procedures for sales of shares into the public markets. The investors are the beneficiaries of these clauses; sometimes the founders are as well.

These agreements provide for two different kinds of registration rights: demand rights and piggyback rights.

Demand rights entitle the investors to require the company to file a registration statement for all or a portion of their shares so they can sell them without restriction to the public. These rights usually become effective 180 days after the company's IPO, effectively building in a lock-up for the investors that underwriters in an IPO would normally require in any event. Demand rights sometimes purport to allow investors to force the company to do an IPO after a period of several years. There is then a battle over the appropriateness of this clause. As a practical matter, it is not possible to force a company to do an IPO (the participation of management is critical), so the battle (on both sides) should be saved for something else.

Once the company has been public for a period of time (currently one year), the company becomes S-3 eligible and is permitted to file a short-form registration statement with the Securities and Exchange Commission. Because the S-3 form procedures are streamlined, it is not uncommon for VCs to require unlimited demand rights on Form S-3, typically with a minimum dollar amount of the securities required to be registered. Because the typical VC fund will have already distributed its company securities to its investors by the time the company is S-3 eligible, and because of the low cost of an S-3 registration statement, this clause is another one that is not worth battling over (by either side).

Piggyback rights allow the investors and sometimes the founders to add a portion of their shares to a registration statement filed by the company at its own initiative.

Because the sale of these secondary shares is a sensitive marketing issue in an IPO, registration rights agreements universally have a so-called underwriter cut-back provision. This provision cedes to the underwriters the determination of whether inclusion of secondary shares in the offering is feasible from a marketing point of view. If, in the lead underwriter's judgment, only a portion of the requested shares can be included, the registration rights agreement frequently contains a priority allocation scheme among various tiers of investors and sometimes even among the founders.

These agreements also contain elaborate provisions dealing with registration procedures, indemnification for securities laws liabilities, and similar matters. These provisions are relatively standard and noncontroversial. Indeed, the registration rights agreement itself should not become the focus of too much attention or loss of goodwill. In an IPO or other public offering, as a practical matter, the underwriters call all of the shots, and the registration rights agreement is rarely taken out of the drawer other than to waive provisions objected to by the underwriters.

Other Agreements.   Other agreements required by VCs include:

- Employee confidentiality and invention assignment agreements. These agreements require all employees to maintain the confidentiality of the company's confidential information and to assign to the company, at no cost, all inventions made by the employee that are related to the company's business or that were made on company time or with use of the company's resources.
- Noncompetition agreements from the founders and key managerial and technical personnel.

SUBSEQUENT FINANCING ROUNDS.   From a practical and legal perspective, subsequent convertible preferred stock financings should be, and usually are, less time-consuming and costly than a first-round financing. Typically the spoken or unspoken commitment on both sides is to complete the deal as expeditiously and simply as possible. It is hoped that most of the major contentious legal issues already have been worked out in the first round. It is usually agreed among counsel, particularly if the investors are largely the same as in the first round, to use the same forms of documentation agreed upon in the first round. Normally, in order to keep the company's compliance requirements as simple as possible, all of the principal agreements are amended and restated and signed by all parties so that there is one integrated, completely consistent set of documents. In the corporate charter, the documentation merely requires adding the new series into a handful of appropriate points.

There are, however, a few new issues that arise in connection with a subsequent-round financing. First, the relative priority of the two series of preferred stock must be agreed upon—that is, whether the new series ranks equally, or *pari passu*, with the prior series with respect to liquidation, dividends, and the like. Also, the board composition must be agreed upon to include one or more designees of the new investors. Last, the various affirmative and negative covenants negotiated for the benefit of the first-round investors must be integrated into the new documentation. The preferred alternative for the company in that respect is to have only one set of covenants, which can be waived by a specified percentage of the old and new investors as a group. The new investors may insist on their own separate set of covenants waivable only by a specified percentage of the new investors. In our view this is a short-sighted approach. In most cases any advantage to the new investors in having their own covenants to block certain actions that they disagree with will be outweighed by the ability of the other series of investors to block a transaction favored by the new investors. The best approach, is to integrate the covenants and provide for a waiver that allows an action to proceed if a majority (or if necessary a supermajority) of investors favors the action.

CONCLUSION.   The legal aspects of venture capital investments are perhaps the least important. The most important aspects are to secure a sound financing platform for the company's growth with investors whom the founders believe they can work with and trust. The advantages gained or lost in the legal details rarely affect the success or failure of the investment from either the company's or the investors' point of view. That is not to minimize the key legal and economic provisions of a venture capital financing—valuation, board control, antidilution, and so forth—but rather to point out that most of the documentation has become fairly standardized. The effort of all parties should be to focus on those few issues that are negotiable and reach a prompt agreement on them so that everyone can get back to business.

BASICS OF DEBT FINANCING

Private technology companies do debt financings only in two situations: bridge loans from current or prospective investors and asset-backed bank financings when they become a bit more established and have accounts receivable and inventory. Private companies also occasionally use debt to fund a portion of the acquisition price of companies they acquire. Thus it is important to have at least a basic working knowledge of some of the principles of debt financings. The principal issues in debt financings, other than the basic economic terms such as maturity date, interest rate and required principal and interest payments, revolve around the rank or seniority of the debt vis-à-vis other company debt. Rank means who gets paid first on liquidation. By "liquidation," we mean the company goes under and voluntarily distributes its assets to creditors and stockholders, or the company voluntarily or involuntarily is put into bankruptcy and the distribution takes place under the jurisdiction of the bankruptcy court. If one class of debt is entitled to be paid before another, it is senior and the other class is junior. If two classes of debt are of equal rank, they are also called *pari passu* with one another. The ranking of debt is determined by the contractual provisions of the debt—contracts that may be just between the debtor (i.e., the company) and the lenders and contracts between lenders known as subordination agreements or intercreditor agreements.

In a complicated private company capital structure (say following an LBO), these elements may be present:

- Senior secured debt.
- Subordinated secured debt.
- Senior debt (someone has subordinated to a senior creditor).
- Senior subordinated debt (not a contradiction in terms—a junior creditor has subordinated to a senior creditor and an even more junior creditor has subordinated to the first junior creditor).
- Subordinated debt (frequently convertible).
- Preferred stock.
- Common stock.

CORPORATE FINANCE AND DEBT FINANCING BASICS. Before discussing subordination and intercreditor agreements, we begin with a discussion of certain basics of corporate finance and definitions of certain terms.

The capitalization of a company consists of equity and debt for borrowed money. Equity generally consists of common stock and/or preferred stock, which generically is referred to as capital stock. Debt for borrowed money is a promise to repay the amount borrowed (principal), with fixed or variable interest, on a specified date or dates (the maturity date). Principal may be paid only at maturity (a balloon payment) or may be amortized by multiple payments. The debt may or may not be prepayable (or perhaps prepayable with a premium or a prepayment penalty). Debt may be straight debt or debt with equity features (convertibility into common stock or with accompanying warrants to buy capital stock at a fixed price). The company will also have other debt (e.g., trade debt) that is not considered capital.

The equity value of a company is the value of the company's capital stock, which is equal to what all of that stock can be sold for. The majority owner of a company may, upon a sale, receive a control premium on the sale, or a greater price than a minority investor could receive. Conversely, the minority investor's shares are subject to a minority discount.

The enterprise value of a company is the value of the company's capital stock plus funded debt or debt, particularly long-term debt, for borrowed money, usually net of cash. Equity value, in academic theory, is the present value of the future net cash flows of the company available to the equity holders, that is, the theoretical amount of all future cash flows, including the incurrence or repayment of debt, discounted to the present to reflect the time value of money. The stock market looks at equity value, and a company's market capitalization (or market cap) is equal to the number of shares outstanding multiplied by the price per share. Public companies are valued (trade) in significant part on a multiple of earnings per share (EPS). Earnings and EPS are determined in accordance with generally accepted accounting principles (GAAP). The price-to-earnings ratio (P/E ratio or multiple) is the market's way of valuing the expected growth in EPS.

Why and when do companies use debt in their capitalization structure? Basic modern corporate finance strategy is to maximize earnings per share within acceptable risk parameters. Increasing EPS increases the value of the company, all else being equal. EPS can be increased with the prudent use of debt in the right circumstances, which are that the company can generate incremental earnings with the cash proceeds of the debt that are greater than the interest paid on the debt. No shares of capital stock are issued with straight debt, so by definition EPS goes up under these circumstances. EPS can also increase when a public company buys back its own stock. In that case, the company has excess cash generating relatively low interest or other investment income, and EPS will go up by buying back a portion of the stock outstanding.

If sold at the right price, sales of additional equity can increase EPS as well. The company expects, either in the short or long term, to be able to grow its business and earnings from the sale of additional shares of capital stock so that after the growth occurs, EPS will go up even though more shares are outstanding.

How do lenders assess risk when a company wants to do a debt financing? Lenders assess risk based on a borrower's balance sheet: its assets and liabilities and the excess of liabilities over assets (or stockholders' equity). Stockholders' equity combines the cumulative amount of the company's past earnings with the proceeds of the issuance of capital stock. Lenders also assess risk based on the borrower's income statement and statement of cash flows (i.e., the borrower's ability, on a reasonably predictable basis, to generate earnings and cash flows sufficient to repay the debt).

The safest loans are usually asset-based, which is debt secured by (i.e., has a lien on) the assets of the company, including accounts receivable and inventory. The amount that can be borrowed under a typical asset-based line of credit are specified percentages of the borrowing base of eligible accounts receivable (i.e., receivables that appear to be collectible and not delinquent) and inventory. The debt terms that the company receives (interest rate, etc.) are a function of perceived risk by the lender. Risk is based partly on anticipated company performance and the tier that the debt is in. Lenders like a lot of debt "underneath" them in a lower tier, such that the company is *well capitalized.*

Both senior lenders and junior (subordinated) lenders attempt to mitigate risk by debt covenants and rights to accelerate the scheduled payment of the debt on default. That is necessary because the interests of the equity holder and the holders of the debt diverge; equity holders and debt holders make different trade-offs on risk versus growth. Sample debt covenants include:

- Limits on the amount of other debt that the company can incur.
- A prohibition on dividends to the equity holders.
- No prepayments of other debt, particularly junior debt that serves as a cushion for the senior debt.

- A prohibition on granting liens to other debt holders.
- A prohibition on the issuance of debt of equal or greater rank.
- The maintenance of specified financial ratios or measures of financial health.
- No transfers of assets to subsidiaries.

Events of default include nonpayment of the debt when required, a breach of the debt covenants, and defaults (cross defaults) on other debt.

SUBORDINATION. Subordinated debt is debt that gets paid after debt that is senior to it gets paid in full first. Subordination must be created by the junior creditor entering into a subordination agreement. Subordination also can be part of the terms of the note or other debt instrument that the junior creditor receives. This latter approach is used in situations where the company does not have any senior debt but expects to have some in the future and wants this particular issue of debt to be subordinated to unspecified future debt. This works fine and binds the junior creditor, but where the senior creditor is identified at the time the junior debt is issued, the senior creditor usually will insist that the junior creditor sign a subordination agreement directly with it.

HOW DEBT TIERS ARE CREATED OTHER THAN BY SUBORDINATION.
You can agree to subordinate to another creditor and another creditor can agree to subordinate to you. But you cannot subordinate another creditor to you, other than via a security interest.

Unlike subordination, a company and its creditors can make one class of debt senior to other classes of debt by securing the debt by a security interest. Unlike subordination agreements, which are fairly complicated and involve a range of issues other than mere rank in liquidation or bankruptcy, a security interest and the associated senior debt cannot affect any of the terms of the junior debt, other than its rank, in the absence of a subordination agreement where such rights are voluntarily affected.

In a corporate structure that involves subsidiaries, there is also something called structural subordination. What that means is that if a creditor lends money to the parent in a parent-subsidiary structure, in a liquidation scenario, the creditors of the subsidiary, no matter how junior, are all senior to all of the creditors of the parent. The reason is that the only way the creditors of the parent can get their hands on the assets of the subsidiary is via a dividend from the subsidiary to the parent. Because stock is equity, it is junior to the debt of the subsidiary, and the creditors of the subsidiary have priority over the parent as a stockholder and not a creditor of the subsidiary—hence the term "structural subordination." Creditors of the parent try to circumvent structural subordination by having the subsidiary guarantee the parent's debt to them, thereby creating creditor status vis-à-vis the subsidiary. These arrangements can be effective but may be overridden in bankruptcy or otherwise by virtue of fraudulent conveyance laws and provisions of the bankruptcy code that are designed to protect creditors from the debtor incurring debt obligations without getting anything, or getting enough, in return.

There is also a concept in bankruptcy called equitable subordination. Equitable subordination arises in situations where because of a creditor's inside status or where there is abusive behavior by the creditor, the court equitably subordinates the otherwise senior or *pari passu* debt to other debt of the company.

To understand better how subordination works in liquidation or bankruptcy, it is helpful to lay out the sequence of the distributions to creditors out of bankruptcy. First, the secured debt is paid or otherwise taken care of. The balance is then distributed to the unsecured creditors pro rata to the amount of debt owed to them. Then, if there are subordination agreements in place among the debt holders, the junior creditors turn over their payouts to their respective senior creditors until those senior creditors are paid in full. An example of a turnover appears in the chart below There exists something called senior subordinated debt, which seems at first to be a contradiction in terms. Senior subordinated debt is debt that is senior to one or more classes of debt in a company but is also subordinated or junior to other classes of debt in the same company (i.e., even though the debt in question is junior to someone, there are other debtors who are subordinated to it). This discussion is a bit oversimplified; in bankruptcy, the bankruptcy laws create tiers and priorities.

Here is an example of how assets are distributed in a liquidation:

EXAMPLE OF A TURNOVER

Balance Sheet
$600,000 in assets
No secured debt
$500,000 in senior debt
$500,000 in sub debt
$500,000 in trade debt

Who gets what?
Senior debt gets $400,000: $200,000 in the initial allocation and $200,000 in turnover from the subordinated creditors.
Sub debt gets nothing: They had to turn over everything until the senior debt was paid in full.
Trade debt gets $200,000: $200,000 in the initial allocation and no obligation to turn over.

One of the more complicated disclosures in public subordinated debt financings is this customary sentence, which we hope will be meaningful at this point.

By reason of such subordination, in the event of insolvency, [unsecured] creditors of the Company who are not holders of Senior Indebtedness of the Company may recover less, ratably, than holders of Senior Indebtedness of the Company and may recover more, ratably, than holders of the [subordinated] Notes.

OTHER ASPECTS OF SUBORDINATION. There is much more in a subordination agreement than the liquidation priority provisions. (See the sample subordination provisions in Appendix 2D.)

The reason for this complexity is that in a situation that has become precarious from the creditors' point of view, the senior lenders want to have a lot more control than simply waiting for a liquidation. Subordination agreements deal with three principal issues: priority in liquidation, payment blockages, and the right to pull the plug or remedy bars. That is why merely getting a security interest in the assets of a debtor is often not sufficient in the eyes of the senior creditor; the senior creditor wants a subordination agreement even though it does not need one to have priority in liquidation—it wants the control represented by payment blockages and remedy bars.

The terms under which the subordinated debt can get paid out generally are hotly debated terms in subordination agreements. In deep subordination or complete subordination, the subordinated debt can get paid out only when the senior debt has been paid in full. Obviously, senior debtors love this, and get it when they hold the cards. More common, however, are provisions that provide that the junior debt can get interest paid to it by the company (and sometimes interim principal payments and payments on maturity) but only if there is no default or event of default on the senior debt. These last two terms mean that there is no actual default in the senior debt, or "event which with the giving or notice or the passage of time would become a default." Another, less restrictive form of this provision is that no payments can be made to the junior debt "upon the maturity of the senior debt, by acceleration or otherwise," until the senior debt has been paid in full. That means that the junior debt can receive its normal payments even if there is a default or an event of default, but only until the senior debt exercises its remedies and accelerates, or calls due, the senior debt.

Where the junior creditors have some cards to play, they argue that this blockage from getting paid should not be allowed to last forever; the senior creditor has to *fish or cut bait* after some period of time (i.e., if the senior creditor does not accelerate the debt for some period after a default, say six months, then the payment blockage goes away).

A related concept is the remedy bar, a provision that says that not only cannot a junior creditor receive normal payments upon a default or whatever provision was negotiated, it also cannot exercise its legal remedies and sue the company because it has not received payment. In other words, even though the junior creditor has agreed to a payment blockage for the benefit of the senior creditor and agrees to turn over anything it gets on a liquidation or contrary to the payment blockage to the senior creditor, that does not mean that the junior creditor has waived its right to sue the company for nonpayment to what is owned to it. Senior creditors usually insist on remedy bars because these provisions give them more control over a deteriorating situation—only the senior creditor can pull the plug while the company and its creditors are trying to work their way out of the mess.

Some debt indentures or other debt documents have a clause that essentially acknowledges that there are no remedy bars agreed to, even though the junior creditor is subordinating to the senior debt in liquidation. Here is another extract from a debt document that we hope will make sense as well:

> These provisions are solely for the purpose of defining the relative rights of the holders of Senior Debt, on the one hand, and Subordinated Debt, on the other hand, against the Company and its assets, and nothing contained herein shall impair, as between the Company and a holder of Subordinated Debt, the obligation of the Company, which is absolute and unconditional, to perform in accordance with the terms of the Subordinated Debt, or prevent the holder of Subordinated Debt, upon default thereunder, from exercising all rights, powers and remedies otherwise provided therein or by applicable law, all subject to the rights of the holders of Senior Debt under this agreement to receive cash, property or securities otherwise payable or deliverable to the holders of the Subordinated Debt.

BRIEF INTRODUCTION TO THE STRUCTURE AND OPERATION OF VENTURE CAPITAL AND BUYOUT FUNDS

The growth of the venture capital industry and of the technology economy is staggering. The world is a very different place from what it was 25 years ago, in significant part due to the way technological innovations have changed the way we live and work. For example, it is hard to believe that 30 or so years ago, word processing had not been invented. The growth has been driven by the urge to invent and also by the urge to make a lot of money. Most of the significant fortunes that have been accumulated since the 1970s have been by technology entrepreneurs. The venture capital industry has been the principal source of financing for technology entrepreneurs. The more successful VCs have also made staggering fortunes for themselves.

From a legal point of view, the structure and economics of the venture capital industry has become largely standardized. There is a relatively small group of lawyers that specialize in the field called venture fund formation, which is a legal specialty in and of itself despite the standardization just referred to.

The central legal entity in a venture capital operation is the venture fund itself. The venture fund is simply an investment partnership, generally organized as a limited partnership, the money of which is invested in start-ups and other private technology companies.

The limited partners put up the capital for the venture fund, and the general partner of the venture fund (generally organized as an LLC [GPLLC]) decides where to invest and manages the fund's investments. The managing members of the GPLLC are the individuals who are the founders of the fund complex or senior managers brought in to help run it. The larger fund complexes also have nonmanaging members who participate in the profits of the GPLLC on a limited basis. These people range from successful entrepreneurs/gurus who need a home to the equivalent of senior and junior associates in a law firm or consulting firm.

The fundamental economics of a venture fund are quite simple. The GPLLC is entitled to 20 percent of the cumulative profits of the fund over its life. That is called a *carried interest*. LBO funds have similar economics. Hedge funds also have carried interests, but the economics are not necessarily a simple percentage of cumulative profits. (Hedge funds are private investment partnerships that invest mostly in publicly traded securities, and LBO funds generally invest in leveraged buyouts of nontechnology companies.)

Drafting an agreement where the GPLLC has a carried interest equal to a percentage of cumulative profits is not that simple. That goal could be accomplished easily if the GPLLC were required to wait until all the results were in to take its cut. But the managers do not want to wait that long. Also, tax rules require the interim allocation of profits to the GPLLC, and because the limited partnership is a tax flow-through entity, distributions have to be made to the GPLLC in order to help its members pay their taxes.

Interim allocations and distributions themselves are complicated because the success of a venture capital fund is rarely a straight line upward; there are multiple winners and losers in the portfolio. Often the winners occur early and the losers occur late. If the fund allocated and distributed to the GPLLC its full 20 percent cumulative carried interest on the profit from the early winners, over the life of the fund the GPLLC will have gotten too much allocated and distributed to it once it has lost money on the later losers. To take a simple example, if the venture fund makes only two investments and the first investment makes a $100 profit and the fund subsequently realizes a loss of $100 on the second investment, the general partner is entitled to nothing because there is no cumulative profit. If 20% of the $100 profit has already been distributed, there needs to be a mechanism to recapture this distribution once the fund has lost the $100 on its second investment. There are multiple drafting techniques to deal with this basic structuring problem—including the infamous claw-back, or a clause that says the GPLLC has to give back profit to which it was not entitled calculated on a cumulative basis. The problem with the claw-back is that the members of the GPLLC may have already bought their personal jets. This potential for being unable to find the cash for claw-backs has led to the development and standardization of additional protective measures, such as escrows of all or a portion of the carried interest to personal guarantees by the managers of the GPLLC.

There are other entities in the fund complex other than the fund itself and the general partner. In addition to these entities, the venture fund complex also includes a management company, which generally is a corporation that gets a current management fee for running the fund, generally around 2 percent of managed assets per year. It is comprised basically of the same people who are members of the GPLLC.

Exhibit 2.2 shows the structure of a typical fund complex.

FURTHER EXPLANATION OF THE ORGANIZATIONAL STRUCTURE. Venture funds are organized as limited partnerships (or occasionally LLCs) principally for tax reasons. These flow-through entities pay no tax, and the taxable income and gain flow through to its partners or members: the GPLLC (and then to its members) and limited partners. In addition, in a limited partnership or an LLC, investment securities can be distributed tax-free to the partners (unlike an S corporation). If the fund were organized as a corporation, the fund would pay tax on gains from the portfolio, and the partners would pay another tax on distributions to them. If portfolio securities were distributed to the shareholders rather than sold, there would also be a corporate-level tax on distributions. In addition, of course, a limited partnership provides limited liability to the limited partners.

Because income and gains are taxed to the partners rather than the fund, the fund commonly will be required to make a distribution of cash to the partners to allow them to pay taxes on their share of the profit. In addition, when portfolio investments are sold or become publicly traded, the fund generally is obligated to distribute those securities to the partners.

The management company typically is organized as a corporation that provides administrative services (offices, administrative personnel,

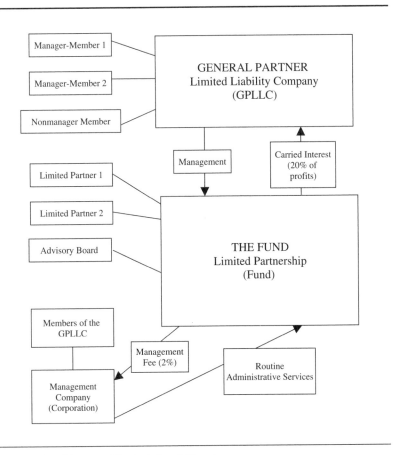

EXHIBIT 2.2   Venture Capital Fund Structure

etc.) to the fund. A corporation is adequate for this purpose because the income can be zeroed out by operating expenses (rent and overhead) and by salaries and bonuses. The corporate structure is also useful since it can provide certain tax benefits, such as pension plans, 401(k) plans, and the like.

ADDITIONAL DETAILS ON THE ECONOMIC TERMS OF VENTURE CAPITAL PARTNERSHIPS.   A summary of the principal economic and legal terms of a typical venture capital fund follows.

- **Capital commitment by the investors/limited partners.** The limited partners typically make a capital commitment for a specified amount of money to be contributed to the fund. Only a small portion of the committed funds are paid at the formation of the fund in order to pay organizational costs and to prepay a portion of the management fee. As funds are needed to make investments and to pay expenses (including the management fee), the commitments are called by the GPLLC in an amount sufficient to meet those obligations.

The commitment period is typically between three and seven years, depending on the nature of the venture fund, with some provision for extensions and for additional required investments in companies in the fund's portfolio. When the commitment period ends, no further capital calls can be made.

There is also some mechanism for the limited partners to terminate their commitments (e.g., by a supermajority vote.) Provisions to penalize limited partners who do not meet their funding obligations exist; these default provisions are usually severe.

- **Investment limitations.** Frequently there are limitations on the kind of investments that the venture fund can make. These may include size of any one investment, industry focus, and geographic limitations.

- **Carried interest variations.** The historical split of profits between the limited partners and the general partner is 80/20. As the industry matured, certain allocation schemes from the large buyout funds crept into venture fund terms. The three principal variations are:

  1. **Simple carried interest.** 80/20 split of cumulative profits.
  2. **Hurdle rate.** The GPLLC gets a share of the cumulative profits above a preferred return to the limited partners. This is rare.
  3. **Disappearing hurdle rate.** The GPLLC is entitled to a full 20 percent carried interest only if the limited partners' 80 percent share provides a specified preferred return to the limited partners. If the hurdle rate is not met, the GPLLC's percentage is reduced until the specified return is met. This method has become relatively standard, except perhaps for the most successful venture funds.

- **Exclusivity.** The individual managers make commitments as to the amount of time they will spend on the venture fund's affairs and agree that they will not form any additional investment funds until it has been fully or nearly fully invested.

- **Advisory committee.** An advisory committee sometimes is formed with representatives of the limited partners. The committee offers advice to the GPLLC and plays a role in resolving conflict of interest situations.
- **Removal of general partner.** The limited partners sometimes are given the right to remove a general partner. This right is usually severely limited, usually to fraud, breach of duty and the like, or a supermajority vote.

APPENDICES

These appendices are located on the Web site that accompanies this book. For information on the Web site, see the "About the Web Site" section.

CHAPTER 3

INTELLECTUAL PROPERTY PROTECTION

BASICS OF INTELLECTUAL PROPERTY PROTECTION

Intellectual property (IP) is any intangible asset that consists of human knowledge and ideas, or a real-world representation of them. The forms of IP most often encountered when representing start-ups are: patents; copyrights; trade secrets; and trademarks, service marks, and trade names.

PATENTS. A patent is a grant from the government conveying and securing for the owner of an invention the exclusive right to exclude others from making, using, selling, offering to sell or importing the invention.

The "right to exclude others" is a significant phrase. Unlike other forms of IP, a patent does not give anyone a right to do anything. Rather, it merely gives the owner of the invention the right to exclude others from practicing the invention. For example, if you invented and subsequently obtained a patent on rocking chairs, and another party held the patent on chairs (upon which your rocking chair is an improvement), you would not be able to make, use or sell rocking chairs without a license to do so from the owner of the chair patent. You could, however, exclude others (including the owner of the chair patent) from making, using, or selling rocking chairs unless they obtained a license from you.

A patentable invention may consist of a process, machine, manufacture, or composition of matter, or any improvement thereof; an ornamental (nonfunctional) design for a manufactured article; a business method; or a distinct variety of an asexually reproduced plant or organism. Printed matter, algorithms, natural substances, and scientific principles are not patentable.

For a patent to be issued, the invention must be novel, useful, and nonobvious. With respect to novelty, the United States uses the first-to-invent approach; that is, prior to being invented by the inventor, the invention must not have been used by others in the United States, or patented or described in a printed publication in the United States or in a foreign country. By contrast, most countries use a first-to-file approach. (The United States, however, is considering moving to the first-to-file approach.) With respect to usefulness, an invention must have a beneficial use. Finally, an invention must not be obvious to one skilled in the relevant technology. This is often the most difficult of the three tests for a layperson to predict; often an inventor will assume that, since the invention was "obvious" to him or her, it would be obvious to others skilled in the technology. However, nonobviousness is a legal determination, and an examining attorney from the U.S. Patent and Trademark Office (PTO) may have a different view of the obviousness of an invention from its inventor. Accordingly, it is advisable to obtain input from experienced patent counsel before disregarding the possibility of patenting an invention based on its presumed nonobviousness.

A trap for the unwary is the so-called on-sale bar: An invention must not have been in public use or on sale in the United States more than one year prior to the filing date of the U.S. patent application. Similarly, an invention must not have been patented or described in a printed publication in the United States or in a foreign country more than one year prior to the filing date of the U.S. patent application. Often such premature publication occurs when a company's marketing or business development departments are eager to publicize a product in advance of its launch or when inventors describe the invention in academic publications or at trade shows.

A patent is issued to the inventor of the subject invention, unless the inventor has expressly assigned or is under an obligation to assign his or her rights in and to the invention (e.g., to an employer under an employment agreement) or if there is an implied assignment (e.g., where an employee was hired to invent). Where an assignment (express or implied) is not found, but the inventor utilized the employer's resources to develop an invention, the employer is given a "shop right"—a nonexclusive, nontransferable right to practice the invention. In such a case, the inventor retains ownership of the patent rights in the invention.

A U.S. patent, and thus the right to exclude others from practicing the subject invention, continues for a period of 20 years from the filing date. This period may be extended by the PTO for delays in PTO processing and, if applicable, federal Food and Drug Administration approval, for example.

Patents are relatively expensive to obtain, maintain, and defend. Attorneys' fees at a medium to large patent firm for the preparation and prosecution of a patent application can range from approximately $7,500 for relatively simple invention to $15,000 to $20,000, or perhaps much more, for a complex invention. As of May 1, 2007, filing fees are $500 for small entities (fewer than 500 employees) and $1,000 for large entities; issuance and maintenance fees (for utility patents) are $450 (due at 3.5 years), $1,150 (due at 7.5 years), and $1,900 (due at 11.5 years) for small entities and $900 (due at 3.5 years), $2,300 (due at 7.5 years), and $3,800 (due at 11.5 years) for large entities.

To protect their patents, businesses should consider at least:

- Requiring all employees and consultants to enter into invention assignment (and nondisclosure and noncompete) agreements.
- Educating staff using policies, handbooks, and training.
- Requiring all technical/inventive personnel to keep dated notebooks/logs of inventions in which:
  - All entries are written in permanent ink, and tampering with or destroying notebooks/logs is prohibited.
  - All pages in the notebooks/logs are witnessed and dated by someone other than the inventor.
- Requiring invention disclosure forms.
- Conducting periodic legal and technical review of possible inventions.
- Involving experienced patent counsel at least three months before using, selling, offering to sell or publicizing inventions.
- Applying to protect potentially valuable innovations.
- Using notices on issued/applied for patents: "Patent No." or "Patent Pending."

COPYRIGHTS. Copyright protection subsists in original works of authorship fixed in any tangible medium of expression.

"Works of authorship" may include literary, musical, dramatic, pictorial, graphic, and sculptural works; motion pictures and other audiovisual works; sound recordings; architectural works and other works fixed in tangible form. Works of authorship may include a company's software, as well as its documentation, technical drawings, Web site, advertising, marketing materials, white papers, research reports, and databases.

Copyright protection does not extend to any idea, procedure, process, system, method of operation, concept, principle, or discovery, regardless of the form in which it is described, explained, illustrated, or embodied in a work of authorship.

With respect to originality, a work is "original" if it owes its creation or origin to the author, which in turn means that the work must not be copied from another source. Thus, original creation is a defense against a claim of copyright infringement, even if the second work happens to be identical to or substantially similar to the first work.

The owner of a copyrighted work has the exclusive right to do, and to authorize others to do, any of the following actions with respect to the copyrighted work: reproduce, prepare derivative works, distribute, publicly perform, and publicly display.

A copyright is owned by the author of the work upon its creation, unless it is created in the scope of the author's employment or pursuant to a written work-made-for-hire agreement. Regarding the former, because an independent contractor is not an employee, the contractor would own the creative work unless otherwise agreed to in writing. Accordingly, a company should enter into a written agreement with each party it engages to develop creative works that expressly assigns to the company all rights in and to such works. Since, technically, a work-made-for-hire agreement is effective only for the nine specific types of works delineated in the Copyright Act (none of which is of the type most likely to be created for most companies, including software), it is not sufficient for a development agreement to simply recite that the work is a work made for hire; rather, the agreement must expressly state that all rights in and to the work are assigned to the company.

Copyright rights extend for the life of the author of the work plus 70 years. In the case of a work made for hire, copyright rights extend for the shorter of 95 years from the date of publication or 120 years from the date of creation.

Copyright registration is not required for copyright protection; rather, copyright protection is automatic. That is, as soon as an original work of authorship is fixed in a tangible medium of expression, the work is protected by copyright. However, in the United States, registration is a precondition to the filing of a copyright infringement action in federal court, and it also affords certain benefits to the owners of copyright registrations. Specifically, the owner of an infringed copyright work may be entitled to statutory damages of up to $30,000 (up to $150,000 if the infringement was found to have been willful) plus attorneys' fees. Additionally, if it occurs within five years of publication of the work, registration acts as prima facie evidence of the validity of the stated facts (including the date of creation of the work). Copyright registration is inexpensive—Government registration fees are $35.00 and, as the copyright registration process is largely ministerial, attorneys' fees are nominal.

To protect their copyrights, businesses should consider at least:

- Using copyright ownership/assignment agreements with employees and (especially) contractors.
- Educating staff on the importance of the company's copyrights and other intellectual property.
- Including copyright notices on all significant original works, including software, manuals, and advertisements.
- Similarly marking all web-posted or publicly distributed works.
- Obtaining copyright registration for valuable works, especially those likely to be infringed (e.g., consumer software or lyrics to a song).

TRADE SECRETS.   Trade secrets consist of valuable and confidential business information. The most widely used definition of a trade secret is found in the *Restatement of Torts*, Section 757, comment b:

> A trade secret may consist of any formula, pattern, device or compilation of information which is used in one's business, and which gives him an opportunity to obtain an advantage over competitors who do not know or use it. It may be a formula for a chemical compound, a process of manufacturing, treating or preserving

materials, a pattern for a machine or other device, or a list of customers.

Trade secrets may include any of these items, whether patentable or not: ideas, inventions, discoveries, developments, designs, improvements, formulae, compounds, syntheses, know-how, methods, processes, techniques, product specification and performance data, other data, computer programs, business plans, marketing and sales plans, research and development plans, manufacturing and production plans, pricing and other strategies, forecasts, products, financial statements, budgets, projections, licenses, prices, costs, customer and supplier lists, the terms of customer and supplier contracts, personnel information, and compilations of such information.

Since ideas, in and of themselves, are neither patentable nor copyrightable, to be afforded protection against their use by others, they must be protected as trade secrets or confidential information. Moreover, trade secret protection is in some ways superior to the protection afforded by copyright or patent because the subject remains—by definition—secret. To obtain a patent, an applicant must disclose the best way to practice the patent. Copyright prohibits copying of the copyright owner's work but in itself does not provide for the confidentiality of the work.

Trade secret rights are neither conveyed by a grant from the government (like patent rights) nor arise as a result of the creation of a work (like copyright rights). Rather, trade secret rights arise as a result of the value of the information and the maintenance of its secrecy. Specifically, in most states, confidential business or technical information is protected as a trade secret if it is not generally known in the industry, it has value (i.e., it gives its owner a competitive advantage) in part because it is not generally known, and it has been the subject of reasonable measures to maintain its secrecy. Reasonable efforts to maintain secrecy are often cited as the most important element of a valid trade secret. The *Restatement of Torts* sets forth these factors as those that must be considered in determining whether particular information is a trade secret:

- The extent to which the information is known outside the owner's business.
- The extent to which it is known by employees and others involved in the owner's business.

- The type of measures taken by the owner to guard the secrecy of the information.
- The value of the information to the owner and to competitors.
- The amount of effort or money expended by the owner in developing the information.
- The ease or difficulty with which the information could be properly acquired or duplicated by others.

Like patent protection, trade secret rights permit the owner to exclude others from using or maintaining control over the trade secret, if the secret was learned improperly. A trade secret is misappropriated if it is knowingly taken or used without authorization from the owner. Trade secret misappropriation remedies may include substantial damages and injunctive relief.

It is not misappropriation if a secret is discovered through independent creation and rightful discovery. Specifically, it is legally permissible to discover a trade secret by obtaining a product and reverse engineering it. However, many products are obtained not by purchase but by license, and many licenses (including most software licenses) include provisions prohibiting the user from reverse engineering the product. Such prohibitions are generally enforceable under U.S. law, except there is a carve-out for interoperability purposes in the software arena (but not necessarily elsewhere; e.g., a European Union Directive ensures certain reverse engineering rights that cannot be waived by contract in member states).

Employers own the trade secrets developed by their employees (at least those paid to create information). As with patents, courts may also award shop rights.

Trade secret protection continues until the information is no longer secret. Thus, a trap for the unwary disclosing party is entering into a nondisclosure agreement of limited duration. Receiving parties often try to limit the duration of nondisclosure agreements to a finite period of time after disclosure, typically three to five years, for administrative as well as liability limitation purposes. Disclosing parties routinely enter into such agreements without much thought. However, once the nondisclosure covenant expires, it can be argued that the information disclosed is no longer protected as a trade secret vis-à-vis the receiving party or any other party.

Although the legal fees involved in the protection of trade secrets are generally low to moderate, the total cost to the client of maintaining its trade secrets could be quite high, given the proactive conduct required by the client, as recommended next.

To protect their trade secrets, companies should consider at least:

- Performing predisclosure due diligence on prospective partners and employees.
- Using nondisclosure agreements and exit interviews with employees and contractors.
- Entering and enforcing noncompetition agreements with key employees.
- Considering nonsolicitation (no employee "poaching") agreements when contracting with competitors or others in closely related fields.
- Limiting access to those who "need to know."
- Responding to raids on employees by competitors.
- Destroying (shredding) unnecessary media containing trade secrets.
- Controlling access to computers and networks.
- Screening potential business partners, vendors, and customers for legitimacy and reputation.
- Marking all confidential materials as "Confidential" and using more elaborate notices where appropriate, e.g., for business plans:

> The information contained in this business plan is confidential and is intended only for the persons to whom it is transmitted by Acme Corp. (the "Company"). Reproducing this business plan in whole or in part, or divulging any of its contents, without the written prior consent of the Company, is prohibited.
>
> This business plan has been prepared by the Company and remains the Company's property. The recipient agrees to return this plan and any copies it makes to the Company upon request.
>
> © Acme Corp., created in 2007. An unpublished work. All rights reserved.

- Not marking nonconfidential material as confidential.

- For highly sensitive materials, the following additional procedures should be used:
  - Keeping them under lock and key.
  - Limiting copying, numbering copies, and keeping distribution and disclosure records.
  - Where appropriate, requiring passwords.

TRADEMARKS. A trademark includes any word, name, symbol, or device, or any combination, used, or intended to be used, in business to identify and distinguish a company's products or services from products and services sold by others, and to indicate the source of the products and services. In short, a trademark is a brand name. For the purposes of this discussion, the terms "trademark," "service mark," and "mark" will encompass both trademarks and service marks. A trademark may be virtually any kind of symbol, including a word, letters, numbers, a tagline, a design, a shape, an object, a sound, a telephone number, a domain name, a color, or a smell.

Trademarks should not be confused with trade names. While a trademark designates the source or origin of a product or service, a trade name designates a company or entity. For example, the name XEROX, when used in the phrase "XEROX copiers," is a trademark, whereas when used in the phrase "XEROX makes the best copiers," it is a trade name.

Trademark law is founded on the right of the owner of a mark to protect and profit from the goodwill represented by the mark. Trademark law permits the owner of a trademark to exclude others from using the same or a confusingly similar mark in connection with identical goods or services, or goods and services that are so closely related to the owner's goods and services that confusion in the market is likely. Trademark rights are territorial; use in commerce gives rise to rights at common law in the geographic region where the mark is used, whereas federal registration affords national rights without respect to where the trademark owner actually uses the mark.

Additionally, if the goods or services are not so closely related that confusion is likely, but the mark is famous, the owner may be entitled to exclude others from using the mark (or a similar mark) under the theory that the other party's use of the mark dilutes the strength of the mark (i.e., the other party's use blurs or tarnishes the mark).

The strength of a mark depends on whether it is generic, descriptive, suggestive, arbitrary, or coined. A generic mark is one that is the thing itself, such as the mark WATER for the liquid you drink. You can never obtain trademark protection for a word that is generic. A descriptive mark is one that conveys an immediate idea of the qualities or characteristics of a product or service, such as GOOD JUICE. You cannot obtain trademark protection in a descriptive mark unless it has obtained secondary meaning, that is, it has been used in such a way that, while its primary significance in the minds of prospective purchasers remains the quality or characteristic of the product or service, a secondary significance in the minds of prospective purchasers has developed that serves to identify the source of the product or service. A suggestive mark is one that requires thought, imagination, and perception to reach a conclusion as to the nature of the product or service, such as VERYFINE. Suggestive marks are of moderate strength. Arbitrary or fanciful marks are ordinary words used in an unusual way, such as the mark APPLE for computers. Arbitrary and fanciful marks are very strong. The strongest of marks are coined marks, which are original, made up, or fabricated words, such as XEROX.

Trademark rights arise under common law based on use in commerce, so federal or state registration is not required. However, registration does afford a mark owner certain valuable benefits. Federal registration provides prima facie evidence of the validity and ownership of the mark and of the exclusive right to use the mark throughout the United States in connection with the goods or services identified in the certificate of registration. It also acts as constructive notice throughout the United States of the mark owner's claim, permits the owner to establish incontestability after five years of continuous and exclusive use, can serve as a basis for obtaining registration in foreign countries, and may be registered with the U.S. Customs Service to assist in preventing illegal importation of counterfeit goods. Federal trademark registration also permits owners to invoke the jurisdiction of the federal courts and may entitle owners to recover damages and costs from infringers' profits, including treble damages and, in exceptional cases, attorneys' fees. For owners unable to obtain federal registration (e.g., if they are unable to satisfy the federal "use in interstate commerce" requirement), state registration may be beneficial. State registration is generally easier to obtain and provides some of the same benefits as federal registration (albeit only within the borders of the state) and can also act as evidence of mark ownership.

Trademark rights can be lost if the mark is abandoned or becomes generic. Abandonment can take place when the mark is no longer used, when an attempt is made to assign the mark without its attendant good-will, or if a mark owner licenses the mark but fails to maintain adequate quality control over the goods or services in connection with which the mark is used. A mark can become generic when it starts to be used by the general public to describe the goods or services themselves, as opposed to their source or origin. For example, the ASPIRIN, CELLO-PHANE, and ESCALATOR marks were once enforceable marks but have since become so widely used by the general public to identify not the source but the thing itself that the marks are no longer protected. Xerox Corporation spends a lot of time and energy educating the public that the term "xerox" is not a synonym for "copy" but is rather a brand, by, for example, publishing notices to this effect in newspapers.

Common law trademark rights are indefinite in duration; they last until the mark is abandoned or becomes generic. Federal registration initially lasts 10 years but can be renewed indefinitely.

The costs of obtaining and maintaining a federal trademark registration are moderate. As of May 1, 2007, the filing fee was $325 for electronic filing and $375 for paper filing per mark per class. Legal and third-party search fees for clearance, filing, and prosecution are typically on the order of $2,000.

To protect their trademarks, companies should consider at least:

- Performing a clearance search before adopting a mark: Check marks, business names, domain names, and Web site content.
- If possible, federally registering the mark based on use or intent to use.
- Providing trademark notices: ® for federally registered marks, ™ or ℠ otherwise.
- Using the mark properly:

  o Trademarks should always be used as proper adjectives, specifically:

    ◊ They should be capitalized or italicized or in some way stand out from the surrounding text.

⬧ They should be used as a proper adjective modifying a generic term, for example:

◆ Pampers$^{®}$ disposable diapers

◆ Xerox$^{®}$ photocopy machines

- Adhering to proper licensing practices; in particular, no uncontrolled licenses.
- Squelching infringement
  Online, companies should consider:

  ○ Monitoring the Internet, domain names, and metatags for infringement.
  ○ Reserving marks as domain names (and vice versa).
  ○ Reserving marks under other available Top Level Domains (e.g., *.org*, *.net*, and foreign national TLDs).

CHECKLIST OF STEPS TO PROTECT INTELLECTUAL PROPERTY.   One way to look at whether you are properly protecting your IP is to look at your IP protection practices as others will look at them when deciding to invest in your company or acquire it. A so-called due diligence checklist of items that lawyers for a potential investor or acquiror might use in examining the strength of a company's IP portfolio follows.

Patent Due Diligence Checklist

☐ Identify all patents, patent applications, and invention disclosures, including the countries, inventors, assignees, dates, application or patent numbers, and actual inventions covered.

☐ Search PTO records, as well as state and local registries, to be sure that all patents and applications are in the company's name and that no assignments, liens, or encumbrances have been recorded (and not properly discharged).

☐ For important patents, conduct a validity study, including an evaluation of prior art searches, prosecution history, and other available data. Confirm that all inventors are properly named and that all have assigned their interests, by affirmative action or operation of law, to the company. Search for third-party patents that might cover the company's intended uses of its important technology and IP.

☐   Review any claims, suits, proceedings, or other potential challenges to full ownership rights, including demand letters, pleadings, or other sources of such information.

☐   Determine if any action is needed immediately or in the near future to respond to a claim or maintain the applications or patents.

☐   If desired, arrange for a valuation of important patents.

☐   Make sure to check into "pitfall" information.

    ☐   Were all inventors employees of the target company? If not, did they properly assign the patent in writing?

    ☐   Are all inventors named?

    ☐   Was the application filed in the United States within one year after the first sale or publication of the invention?

    ☐   Was the application filed in foreign territories in a timely manner (which may be before any sale or public descriptions)?

☐   Has the company granted any licenses to this patent? If so, be sure they are reasonable—and not detrimental to the acquiror's plans—regarding scope, territory, duration, maintenance obligations, counterrestrictions, and other important aspects.

☐   Did the company have all employees and inventors execute agreements on confidentiality, invention, assignment, and, ideally, noncompetition and nonsolicitation? Collect and inspect all signed agreements.

☐   Did any of the contractors used to develop important IP use subcontractors? If so, inspect the subcontract documents to be sure that IP ownership was properly transferred.

Copyright Due Diligence Checklist

☐   Identify all significant copyrightable works owned by the company and determine if copyright applications have been filed in any jurisdictions. (The United States is the key and often the only relevant jurisdiction with a copyright registration process.) Consider whether any copyrighted works that have not been registered ought to be.

☐   Conduct a U.S. Copyright Office records search to be sure that all significant copyrights are in the company's name; check these records as well as state and local registries to confirm that no assignments, liens, or encumbrances have been recorded (and not properly discharged).

☐ Confirm that all significant copyrighted works used in the target company's business (or considered by the buyer to be a part of the value being acquired) have been created by employees within the scope of employment and/or under written work-made-for-hire agreements, or by contractors who have executed work made-for-hire or assignment-of-rights contracts. If any contractors have used subcontractors, inspect the subcontract documents to be sure IP ownership was properly assigned.

☐ Review any claims, suits, proceedings, or other potential challenges to full ownership rights, including demand letters, pleadings, or other sources of such information, and determine if any action is needed immediately or in the near future to respond to a claim or maintain the copyright.

☐ If desired, arrange for a valuation of the important copyrights, which can now be based on information that may not have been known prior to due diligence.

☐ For important works, note the term of protection (in a corporate environment, generally 120 years from creation or 95 years from first publication). Consider that any works owned by "assignment" (which does not include works made for hire) are subject to the author's right to terminate that assignment during the 35th to 40th years after the grant; since notice of termination can be given 10 years in advance, the company should be asked to represent that it has received no such notices of termination.

Trade Secret Due Diligence Checklist

☐ Identify trade secrets and other confidential information of value.

☐ Investigate and evaluate procedures followed to protect such information from unauthorized transfer, disclosure, and use.

☐ In particular, determine if all employees and contractors with access to secrets have been required to sign nondisclosure (and perhaps nonsolicitation and noncompetition) agreements. Collect and review these agreements. Does the company conduct project termination and exit interviews with contractors and employees to ensure that trade secret materials are surrendered and that these individuals appreciate their obligation of continuing secrecy? If not, consider taking corrective action.

☐ Evaluate all license and nondisclosure arrangements in which critical secrets were disclosed to third parties. Were proper procedures followed? What is the current status of the relationship? If the relationship ended, were the proprietary materials returned and did the recipient confirm that it retained no copies?

☐ Does the company have procedures in place—such as policy statements and provisions in employment contracts expressly prohibiting misuse—to ensure that its personnel do not misappropriate the trade secrets of other businesses, especially those of prior employers?

☐ Check state and local registries to determine if any security interests or other liens or encumbrances that limit the company's rights to its trade secrets have been filed (and not discharged).

☐ Identify any pending offensive or defensive trade secret litigation and assess its significance.

☐ What procedures does the company use to prevent unauthorized access to its computer systems, particularly in light of existing intranets, extranets, and other forms of Internet access?

☐ Specifically, does the company allow use of laptops at work? Can these be removed from the company's premises? What procedures exist to ensure that the laptops have not been and cannot be a source of trade secret leakage?

☐ If employees or contractors can connect to the company's internal computer system from home or other outside locations, what procedures are in place to prevent unauthorized access and misappropriation?

☐ If the company has a Web site, does it allow access to any confidential information? If so, what procedures are in place to keep such information away from the wrong hands and eyes?

Trademark Due Diligence Checklist

☐ Identify all significant trademarks, service marks, trade dress, trade names, and domain names.

☐ Determine if these were "cleared" for use—that is, determine the extent of research performed to confirm that no third party had rights (by use or application) to a confusingly similar mark

at the time the target company adopted the mark (or significantly expanded its use of the mark).

☐ Determine if marks have been used properly, as proper adjectives generally coupled with the generically identified product
or service type (e.g., Rollerblade® brand inline skates) and
including proper markings (® for federally registered marks
and ™ or SM and superscripts for unregistered or state-
registered trademarks and service marks). Review procedures
in place to ensure correct use of trademarks by the company
and its licensees and representatives.

☐ Determine whether all important marks, as just identified,
including all features and aspects capable of trademark protection, are covered by existing registrations or applications.

☐ Review PTO records to ensure that ownership is properly characterized and that any assignments to the company have been
properly recorded. Examine both PTO records and state and
local registries to determine if any security interests, liens, or
encumbrances have been recorded (and not discharged).

☐ Review contracts that relate to trademarks, such as assignments, design and development agreements, and employment
contracts for graphic artists, to ensure that any resulting marks
are owned by the target company.

☐ Specifically consider the implication of the copyright owner's
right to terminate assignments on any graphics or designs com-
missioned from third parties.

☐ Review procedures for ensuring timely PTO filings, including
responses to office actions, Section 8 and Section 15 affidavits,
responses to opposition, and cancellation proceedings, as well
as renewal applications. In particular, identify any filings that
will be required within the next few months and be sure they
will be attended to; docket as appropriate.

☐ Evaluate the extent of global use to ensure that marks have
been cleared in all relevant territories and that necessary foreign
registrations have been sought or obtained.

☐ Review the company's existing Internet domain names (DNs)
to be sure that these are in the company's name, are transferable, and will be transferable to the acquiror. Identify any other
DNs that may pose problems (e.g., if the company adopted

the "company.net" Web address because a third party already owned "company.com"). Determine whether additional DNs should be obtained or other protective efforts deployed.

☐ Review existing license agreements, including oral or implied licenses, to ensure that existing licenses provide sufficient quality control.

☐ Procedures are in place to ensure that the right to control quality is exercised—for example, by periodic inspections of licensees' products and advertising.

☐ Have any known infringements occurred? Have these ceased (or been otherwise resolved), or do they continue? Identify major outstanding infringement and litigation issues, including pending claims, action plans in place, and any changes to the plans you believe are required.

LICENSE AGREEMENTS

A license is an agreement whereby the person or entity that owns or rightfully controls certain (generally intangible) property (the licensor) grants to another person or entity (the licensee) the right to use the property pursuant to certain terms and conditions, or contractually agrees not to sue the licensee for its proper use of the property. A license does not transfer ownership in the property. Licenses are used, in part, to impose restrictions on the use of property that legally cannot be imposed if ownership is transferred instead of licensed.

MAJOR PROVISIONS OF A LICENSE AGREEMENT.   Although license agreements can be extremely flexible and tailored to the parties' interests in a virtually unlimited variety of ways, most licenses contain several key provisions, as described next. For the sake of simplicity, we describe these provisions as they relate to one of the most common forms of license agreement: the software license. Special considerations relating to biotechnology licenses are discussed in "Technology Licensing: Advanced Topics."

Identification of the Parties.   While this point may seem self-evident, great care should be taken to ensure that the license agreement is being entered into between or among the proper parties. This is particularly true with respect to the identification of the licensee. Should the grant of rights be restricted solely to the party identified as the licensee? Or should the licensee's subsidiaries or affiliates also be entitled to benefit from the rights being granted? A party may be organized such that intellectual property must be licensed into an IP holding company and then sublicensed to the affiliate within the organization tasked with exploiting the property. By contrast, the economic terms of an end user license may be predicated on the subject IP being used only by a particular company or division within a conglomerate, as opposed to all of the companies that comprise the conglomerate. For example, if a licensor licenses its software to Acme U.S., Inc., and the licensee is not authorized to grant its affiliates the right to use the software, the licensor may have the opportunity to enter into an additional license with Acme U.K. Ltd. The automatic right to sublicense to affiliates (i.e., related parties) of a licensee is not well advised, given the uncertainty of identifying the affiliates. If a licensee operates as essentially one business conducted through subsidiaries, the term "subsidiary" should be used rather than "affiliate." If a sublicense is permitted to subsidiaries, care must be taken to ensure that the sublicense expires at the time the subsidiary no longer qualifies as such with respect to the licensor (i.e., the licensee cannot sell the subsidiary and have the license survive the sale).

However, if a licensor has concerns about the financial wherewithal of a licensee, it may require that certain of the licensee's affiliates or shareholders be a party to the agreement to guarantee the payment provisions or to guarantee the representations, warranties, and indemnifications.

Description of Licensed Property.   Great care should be given to the description of the property being licensed. The licensee should ensure that it is getting all of the property it needs for its intended use. For example, the licensee may argue that it should receive bug fixes, maintenance releases, and minor updates at no charge. By contrast, the licensor should ensure that it is not licensing more than it intends to, particularly if this could mean lost revenue opportunities. For example, a licensor may want to ensure that major updates, upgrades, and new versions of the software are excluded from the definition of licensed property unless the licensee pays additional fees. The terms and conditions upon which major updates, upgrades, and new versions of the software are provided are themselves a major contractual issue, including the definition of these terms and their price and timing.

The description of property should also describe the form of the property being licensed. This is particularly important with respect to software: Is the software being licensed in object code only, or is the source code (which may expose to the licensee to the licensor's valuable trade secrets) being licensed as well?

Scope of License
LICENSE GRANT

It is important to take great care in describing the limitations of the license grant in terms appropriate for the types of IP rights embodied in the licensed property.

For example, if the licensed property is afforded copyright protection, the grant of license should expressly state which of the copyright "bundle of rights" is being granted. That is, is the licensee permitted to reproduce, prepare derivative works of, distribute, publicly perform, and/or publicly display the licensed property or permitted to conduct a limited set of these activities?

If the property is the subject of a patent, the grant of rights should expressly state to what degree the licensee may make, use, offer for sale, sell, and/or import the subject invention. Note that the right conferred to a patent owner when it is granted a patent is, in the language of the statute and of the grant itself, the right to exclude others from making, using, offering for sale, or selling the invention in the United States or importing the invention into the United States—not the right to make, use, offer for sale, sell, or import the invention. Accordingly, a properly drafted patent license merely grants the right to practice the subject invention without being sued by the licensor; it should avoid the suggestion that the licensor is granting all of the rights necessary for the licensee to practice the subject invention without infringing on a third party's intellectual property rights.

PERMITTED USES AND LICENSE RESTRICTIONS

In addition to carefully describing which statutory rights are being granted, the license grant should describe the specific uses for which such rights may be employed. For example, a software license may permit the licensee to use the software to do (or prohibit it from doing) some or all these: evaluation, internal operational purposes, internal use to provide revenue-generating services to third parties, and product development or distribution to end users or to a chain of third parties for ultimate distribution to end users.

The agreement should also specify any restrictions on the use of the licensed property, such as limitations on the number of users or computers on which the software may be installed. If the rental, lease, or service bureau or timesharing use of the licensed property is prohibited, this fact should be expressly stated. The agreement should also expressly prohibit the reverse engineering of the software (to the extent that this restriction is not prohibited by law) and the removal or alteration of proprietary notices contained in the software, and should also state any compatibility requirements.

EXCLUSIVITY

All licenses should expressly state whether they are exclusive or nonexclusive. In an exclusive license, the rights are granted to the licensee to the exclusion of all other parties, including the licensor. Since exclusive grants limit future business options, prior to granting an exclusive license, a licensor should give a great deal of thought to its long-term effects on the licensor's business; an exclusive deal that seems attractive to a cash-strapped start-up licensor in the short run (e.g., one that provides for a substantial up-front payment) may exclude the licensor from entering into a more attractive deal in the future. Moreover, exclusivity provisions usually are closely examined as part of merger or acquisition due diligence.

For these reasons, if a licensor grants a degree of exclusivity, often it tries to limit the exclusivity by granting it solely within a particular geographic territory, market, or field of use; limiting it to a particular period of time; or making continued exclusivity subject to performance by the licensee of certain objectives, such as the achievement and maintenance of a certain level of sales or the payment of minimum royalties.

TERRITORY

Licenses may be worldwide or limited to a particular geographic territory. The geographic scope of the license may be driven by any number of factors, including in which countries the licensor has obtained patents in the licensed property and where the licensee has sufficient presence.

MARKETS/FIELDS OF USE

Similarly, licenses (particularly resale or distribution license agreements) may be limited to a particular vertical market or field of use. This limitation may be driven by the licensee's expertise in a particular field or presence in a particular market.

DURATION

License terms may be of a fixed duration or "perpetual." In either case, the duration, or "term," should be expressly stated. If a fixed term is renewable, the agreement should describe whether it automatically renews upon the expiration of the then-current term (subject to either party providing notice that it declines to renew) or the parties need to expressly agree to renew the agreement. In most cases, the term of the license is subject to the termination provisions of the agreement, as further discussed later in this chapter.

A note of caution regarding perpetual licenses: Since copyright and patent rights are of a limited duration, it is technically not possible to license these rights perpetually. With respect to copyrights, a "perpetual" license is generally interpreted as a license continuing for the remaining term of the copyright. With respect to patents, however, a royalty-bearing patent license that extends beyond the life of the patent could be found to be a restraint of trade and thus a violation of antitrust laws.

There is a distinction between perpetual licenses and irrevocable licenses. "Perpetual" describes the term of the license; "irrevocable" means that the license cannot be revoked during the term. In the event of a breach by the licensee of an irrevocable license, the licensor can sue for damages for the breach but cannot revoke the license. If a breach is meant to give the licensor the right to terminate, the licensor should provide in the granting clause that the perpetual or irrevocable nature of the license is in each case subject to the further terms of the license, particularly including the termination provisions.

RIGHT TO SUBLICENSE; RIGHT TO DISTRIBUTE

The agreement should expressly state whether the licensee is permitted to sublicense any of its rights to a third party, including, as discussed, any or all of its subsidiaries or affiliates. If it is not permitted to sublicense its rights (e.g., if it's permitted use is limited to its internal data processing purposes), the right to sublicense expressly should be excluded. If the right to sublicense is necessary for it to use the licensed property as contemplated by the parties, the scope of its right to sublicense should be defined and all other sublicense rights should be expressly excluded. For example, if a hardware manufacturer wants to include the licensor's software on its hardware for distribution to end users, the grant of license should permit the manufacturer to sublicense the software to end users solely as installed on the licensee's hardware, and it should expressly exclude the right to sublicense the software apart from the hardware.

Licensees should be required to impose on their sublicensees restrictions on the use of the licensed property sufficient to protect the property at least to the extent required under the prime license. The licensor may require the licensee to use the licensor's form of end user license agreement (EULA), permit the licensee to use a form of EULA agreed to in advance by the licensor, or dictate terms that the licensee must include in its EULA.

Similarly, the licensor should be explicit that, besides not being able to sublicense, the licensee has no right to assign the license to a third party. Licensees will push back on this limitation, asking that the license be assigned in connection with the sale of the business. The license may become integral to the licensee in the operation of its business, and if it cannot be assigned, the value of the licensee's business may be significantly diminished. Even if the licensor permits the license to be assigned in connection with the sale of the licensee's business, the licensor may want to restrict the license from being transferred to certain third parties, such as competitors. Also, if the license is permitted to be assigned, should the right to sublicense to subsidiaries or affiliates of the buyer be included? It may be one thing to allow sublicensing to the worldwide subsidiaries of a small company and quite another to allow sublicensing to the worldwide subsidiaries or affiliates of a giant multinational corporation.

Payment Provisions.   A license may be royalty-free, but typically in consideration of the rights granted to it a licensee will be obligated to pay the licensor a license fee or royalty. A license fee is a predefined amount payable in a lump sum or in periodic payments. A royalty is a running fee typically used with distribution licenses and is dependent on the level of sales of the product incorporating the licensed property. A running royalty may be a per unit fee or a percentage of gross or net revenues. Net revenues are the amounts received (or invoiced) by the licensee minus certain defined costs of doing business, such as credits and refunds, discounts, bad debt, sales and use taxes, customs duties, and costs of collection. Since these deductions are sometimes difficult to define and often difficult to verify, many licensors prefer to be paid royalties on gross revenues. If the royalty is on sales of products that use the licensed technology, provision usually is made to deal with situations in which the product or component is only a part of the product ultimately sold.

Royalties may be paid in advance or in arrears. Often, upon execution of a license agreement, a licensee is required to pay a substantial advance against royalties. Such an advance is recoupable against royalties actually accrued but often is nonrefundable if never recouped. A license agreement may also call for minimum royalties to be paid over a defined period of time. This agreement may include minimum royalties payable at defined intervals throughout the term of the license (e.g., monthly, quarterly, or annually) or upon expiration of the term. In the first case, the agreement should define the penalty for failure meet the minimum royalty: Should the license terminate? Should the licensee lose its exclusivity? Can the licensee retain its rights by paying the shortfall? If so, for how long?

Late payments typically are subject to the imposition of interest by the licensor.

If the licensee is paying royalties, it is customary to require it to provide with royalty payments reasonably detailed reports showing the basis of the calculation of the royalties (such as units sold, revenue received, and permitted deductions made) and to maintain records supporting such reports throughout the term of the license and for a period of time thereafter. It is also customary for the licensor to be permitted to audit such records at its own expense; if the audit reveals a material discrepancy, the licensee must reimburse the licensor for the cost of audit plus any shortfall and applicable late fees.

Ownership. Even though implied by the nature of the agreement, a license agreement often requires the licensee to acknowledge that the licensor (or its licensors) owns the licensed property and retains all rights in it not expressly granted in the license agreement.

If the licensee is permitted to make derivative works or improvements to the licensed property (or if the licensor is required to make the same for the licensee), the agreement should specify who owns such derivative works or improvements and any inventions created in the process of making the same (collectively, "modifications"). This area is often the subject of intense negotiation and is highly dependent on the facts driving the arrangement, including the nature of the modifications. If the modifications are highly specific to the licensee's environment, it may be appropriate for the licensee to own them. If the modifications improve on the functionality or cannot be used independent of the licensor's property, it may be appropriate for the licensor to own them. If it is a collaborative effort, the parties may agree to own the modifications jointly.

Representations and Warranties.   Representations and warranties are statements of fact about the transaction or the licensed property that speak as of a moment in time, or assurances about the performance or status of a licensed property. Representations and warranties can be express or implied.

License agreements often contain IP representations and warranties. Such representations and warranties typically provide that the licensor has all rights in and to the licensed products necessary for it to grant the licenses contained in the agreement and that the licensed property does not infringe on third parties' IP rights. Care should be taken in describing the forms of IP covered by the representations and warranties. For example, since patent due diligence is extremely costly and time consuming, particularly for foreign patents, a software licensor may wish to limit the IP representations and warranties to copyrights; or, if it includes patents, it may exclude unissued patents and all patents issued outside of the United States.

Software licenses often include representations and warranties regarding software performance. From a licensor's perspective, the performance should be measured against a well-defined, objective standard and exclude nonmaterial failures to perform. For example, a licensor may wish to state no more than that the software will operate in material conformance with the specifications furnished to the licensee by the licensor. Generally, a licensor will want to limit such representations and warranties to a defined period of time; a licensee may wish for such representations and warranties to last for the duration of the license. Not all license agreements include all of these representations and warranties. Some or all of them may be excluded on the basis of the economics or subject matter of the deal or the parties involved. For example, it may be appropriate to exclude IP and performance representations and warranties from beta or evaluation license agreements, and it may be possible to exclude IP representations and warranties from end user license agreements for relatively inexpensive software products.

If representations and warranties are provided, the remedies for their breach should be specified. The remedies for breach of the IP representations and warranties typically include the obligations on the part of the licensor to some or all of these issues:

1. Obtain for the licensee the rights necessary for it to continue its enjoyment of the rights granted to it under the license agreement.
2. Modify the software so it becomes noninfringing.
3. Replace the software with noninfringing software.
4. If none of these alternatives is available on commercially reasonable terms, terminate the license and refund to the licensee all or a portion of the fees paid.
5. Indemnify the licensee (as described next).

The remedies for breach of the performance remedy typically include one or more of the repair or replacement of the software, money damages, and termination of the license and a full or partial refund of the license fees. Licensors typically state that the delineated remedies are the licensor's sole obligations and the licensee's sole remedies with respect to a breach of licensor's representations and warranties.

The licensor typically expressly excludes and disclaims all representations and warranties not expressly described in the agreement. These areas may include implied representations and warranties of noninfringement, merchantability, and fitness for a particular purpose. The licensor also typically will state that its representations and warranties do not apply to the use of the software in combination with any software or hardware not authorized by the licensor, any modifications of the software not made by the licensor, and the licensee's failure to use the latest commercial release of the software.

Indemnification. License agreements generally include an indemnification provision, which describes the parties' respective obligations and remedies if certain things go wrong.

If the licensor provides IP representations and warranties (and often even if it does not), it is usually required to indemnify, defend, and hold harmless the licensee against third-party IP infringement claims. As discussed earlier with respect to IP representations and warranties, great care should be taken in defining the forms of IP that give rise to the licensor's indemnification obligations (e.g., excluding all patents, non-U.S. patents, or pending patent applications).

As with the licensor's representations and warranties, there are typically certain exclusions from licensor's IP indemnification obligations. Specifically, the licensor typically is not required to indemnify the licensee against third-party claims arising due to licensor's compliance with the licensee's functional specifications, from the licensee's failure to use the current commercial release of the software, or from the licensee's use or distribution of the software or the combination of the software with the licensee's or other parties' products. The licensor typically is not required to indemnify the licensee against claims for which the licensor does not receive adequate and timely notice and opportunity to defend or appropriate cooperation from the licensee.

Licensees typically are required to indemnify the licensor against losses suffered because of any of the activities described in the preceding paragraph as creating exceptions to the licensor's indemnity obligations. A licensor may also try to require the licensee to indemnify the licensor against losses suffered because of the licensee's breach of the agreement. If the licensor has ongoing obligations to the licensee, it may be the licensee who requires this indemnification from the licensor. Often reciprocal indemnification occurs. This is a trap for the unwary. Since, as will be discussed, indemnification obligations typically are excluded from exclusions of indirect damages and limitations of liability, such an indemnification obligation could result in the exception swallowing the whole by eviscerating the indemnifying party's exclusions of indirect damages and limitations of liability.

Indemnification provisions should spell out the mechanics and procedures for obtaining indemnification, including the obligations on the part of the indemnitee to provide prompt notice and to cooperate with the indemnifying party's efforts to resolve the problem (at the indemnifying party's expense), and should allow the indemnitee to be represented by independent counsel, generally at its own expense.

Limitations of Liability.   Most license agreements include a provision limiting the parties' exposure to liability and excluding certain types of damages. It is common practice for both parties to exclude all damages other than direct damages, including incidental, consequential, special, and punitive damages. Since in certain situations such an exclusion could significantly impair a claimant's ability to collect meaningful damages (e.g., consequential damages may be the only effective remedy for a claim of misappropriation of confidential information), certain types of claims may be carved out of the exclusion of indirect damages. These claims include IP indemnification obligations and other claims covered by the indemnification provisions and misappropriation or unauthorized disclosure of confidential information.

It is also common practice to place a cap on the maximum liability of the parties under the agreement. This amount may arbitrary amount or an amount received by the licensor over a specified period of time. In either case, the licensor should be careful to ensure that if the claim relates to the licensee's failure to make payments, the cap should not have the effect of limiting the outstanding amounts payable by the licensee. Also, as with the exclusion of indirect damages, certain types of claims may be carved out of the liability cap or subject to a higher cap.

Confidentiality.   Because of the nature of license agreements, confidential information, including that included with or embodied in the property that is the subject of the license, often is disclosed between the parties. As a result, most license agreements contain confidentiality provisions (or, if the parties are subject to a separate nondisclosure agreement, provide that such agreement covers the information disclosed in connection with the license agreement).

If only one of the parties will be disclosing confidential information, it may be appropriate for the confidentiality provisions to be unilateral. However, in most license arrangements the relationship is sufficiently complex to warrant bilateral confidentiality provisions.

"Confidential information" can defined as narrowly as written information marked as confidential, more broadly also to include information disclosed orally if later identified in writing to be confidential, or as broadly as all information disclosed by either party, whether written or oral and whether marked confidential or not. If the last in this list is unpalatable, one of the first two definitions can be used with the addition that the confidentiality obligation also covers verbal information that is technical and ordinarily considered to be confidential. Naturally, the party most likely to be the disclosing party would prefer the broadest definition, while the party most likely to be the recipient would prefer the narrowest definition.

In any case, such definition typically is subject to some or all of these carve-outs:

- If the recipient had prior knowledge of the information (though often only to the extent that the recipient has documentation to prove this).
- If the recipient received such information from a third party not under obligation of confidentiality.
- If the information is publicly available or becomes publicly available through no fault of the recipient.
- If the information is independently developed without use of or reference to the disclosing party's confidential information.

The party invoking any of these exceptions has the burden of proof. In addition, often it is stated expressly that a party may disclose confidential information as required by a law or court order, provided that the recipient gives the disclosing party advanced notice and acts reasonably to maintain confidentiality, such as by seeking protective orders.

Confidentiality provisions generally provide that the recipient cannot disclose the confidential information except to its employees and contractors who are subject to confidentiality obligations and who have a need to know. They further provide that the recipient may use the confidential information only for permitted purposes and must safeguard the information according to a defined standard of care (typically no less than it provides for its own confidential information). Generally such provisions provide that confidential information must be returned or destroyed upon expiration or termination of the agreement.

Confidentiality obligations typically survive the termination of the license for a defined period of time or indefinitely. A note of caution is warranted with respect to trade secrets included in the confidential information. Since trade secret protection continues only for so long as the information is maintained as secret, the disclosing party should ensure that the confidentiality provisions last indefinitely with respect to any trade secrets.

Termination. One or both parties may have the right to terminate the agreement prior to the expiration of the term. The types of termination fall into two broad categories: termination for cause and termination for convenience (or without cause).

License agreements typically provide that the agreement can be terminated for cause. In such cases it is good practice to define "cause." The definition may include the material breach of the agreement that remains uncured after notice (as further discussed later), the change of control of a party, the bankruptcy of a party (though such an "ipso facto" clause is generally not enforceable in bankruptcy under federal law), the failure by a party to achieve certain milestones or other targets, or other causes that the parties agree on.

Depending on the nature of the license, a license agreement may also provide for termination for convenience. As the name implies, a party with the right to terminate for convenience generally can terminate the agreement at any time, whether the other party has done anything to warrant termination or not. In most cases a licensee would not want the license agreement to permit the licensor to terminate without cause, since the licensee may be relying substantially on the existence of the license for internal data processing purposes or as part of its business objectives. However, licensors may want to provide that the license expires if the licensee ceases to conduct business related to the licensed property or ceases operations entirely. That would be particularly important in the case where a license is exclusive and fully paid up; in that case, a cessation of business would not necessarily implicate other provisions that would allow termination by the licensor.

A license agreement should specify the procedure for termination. Typically the party seeking to terminate is required to provide written notice of its intent to the other party. The agreement should specify the period of time prior to the effective date of termination during which the party wishing to terminate must give notice. The notice period for terminating for convenience is typically longer than that required to terminate for cause. With respect to termination for breach, license agreements typically provide a period during which the breaching party is permitted to cure the breach in order to avoid termination (typically coterminous with the notice period). However, if the breach giving cause for termination is not capable of being cured (e.g., misappropriation of confidential information), a cure period (and thus a notice period) may not be appropriate.

A license agreement should describe the parties' respective rights upon the termination or expiration of the agreement. Typically the license terminates, and the licensee must return to the licensor (or destroy and certify to the licensor that it has done so) all materials provided by the licensor. Under certain circumstances, a distributor licensee may be permitted to fulfill orders for the licensed product unfulfilled as of the date of termination or sell off inventory on hand (so long as it does not run up inventory in the period preceding expiration or termination). By their nature, certain rights and obligations of the parties typically survive the expiration or termination of the agreement. These may include the payment of accrued royalties, the payment of royalties on posttermination sales, the right to audit the licensee's books and records, support obligations, confidentiality obligations, and warranty and indemnification obligations. Software end user sublicensees' rights typically are independent of the prime license agreement and thus usually survive its expiration or termination.

Escrow.   Software licensees often request that the source code to the licensed software be placed in escrow, to be released to it upon the occurrence of a release condition (as discussed later). Where the licensor agrees to such an arrangement, the source code generally is deposited with an independent escrow agent acceptable to both parties, subject to a separate escrow agreement by and among the three parties (or by and between the licensor and the escrow agent and naming the licensee as a beneficiary).

Since the source code may embody valuable trade secrets of the licensor, the licensor should carefully consider the appropriateness and necessity of any arrangement whereby another party may have access to the source code, including the deposit of the source code into escrow for the benefit of a licensee. An obvious example of when such an arrangement is not appropriate from the licensor's perspective is where a licensor is not required under an agreement to provide its licensee with support or maintenance of its software (or when such obligations expire).

If the licensor determines that source code escrow is appropriate and necessary, it should take great care in selecting and describing in the escrow agreement the events that must occur or conditions that must be satisfied for the source code to be released to the licensee (release conditions). The licensee usually requests that the source code be placed in escrow to mitigate its concern that the licensor may become unable to support or maintain the software. Accordingly, a licensee generally will request that the release conditions include the licensor's actual or threatened failure to support or maintain the software and the licensor's bankruptcy or insolvency. The licensor, however, would prefer to limit the release conditions to the licensor's actual (perhaps even repeated) material failure to support and maintain the software as required in the license agreement and the licensor's failure to cure such failure after an additional notice period. In any event, the release of the source code from escrow generally is governed by a release procedure defined in the escrow agreement that provides for the notice of a release condition by the licensee, contrary instructions by the licensor, and a procedure for resolution of the matter by third parties.

If a license agreement provides for the escrow of the source code, it should also provide for a limited grant of license to the licensee in and to the source code upon the occurrence of a release condition, precisely describing the permitted use of the source code and any restrictions on such use. It should also make clear that the source code is subject to the confidentiality provisions provided in the agreement.

Dispute Resolution; Venue; Choice of Law.   License agreements often include provisions describing the procedures by which disputes between the parties are to be resolved. If the parties agree to alternative dispute resolution (ADR), the provision should state whether ADR is mandatory or not; describe the escalation path (e.g., commencing with direct discussions, moving to mediation, and ending with arbitration, unless the matter is settled along the way); and state whether any types of disputes should be excluded (e.g., disputes regarding IP and the misappropriation of confidential information typically are excluded from the ADR requirement). ADR provisions should also state the rules and body governing the mediation or arbitration (e.g., the American Arbitration Association), the number and manner of selecting the arbitrators or mediators, and the location of arbitration or mediation.

For disputes or actions not subject to ADR, the agreement should state the venue or venues in which hearings are to be held and whether such venues are exclusive or nonexclusive. If the subject of the license is complex, the licensor may wish to require the waiver of trial by jury.

The license should also state the governing law under which the agreement is to be interpreted. A licensor may argue that since it is its intellectual property that is at stake, it should be entitled to dictate the governing law. However, a licensee of sufficient bargaining position may insist on governing law with which it is more comfortable and familiar.

Assignability.   License agreements should state whether and under what conditions the agreement or any of the rights or obligations under it are assignable by either party. Unlike other types of agreements, certain IP licenses, if silent on the matter, are not assignable.

With IP license agreements, the issue of assignability is very fact-specific and depends in large part on the respective rights and obligations of the parties, in addition to the parties' negotiating leverage. If a licensor does no more than grant a license and collect royalties, a licensee should have little reason to object to it assigning the agreement to another party. However, if the licensor is required to provide customization, maintenance, or support, it may be appropriate for these obligations to be deemed personal to the licensor and thus not assignable. But, as with a licensee, what happens if the licensor is proposing to sell its business?

If a licensee is using the software solely for its internal processing purposes, it may be acceptable to permit it to assign the agreement in the event of a change of control or other merger or acquisition transaction. By contrast, if the licensee is a distributor of the software, it may be appropriate to prohibit the assignment of the agreement to any party unless the licensor has consented to such assignment in writing. The licensor should be able to withhold its consent to assignment if, for example, the licensor has concerns about the proposed successor's ability to perform the licensee's obligations under the agreement or if such party is a competitor of the licensor.

In any event, the provision should state that any purported assignment in violation of the provision is void and of no effect and that the agreement is binding on the parties' successors and assigns.

Miscellaneous.   Finally, license agreements contain a number of miscellaneous or so-called boilerplate provisions. Despite the name, these provisions are negotiable and may be of great importance. Examples of boilerplate provisions include:

- Integration clauses (merging all prior discussions on the subject matter into the "four corners" of the agreement).
- Severability provisions (providing that any provisions held invalid will not effect the remaining provisions).
- Amendment provisions (requiring all amendments to be in writing and signed by the parties).
- Notice provisions.
- Waiver provisions (providing that a waiver of a breach is not to be deemed a continuing waiver).
- Independent contractor provisions (negating any implication of agency between the parties).
- Force majeure provisions (excusing delays in the performance of obligations caused by events beyond the party's control).
- Provisions governing each of the parties' responsibilities with respect to export control.

Checklist for License Agreements.   This checklist summarizes some of the principal issues in negotiating license agreements based on what potential buyers and their lawyers look for in acquisitions.

Licensing-In Due Diligence Checklist

- ☐ Identify all licenses where the company is the licensee (in-licenses) of important intellectual property rights and technology.
- ☐ For each license, identify the:
  - ☐ Scope
  - ☐ Duration
  - ☐ Termination events
  - ☐ Territory
  - ☐ Cost (including, among other elements, installment payments, royalties, support fees, and commissions)
  - ☐ Exclusivity

☐ Rights to sublicense
☐ Liability
☐ Protection against third-party claims (IP indemnification)
☐ Treatment of derivative IP (Who owns it? Must the owner license back or cross-license?)
☐ Assignability

☐ Must any notice be given or approval be obtained to assign this license to the buyer? If so, be sure to follow all required procedures.

☐ Verify with the licensor that the license has not been terminated or modified.

☐ What costs are associated with the license? Are they affordable, or are they too high for the buyer's business plans? Can these costs be decreased, other than through renegotiation? Alternatively, under what circumstances, perhaps including mere acquisition or growth, do these costs increase automatically or at the will of the licensor? (The mere act of making the buyer the new "owner" of the license could have cost implications, e.g., where the in-licensed software is priced on the basis of "seats" or "concurrent users" and the intent of the acquisition is to deploy the software within the merged enterprise.)

☐ Is the scope of the license granted to the target company broad enough for the buyer's business purposes and future business needs? How much more might it cost to expand the license rights for future growth?

☐ What is the term of the license? Does enough time remain on the current term for the buyer's proposed uses? Can the term be extended by the target company? Alternatively, can it be terminated by the licensor as a result of the merger, change of control, or conduct of the licensee? Be sure that the company represents that nothing has occurred, including a breach or misconduct, that would allow the licensor to terminate the grant.

☐ In what territory can the rights be exercised? Is this territory sufficiently broad? Can it be increased? Alternatively, are there conditions under which the licensor can reduce the geographic limits, such as a failure to achieve defined sales or revenue goals?

Licensing-Out Due Diligence Checklist

☐ Identify all licenses of significance where the company is the licensor (licenses-out), with particular emphasis on those not in the ordinary course of business.

☐ Are the "ordinary course" licenses all in substantially the same form? Inspect the form: Require the target company to identify different versions and special deals.

☐ For all out-licenses, consider the same basic issues as for in-licenses:

  ☐ Scope
  ☐ Revenues produced
  ☐ Obligations imposed (such as maintenance, support, and training)
  ☐ Exclusivity (Does combination of scope and exclusivity unduly constrain the buyer?)
  ☐ Assignability
  ☐ Sublicensability (Are there restrictions against use by competitors?)
  ☐ Term and termination rights
  ☐ Rights to improve
  ☐ Allocation of rights to improvements
  ☐ Exposure under warranty, liability, and indemnity provisions

☐ Is notice or consent required in connection with the proposed transaction? If so, be sure to follow all required procedures.

☐ To whom have licenses been granted? Pay particular attention to the definition of the "licensee" and the rules on transferability and sublicensing. Consider whether these may create problems for the merged entity (e.g., by creating a relationship with a competitor, foreign business, or government, the implications of which are unacceptable or require analysis).

☐ Similarly, how broad is the scope and territory? Is the breadth of the scope problematic—for example, creating a potential competitor in a critical territory?

☐ What is the duration of these licenses, and can they be terminated?

☐ Will inheriting these out-licenses impose obligations or restrictions on the buyer—for example, territories it will be prevented from exploiting, customers it will be prohibited from contacting, or maintenance or support that it will be obligated to provide, perhaps at significant cost?

☐ What remuneration, if any, do these licenses provide? Is the remuneration sufficient in light of the obligations the licenses impose?

☐ Have all limitations, restrictions, and obligations that are imposed on licensees been imposed by these licensees downstream (on their sublicensees and subdistributors)?

TECHNOLOGY LICENSING: ADVANCED TOPICS

OPEN SOURCE SOFTWARE TRAPS.   Today there is a vast array of free open source software available, from e-mail programs and desktop publishing to Web server software and content management tools.[1] Open source software has become an increasingly important part of corporate computer systems, shifting the computing approach of many dominant technology companies. This trend has significant legal and business implications for companies, because it turns the traditional software business model on its head by allowing companies to customize open source applications to suit their needs.

The most popular open source program is made available by the Free Software Foundation under its General Public License (GPL). The GPL's attractiveness stems from the fact that it permits free use, modification, and redistribution of the open source software and its underlying source code.

The GPL is also of the most concern to businesses because if, for example, a commercial software vendor wants to modify the open source software using the vendor's own proprietary code, the GPL license requires that the code be licensed under the GPL—or a less restrictive licensing scheme—to the public for free, regardless of whether the vendor intended this result. This could spell disaster for a company that derives a substantial portion of its revenue from licensing its proprietary software. One way to avoid this result is to keep corporate proprietary code separate from the GPL code and to keep

---

1.   This information is taken from materials written by Kimberly B. Herman of Sullivan & Worcester, Boston, Massachusetts.

any modifications made to each fully independent so that proprietary code is not integrated into an open source application.

Critics, including Microsoft, call the GPL license viral because of this characteristic and consider it a serious competitive threat. Open source advocates take the position that the collaborative nature of open source software creates better software for everyone and is less expensive to implement than proprietary, closed-source software applications.

Complicating matters is that the enforceability of open source licenses, including the GPL, has not been tested in a court of law. To date, the only lawsuit dealing directly with open source is the pending multibillion-dollar case between the SCO Group and IBM, where SCO is claiming its proprietary UNIX code was illegally copied into Linux. SCO has since filed lawsuits against large-scale Linux users for misappropriation of intellectual property. These lawsuits may very well represent the start of litigation stemming from use of open source software.

Until the courts determine whether open source licenses are enforceable and the dust settles in the SCO suit, companies should know whether open source applications are part of the commercial software they purchase a license to use—it is common practice for software vendors to embed open source programs into their commercial applications without taking responsibility for it—and should assume that the licenses governing use of the open source are, in fact, enforceable and act accordingly.

A company should take several steps to minimize these risks. First, a company should identify all open source software it is using by making a list of all such open source software. Second, a company should collect the applicable open source license agreements and have legal counsel review them to ensure corporate compliance. Most open source licenses can be found on the Internet at *www.opensource.org*. As part of this step, legal counsel should also determine how open source is being used within the company and whether modifications to the open source have been made. If modifications have been made to the open source code under the GPL license, the license dictates that the modifications also become open source applications.

Once a company evaluates its legal exposure and patches any holes in its processes, it should develop an open source policy (see Exhibit 3.1) that identifies personnel authorized to review and approve

[COMPANY NAME]

POLICY STATEMENT CONCERNING OUR PROCUREMENT
AND USE OF OPEN SOURCE SOFTWARE

WHAT IS OPEN SOURCE SOFTWARE?

Generally speaking, "open source" refers to any software program that is licensed on terms that permit the user to run the program for any purpose, to study and modify the source code of the program, and to redistribute copies of the original or modified program, all without the payment of a fee or royalty to the licensor. Well-known examples of open source software include the Linux operating system, the JBoss application server, the Apache web server, and the MySQL database engine.

SAMPLE POLICY STATEMENT

We, like many other companies, recognize that there are significant benefits to using open source software in our business, including greater reliability, increased performance, improved scalability, and reduced total cost of ownership. In our case, and by way of example, we use the following open source software packages for the following reasons:._____.

While we recognize that there may be many benefits to open source software, we do not believe that the open source licensing model is the best licensing model for our own software products. As you know, we invest heavily in software development, and we remain committed to a commercial licensing model, which allows us to charge a fee for our software products—we believe that this is the most efficient way for us to operate a profitable business and maximize value for our investors. We are, therefore, committed to taking all steps necessary to protect our intellectual property rights in the software that we develop.

It is our policy that open source software may be used in our business so long as its use does not in any way adversely impact our ability to charge a fee for the software that we develop and so long as the acquisition and use of such software otherwise complies with this Policy. Moreover, where we have acquired open source software for use in our business, it is our policy to comply with the license and copyright restrictions applicable to all instances and uses of such open source software. Unauthorized use of open source software is absolutely prohibited. It is the responsibility of all of our personnel to ensure that we comply with the license terms applicable to all open source software acquired by us or used in our business. Any questions or concerns regarding noncompliance should immediately be addressed to [*].

EXHIBIT 3.1   SAMPLE COMPANY POLICY ON OPEN SOURCE SOFTWARE

GENERAL RESPONSIBILITIES

The [[*] Department] has responsibility for the procurement and administration of all open source software acquired by us or used by us in our business. Without the express, prior authorization of the [[*] Department], you should not:

- Order or procure any open source software on our behalf;

- Receive, download or install any open source software on your personal computer or any other computer owned or leased by us; or

- Copy, or modify the source code of, any open source software installed on our computer systems or otherwise maintained by us or on our behalf.

If you believe that you need to take any of the foregoing actions for a legitimate business purpose, you should submit an Authorization Request to [*]. The Authorization Request may be sent via e-mail, fax, or interoffice delivery and, if urgent, should be marked for immediate attention.

ADDITIONAL GUIDELINES RELATING TO RECIPROCAL OPEN SOURCE LICENSES

We believe that so-called "reciprocal" open source licenses pose the greatest danger to our ability to protect our intellectual property rights in the software that we develop. In brief, a reciprocal open source license obligates us to make the software (including source code) that we develop generally available, free of charge, to the extent that this software constitutes a "derivative work" of the applicable open source software held under a reciprocal license. The most popular form of reciprocal license is the GNU General Public License (including the GPL and the LGPL).

Unfortunately, the determination as to what constitutes a derivate work in this context is extremely fact specific and subject to a great deal of interpretation. Accordingly, and as an added means of protecting our intellectual property rights in the software that we develop, we have adopted the following guidelines with respect to the use of open source software held under a reciprocal license:

- You are responsible for making yourself aware of license terms, and ensuring compliance with the license terms and copyright restrictions, applicable to all instances of open source software used by you. If you are unsure as to whether or not a particular software program is held under a reciprocal license, you should contact [*] immediately and, in all events, prior to making any modifications to the source code of the applicable software program.

EXHIBIT 3.1   (continued)

- You should not copy or reinstall any open source softwareheld under a reciprocal license without the prior written authorization of the [[*] Department].

- If, with proper authorization, you are using open source software held by us under a reciprocal license, you should not make any alterations to the source code of such software without first notifying [*] and obtaining explicit written authorization.

- If, as part of your business relationship with us or otherwise using any of our facilities or equipment, you intend to write any new software program, routine, or script (a "New Program") that links to or from, interacts with, embeds (is embedded in), or otherwise incorporates any open source software held by us under a reciprocal license, then you should prepare a written description of the New Program (including a written description of the functionality of the New Program, a list of all dll's and any functions, subroutines, or other procedures upon which it relies). This written description should be first submitted to [*] before you take any action with respect to a New Program.

- You should not take any action with respect to the development of a New Program without the prior written authorization of the [[*] Department].

- Any New Program developed by you with proper authorization should be documented in detail and separately stored in our development environment.

EXHIBIT 3.1   (continued)

the use of open source applications that the company is using or intends to use as well as personnel who have the authority to access the open source code and a narrow set of circumstances under which personnel can modify the open source code. All of these efforts should be carefully documented. Finally, an open source software training program should be instituted to ensure that personnel are aware of the legal risks that may arise through use of open source and threaten a company's critical intellectual property base.

It is clear that the open source movement will continue to pick up speed notwithstanding the legal and business risks, because most people seem to agree that there are many significant advantages in using open source applications, including swift identification and repair of security flaws and rapid innovation. With some caution and some prior planning, implementation of open source can be a success.

BIOTECH/PATENT LICENSING. Here we address contractual and intellectual property considerations that arise frequently in the drafting and negotiation of license agreements in the biotech industry, and in particular license agreements for engineered compounds or biological materials.[2] For ease of reference and in order to avoid becoming bogged down in matters of science (which are beyond the scope of this text), these engineered compounds or biological materials will be simply referred to as the "compound." It is assumed that the licensor has a proprietary interest (either as the patent owner or as the exclusive licensee from a third party) in the compound that is the subject of the license agreement. The topics to be covered are field of use restrictions; compounds with possible multiple applications or the "multipurpose compound"; special issues related to nonexclusive licenses; payment terms; and rights to the drug master file upon early termination of the license.

Field of Use. As the name suggests, a field of use provision in a license agreement limits the licensee's rights in the licensed technology to specified applications. Typically, the field of use restriction first pops up in the definitional section of the license agreement, and is usually called the field. It will then appear in the grant of rights or actual license grant provision, where it serves as a limitation on those rights. For example, a grant clause with a field of use restriction may state that "Licensor hereby grants to Licensee a nonexclusive license of and under the Licensed Patents in the Territory to make, have made, use, sell and import Products for use in the Field."

Field of use restrictions deserve special consideration in biotechnology. Consider a compound that might have potential preventive, diagnostic, or therapeutic uses for several disease indications in both humans and animals. In the absence of field of use restrictions, the licensee would have rights to exploit the compound in all of those fields, and if the license were exclusive, no one else would have those rights. If the license does have field of use restrictions, but they are not carefully considered and drafted, the licensee might not have rights to

2. This information is taken from materials written by Jeffrey Somers of Morse, Barnes-Brown & Pendleton, Waltham, Massachusetts.

do what it wants to do. The goal in drafting field of use restrictions is clear and unambiguous language so each party (and a court, if it ever came to that) knows what is included and what is not.

From the licensor's perspective, it wants the most narrow field of use that gives the licensee what it wants/needs, but also gives the licensor the opportunity to exploit the other potential uses of the compound. For example, suppose that there are early indications in the lab that the compound might have some efficacy for two very disparate diseases, such as brain tumors and stomach ulcers (not likely, but a stark example to make this point). Pharma Company is interested in the compound, but its focus is cancer, and, therefore, its interest is in the potential use to treat brain tumors. It is not likely to invest in the development of the compound for stomach ulcers. If the owner of the compound licenses it to Pharma Company without a field of use restriction to brain tumors, the owner has deprived itself of the opportunity to develop (either itself or through another licensee) the compound for stomach ulcers (or any other use that might be identified through further research). As a result, the best use of the compound may never be exploited. Therefore, it is in the interest of the licensor to give the licensee a field of use that permits the licensee to effectively exploit the compound in its desired field of use, but not to deprive the licensor of the opportunity to exploit the other potential uses. The licensor does not want to put all of its eggs in one basket with a licensee that may not have the resources to pursue multiple potential uses. In other words, the licensor seeks to maximize the potential value of its invention.

The licensee, however, wants as broad as possible a field of use (e.g., therapeutic use in humans or cancer in general) or, ideally, no field of use restriction. Much will depend, of course, on the stage of development of the compound. If it is very early stage, there have been no other licenses, and Pharma Company will fund substantially all of the subsequent development, Pharma Company may want and be entitled to a broad field of use because it is first in line and taking the early risk. It does not want to fund further development (to which the licensor often has access and rights) and then miss out on the potential for a blockbuster use that has not yet been identified but is not included in its field of use. However, if the compound is more fully developed and there are already other licenses in place, Pharma Compound will have to accept a narrower field of use (what has not been taken yet by other licensees).

PRACTICAL TIPS

How can you bridge these conflicting interests? There are a number of possibilities, of which two are often used. The licensor can agree to a broader field of use (or none at all) but have the right to take back fields of use if the licensee elects not to pursue that use. Another solution is for the licensee to agree to a narrow field of use but have a right of first refusal on other uses that the licensor proposes to license to third parties in the future.

Again, it is necessary to be sure that the field of use is as clear and as unambiguous as possible. It will be necessary for each party to get its scientists involved if a field of use is proposed that is technically described.

If the parties have agreed to a limited field of use, it is important to be clear that all others are not included. For example, instead of defining the field of use as "therapeutic use in humans, but not diagnostic use," define it as "therapeutic use in humans but no other use." A belt and suspenders approach would be to add that the licensor "retains all rights in all fields other than therapeutic use in humans."

The terms of the improvements and grantback provisions must be considered in relation to the field of use restrictions. For example, if the license includes a narrow field of use but also includes a grantback to the licensor of any improvements made by the licensee, the licensor could have an enormous windfall. Using the same example, suppose the potential use for stomach ulcers is unidentified at the time of the license, and while the licensee is doing its development work related to brain tumors, it stumbles on this potential use. This would be an improvement that is granted back to the licensor. Suppose further that this proves to be the blockbuster use of the compound. Unless the licensee has some rights in the improvement (beyond the right to use it for the use for which it is licensed), such as a right of first refusal to license the improvement or a participation in the economic benefits from the commercialization of the improvement (e.g., a royalty on sales by the licensor or a third-party licensee), the licensee will have lost out entirely on something it discovered.

Multipurpose Compound.   Suppose that Pharma Company has been sponsoring research at Baby Biotech that leads to the discovery of an engineered peptide that shows some promise. The early indications are possible activity related to stomach ulcers, but it is too early in the research to know if there are any other possible indications or targets. Meanwhile, the clock is ticking under Pharma Company's sponsored research agreement to exercise its option for a license of the patents (at this stage, patent applications) on the engineered peptide. Pharma Company exercises its option. What does it get? A license of the patents for all potential uses (at this stage in the patent prosecution strategy, the patent application would be as broad as possible) or just for stomach ulcers? The multipurpose compound presents many of the same issues and considerations that have been addressed in the discussion of field of use restrictions.

From the perspective of Baby Biotech, the licensor, it would prefer a narrow license in order to maximize the potential of the multipurpose compound through multiple license grants. It would achieve this by carefully crafted field of use restrictions in each license. Through this program, it could achieve concurrent development of the peptide by a number of licensees with available resources, something that a single licensee, especially in the pharmaceutical industry, is unlikely to be able to undertake.

From Pharma Company's perspective, it would like, for all the reasons discussed, a worldwide exclusive license of and under all of the patents related to the engineered peptide. Having paid for the discovery of the multipurpose compound, its position is that it is entitled to all of the potential value of the discovery. Even if it does not have the resources necessary to engage in concurrent development for possible different indications, it would like the right to control and benefit from that process through a sublicensing program.

PRACTICAL TIPS

In the sponsored research context, you may be able to avoid these issues by addressing them in the funding agreement. If Pharma Company is providing all or substantially all of the funding to Baby Biotech for a specific research program, it likely will be able to negotiate for all rights in all discoveries from the program. The funding agreement should be unequivocal if that is the case. If Pharma Company has not provided funding and is negotiating with Baby Biotech after it has made a discovery, Pharma Company will likely not get all fields, but will probably be limited to the uses that are its specialty (most pharma companies focus on one or a few disease indications). If Pharma Company is sponsoring research at a university, its rights are also likely to be limited. The special considerations involved in university licensing are addressed later in this chapter.

Nonexclusive License Agreements.   If the owner of an invention has granted a nonexclusive license of the invention, it has reserved the right to grant one or more other nonexclusive licenses. Unless their licenses are limited by field of use or territory, the licensees under nonexclusive licenses may exploit the subject invention for all uses and everywhere. In other words, they may engage in full-scale head-to-head competition trying the exploit the same invention. Obviously, licensees would prefer exclusivity in order to avoid potential competition, while licensors might prefer nonexclusive licensing in order to maximize the potential of an invention.

In the biotech and pharmaceutical arenas, nonexclusive licensing is generally confined to what we will refer to as peripheral inventions, such as drug delivery systems or discovery methods. Suppose a party has invented a method to formulate certain kinds of small molecules to achieve a sustained, measured release of the small molecule in the patient over a period of time. This party would undertake a program of nonexclusive licensing in order to maximize the value of the invention. In this case, a pharma company licensee is willing to take a nonexclusive license because it will have a legal monopoly as a result of coupling its patented small molecule with the drug delivery system. While a pharma company licensee might wish to monopolize (through an exclusive license) such a drug delivery system because of the competitive advantage it gives to its product, it is not likely that the licensor will agree. The shrewd licensor will stick to nonexclusive licensing, although the aggressive licensee offering the right incentives might be able to negotiate for an "exclusive" in a limited field of use. For example, for more generous economic terms, a pharma company might persuade the licensor to restrict all other licensees from using the invention for products that treat stomach ulcers, which is the pharma company's specialty. Obviously, what any licensee can get is depends to a great degree on what has already been granted to existing licensees.

Due to the prohibitive cost of, and long odds against, developing a pharmaceutical product, nonexclusive licenses of compounds with therapeutic potential are rare because a licensee would not undertake the development without the benefit of the legal monopoly created by an exclusive license. But it should be noted that an exclusive license of a compound that is limited to a narrow field of use, such as a specified disease indication, presents some of the same concerns to the licensee as a nonexclusive license because the licensor can grant "exclusive" licenses for other fields of use. This can be problematic because of the potential for off-label use of pharmaceutical products. To use a stark and somewhat unlikely example, suppose Baby Biotech has granted an exclusive license of its proprietary peptide XYZ to one party, Human Health Products, for "therapeutic use in humans but no other uses." Suppose Baby Biotech then grants another exclusive license of XYZ to another party, Animal Health Products, for "therapeutic use in animals but not other uses." Suppose further that Human Health Products and Animal Health Products proceed to develop the same or substantially the same formulation of XYZ and each introduces a product into the marketplace. Two things are certain: Animal Health has spent far less to develop its product than Human Health has, and the market price of Animal Health's product is much less than the price of Human Health's product. What is to stop potential consumers of Human Health's product from buying Animal Health's product?

From the licensor's perspective, nonexclusive licensing may seem, and often is, the best way to maximize the potential value of an invention. However, a licensor must evaluate certain factors before committing to a licensing strategy. Will any prospective licensee take a nonexclusive license? While multiple nonexclusive licenses are possible, would a single exclusive licensee exploit the invention more fully than multiple licensees? Could value be maximized by multiple "exclusive" licenses in narrowly defined fields of use? The licensor has probably committed to an irreversible strategy when it grants its first license.

From the licensee's perspective, it generally would prefer an exclusive license even if limited to a narrow field of use. The considerations and stakes are very different when the subject matter of the license is a compound as opposed to, for example, a drug delivery system or other peripheral invention. With the latter, exclusivity can be obtained, even under a nonexclusive license, if the drug delivery system is used with a proprietary compound.

PRACTICAL TIPS

An owner of an invention must decide on its licensing strategy before it grants it first license; once an exclusive has been granted (unless limited by field of use or territory), it cannot grant a nonexclusive, and vice versa. A prospective licensee must undertake due diligence with respect to outstanding licenses of the same invention. While it probably would not learn the economic terms of outstanding licenses, the prospective licensee needs to know what has been granted to whom and for what uses in what territories. The prospective licensee needs to know if there is room left for its intended use of the invention. If a prospective licensee is prepared to take a nonexclusive license of a compound or product (or the effective equivalent of an exclusive license with a limited field of use), it must negotiate for an agreement by the licensor that will restrict all other licensees from developing the same or substantially similar formulation that the licensee is developing. Note that this may not be possible if it is not the first licensee. The licensee should require that the license agreement include provisions stating that the grant of rights does not conflict with any outstanding licenses and that the licensor will not grant any licenses that conflict with it.

Payment Terms.   Some or all of these economic terms are common in biotech or pharmaceutical license agreements: a license or signing fee; annual or other periodic fees; milestone payments; percentage royalties, which may include minimum annual amounts; and the expenses of the patent prosecution program. All of these terms are subject to negotiation, and it cannot be said that any amount or rate is right or wrong because much depends, as it always does with business terms, on the relative bargaining power of the parties and their assessment of the potential value of the invention.

The size of a license or signing fee, if any, is almost entirely dependent on the stage of development of the invention. From the licensor's perspective, it is a way to recoup some of its investment to date in the work that has led to the invention. How much it might ask a licensee to pay will be influenced in part by whether it intends to pursue a nonexclusive licensing program or to grant an exclusive license.

From the licensee's perspective, this fee is the cost of admission. If the licensee highly values the potential of the invention, it is getting an exclusive license, and the licensor has invested heavily in development to date, the licensee may be prepared to pay a very hefty signing fee. However, if the licensee has been funding the research work of the licensor and the invention needs an enormous amount of development that will be funded by the licensee, it would be willing to pay only a modest license fee, if any.

Annual or other periodic fees often are used to provide incentives to the licensee to exploit the invention. These fees almost always terminate when percentage royalties (usually based on commercial sales of product) commence. The theory is that the licensee will not be willing to pay annual fees indefinitely if it is not going to exploit the invention. However, a licensee might be willing to do just that in order to prevent third parties from having access to the invention. In other words, the licensee is willing to pay to shelve the invention. Of course, this strategy works only with exclusive licenses. A licensor must be aware of this possibility and negotiate annual fees that have enough bite to discourage the licensee from sitting on the invention or that reward the licensor adequately even if the invention is not exploited. Increasing annual fees are an effective device.

Milestone payments are very common in licenses (whether exclusive or nonexclusive) of compounds or biological materials with potential pharmaceutical applications. They are usually triggered by the typical development benchmarks for a pharmaceutical product, the achievement of which validate the value of the compound or material. The typical milestones are:

- Identification of a lead candidate for development
- Filing of an Investigational New Drug application or equivalent
- Completion of Phase I clinical trials
- Completion of Phase II clinical trials
- Completion of Phase III clinical trials
- Filing of New Drug Application or equivalent
- Approval of New Drug Application or equivalent

If the three phases of the clinical trial process are used as triggers for milestone payments, the license agreement should be clear whether these are achieved by "completion" or "satisfactory completion." The licensee would prefer the latter, as it would indicate that the development is progressing satisfactorily. The licensor, however, would obviously prefer the former because it will be paid the milestone payment even if the licensee is not satisfied with the results of the clinical trial. In order to avoid the possibility of disagreement of what constitutes "satisfactory completion," the license agreement might specify that commencement of the next phase of the clinical trials is deemed to evidence satisfactory completion of the preceding phase (e.g., commencement of Phase II clinical trials means that Phase I clinical trials have been successfully completed).

PRACTICAL TIPS

While every licensing situation is unique, there are some industry standards. For example, the current range for royalty rates is from about 2 percent for a just discovered/engineered compound or material to about 20 percent for a fully developed product approved for sale.

Drug Master File.   The drug master file is the collection of information and data that results from the development process for a potential pharmaceutical product, such as toxicology studies and clinical trial results. The drug development process is highly regulated and structured in the sense that certain types of tests and procedures must be conducted for all potential products, even if the details of those tests and procedures may differ from potential product to potential product. The cost of drug development is prohibitive (current estimates are for $400 to $800 million over up to 10 years, on average), and therefore the drug master file has an inherent value represented by that cost. An important issue to be considered in biotech licensing is the disposition of the drug master file in the event of early termination of the license agreement.

A drug development project can be discontinued even if it has been successful to date. Suppose Pharma Company is the initial licensee of a compound from Baby Biotech. Pharma Company has carried the program though the filing of an IND and has spent a total of $50 million to date. Suppose further that, while the results have been promising to date, Pharma Company decides to abandon the project because it has other more promising projects and insufficient resources to pursue them all. Pharma Company reluctantly decides that it must terminate the license agreement with Baby Biotech. In this scenario, Baby Biotech will likely attempt to license the compound to a third party or pursue the project itself.

    If the license agreement was thoroughly drafted, this eventuality would be addressed, most likely in the termination provision. As an example of one such provision, if after a no-fault termination of the license agreement by Pharma Company, Baby Biotech commercializes a product incorporating the compound, Pharma Company is entitled to compensation, the amount of which depends on the stage of development at which the license agreement was terminated. The compensation is a royalty on sales if Baby Biotech itself commercializes a product or, if Baby Biotech licenses to a third party, a percentage of what the third party licensee pays Baby Biotech in royalties, fees, milestone, and so forth, and reimbursement of a portion of Pharma Company's out-of-pocket expenses for its work. For example, if the no-fault termination takes place during preclinical trials but before the filing of an IND, Pharma Company is entitled to a royalty of 1.5 percent on sales by Baby Biotech; if Baby Biotech licenses to a third party, Pharma Company is entitled to 20 percent of all amounts paid to Baby Biotech by the third party under the license and reimbursement of 50 percent of Pharma Company's out-of-pockets expenses incurred for the preclinical work. If the no-fault termination takes place after regulatory approval of a product, the corresponding amounts are 9 percent royalty, 50 percent of any payments under a third-party license, and reimbursement of 100 percent of out-of-pocket expenses. Thus, the economic terms of the no-fault termination provision recognize the increasing value of the drug master file as the development process continues.

PRACTICAL TIPS

Each party should consider this issue in the course of negotiating the license agreement. From the licensor's perspective, it would like access to and use of the drug master file, ideally at no cost, under any early termination scenario. From the licensee's perspective, it seeks some recovery of its investment in the event the drug master file benefits the licensor or a third party.

SPONSORED RESEARCH AGREEMENTS, UNIVERSITY AND GOVERN-MENT LICENSING, AND CLINICAL TRIAL AGREEMENTS. This material addresses contractual and intellectual property considerations that frequently arise in the drafting and negotiation of sponsored research agreements (SRAs), license agreements with universities (and other nonprofit organizations) and the federal government, and clinical trial agreements.[3] Each of these subjects is addressed separately, but most of the section will be devoted to sponsored research, which is the driver for much of the innovation in the medical and life sciences industries. The next section discusses SRAs in some detail; "University and Government License Agreements" focuses on a few key provisions of license agreements with universities and nonprofits; and "Clinical Trial Agreements" is a very brief overview of clinical trial agreements, the terms of which are frequently dictated by the hospital (especially if it is a prominent teaching hospital) employing the clinical investigator. A disclaimer: The author's background in this practice area is representing the pharmaceutical company. This section is biased toward that perspective.

Sponsored Research Agreements. The term "sponsored research" refers to research (also development) that is paid for by one party (the sponsor) and performed by another party, which presumably has expertise in the subject matter. For its money, the sponsor expects one or more of several things from the sponsored activity: new inventions, proof of concept, corroboration of results, and product improvement, among others. The sponsor typically expects to own or have exclusive rights to the results of the sponsored work. The other party is typically a university or hospital (referred to for simplicity as industry–university arrangements), another commercial enterprise (industry–industry, such as big pharma-small biotech), or the federal government (industry–government).

The work covered by a sponsored research arrangement can range from a one-time, short-term specific task (such as performing toxicology studies for a potential pharmaceutical compound) to a multiyear program related to a more general field of basic research (such as the applicability of variants of a certain category of peptides to

---

3. From materials written by Jeffrey Somers of Morse, Barnes-Brown & Pendleton, Waltham, Massachusetts.

the treatment of various disease indications). The former involves the payment of money by the sponsor for a discrete work product; the latter also involves the payment of money by the sponsor but can also involve collaboration on the research, which can complicate the IP ownership issues.

Sponsored research is always governed by a written agreement. Key provisions, found in almost all SRAs, regardless of the parties, are:

- Scope of work and changes to the scope of work
- Funding terms; budget
- Reporting the results of the work
- Ownership of, and rights in, the results of the work
- Patent filing, prosecution and maintenance
- Publication of the results of the work
- Confidentiality
- Liability, indemnification, and insurance
- Term and termination

INDUSTRY–UNIVERSITY SPONSORED RESEARCH: PRINCIPAL PROVISIONS OF THE SRA

Scope of Work. The scope of work usually is described in some detail in an exhibit to the agreement. Provision should be made to permit the sponsor to change the scope of the work within reasonable limits and, in any event, to approve any change; the university should have limited or no rights to change the scope of work unilaterally. In a long-term collaboration, there may a joint scientific committee made up of representatives of the sponsor and the university. The joint scientific committee monitors the progress of the research and suggests changes to the scope of work based on that progress.

Designate the Principal Investigator. A sponsor usually provides funding to a university because it wants a luminary on the university faculty to conduct or at least oversee the research. The sponsor should have the right to terminate the SRA if the principal investigator (PI) terminates her or his affiliation with the university. Often the university has the option to propose a successor, but subject to the approval of the sponsor.

Funding and Budget.   Usually the funding is tied to an agreed budget, which can be very detailed in terms of full-time employees (FTEs) required to do the work and costs of supplies and other materials. Equipment, which is either loaned or gifted to the university, may also be included in the funding. The sponsor is interested in periodic payments (quarterly is common); the university is interested in a minimum commitment, usually of one year, especially if it is hiring postdoctoral candidates to do much of the work.

"Encumbered" PI.   Most PIs work in a lab with other faculty and/or postdoctoral candidates. Exclusive arrangements (i.e., arrangements where one sponsor funds the entire activities of a lab and, therefore, has rights to all of the output of the lab) with luminary PIs are rare. Most PIs and labs are "encumbered" with concurrent or prior sponsored research arrangements with other industry sponsors or with government funding (federal grants supporting basic research). It is critical to understand what, if any, encumbrances may be on a PI and to take necessary steps to assure that any other arrangements will not adversely affect the sponsor's rights to the results of the work it is funding. Due diligence is very important here.

Ownership of Results.   Most, if not all, universities have policies that provide that all inventions made with the use of university funding and/or facilities belong to the university, even if the funding is provided by a third party. Therefore, in a straightforward money-for-work sponsored research arrangement, the results are owned by the university and the sponsor has an option (usually exclusive) for a license, which may be either exclusive or nonexclusive, of the results of the research. In a collaborative arrangement, where employees of the sponsor are working collaboratively and in parallel with the PI on the research and sharing information, there are likely to be joint inventions. These are generally jointly owned, with the sponsor having the right to license the university's interest. The university generally has no rights in the sponsor's interest in jointly owned inventions, except perhaps a nonexclusive license limited to internal research work, usually within the scope of the request for application (RFA). The sponsor owns any inventions made solely by its employees, with the university generally having no rights. Ownership of inventions generally is governed by the U.S. rules for inventorship of patents (in other words, ownership follows the inventors named in the patent application). A word of caution: Joint inventions may lead to jointly owned patents. In the absence of an agreement to the contrary, each of the owners of a jointly owned patent may fully exploit the patent for its own account without any approval of the other party required.

Sponsor Rights in Results.   Generally, the sponsor is granted an exclusive option to license the results of the sponsored research. The option must be exercised within a defined period of time after a triggering event, which may be the disclosure of the invention or the filing of a patent or other IP application covering the invention. The sponsor would prefer a later triggering event in order to permit more time to evaluate the invention, especially if a license fee is required at the time of signing the license agreement. Most university SRAs provide for the negotiation "in good faith" of a license "on usual and customary terms" (or similar language) at the time the option is exercised.

Reporting Inventions.   The SRA must provide for the reporting of any inventions to the sponsor. Most university policies require faculty to report inventions to a university office, but the sponsor must also receive notice in order to begin to evaluate the invention and to monitor the patent (or other IP protection) process. The SRA should provide that the PI and those working with her or him keep detailed and accurate records of the progress of the research. This is important not only with regard to the issue of ownership of results (especially if the PI is encumbered) but also for patent purposes. Good scientists know the importance of this practice.

Patent Process.   The SRA should specify which party is responsible for the preparation and prosecution of any patent applications and the maintenance of any patents that issue on inventions made during the course of the SRA. (If a license is taken, this subject is picked up in the license agreement.) In general, sponsors would prefer to control this process, but some universities insist that they control the process. If the university is responsible, the sponsor should negotiate for some right to review and comment on filings in advance. In addition, the sponsor should have the right to designate countries in which applications will be filed and, if the university fails or refuses, to undertake such filings (which would be in the university's name). If the university decides to abandon an application or an issued patent, the sponsor should have the right to pick it up. In any event, the sponsor will pay all of the patent costs, including in some situations past patent costs.

Publication of Results.   This subject epitomizes the tension between the conflicting missions of the university and the sponsor. Most if not all universities have policies similar to that stated in the MIT Guide, which states, in relative part, that an overriding policy is the "prompt and open dissemination of the results of M.I.T. research and the free exchange of information among scholars." The guide goes on to state that "technology transfer is . . . subordinate to education and research." Therefore, "dissemination [publication] must . . . not be delayed beyond the minimal period necessary" to protect the rights of the parties (i.e., to file a patent application or make some other protective IP filing). If it had its way, the sponsor would require that all of the results be kept confidential until it chose to make them public. At best, the sponsor can expect to have the right to review and comment on any publication in advance (oral publications are problematic) and to have a delay in publication until protective steps have been taken. Ninety to 120 days overall from the first notice of the proposed publication is about the best that the sponsor can expect.

Representations and Warranties.   Generally, the university disclaims any representations and warranties about the sponsored research other than to pursue the research with reasonable diligence and to conduct the research following current good laboratory practices.

Government Rights.   Many universities receive government funding for research. Therefore, a sponsor is very likely to find that a PI and her or his lab is encumbered because of prior (which may effect the know-how of the lab) and/or concurrent funding in the same field in which the sponsor has an interest. Fortunately, the encumbrance of government funding is not that burdensome. The Bayh-Dole Act (PL 96-517, Patent and Trademark Act Amendments of 1980) created a uniform patent policy among the many federal agencies that fund research, enabling small businesses and nonprofit organizations, including universities, to retain title to inventions made under federally funded research programs. The act encourages universities to collaborate with commercial concerns to promote the utilization of inventions arising from federal funding. The trade-offs for letting universities take ownership of government-funded inventions are that the government retains a nonexclusive license to practice the invention throughout the world and the government retains march-in rights. The march-in rights give the government the right to take back the invention if it is not being effectively commercialized. In addition, the act now requires, as a result of subsequent amendment, that any product covered by a government-funded invention that is sold in the United States must be substantially manufactured in the United States. This may be problematic if the commercial licensee of the university is a foreign entity.

Policies Posted Online. If a party is considering a sponsored research program at a university, one of its first steps should be a visit to the university's Web site. Most universities, especially those actively involved in sponsored research, post their technology transfer policies online. Many also have forms of their agreements online.

INDUSTRY–INDUSTRY SPONSORED RESEARCH

Industry–industry sponsored research typically would be between big pharma, as sponsor, and small biotech or big biotech (one with cash), as sponsor, and small biotech. The principal reasons for the sponsor are generally one or more of these: diversification of research activities, lead compound identification, taking over development of a lead that the other party is unable to pursue, or product diversification. These arrangements are often more collaborative than industry-university arrangements and can involve cross-licensing, comarketing, and division of the research and development functions between the two parties based on their capabilities. The other party, usually a small biotech with one product or some research technology, enters these arrangements for the funding to develop its product or validate its technology. If the arrangement is successful, it can be the springboard to the development of other products and services.

The agreements covering these arrangements are as diversified as the arrangements themselves. One issue that is generally not an issue in industry-industry agreements is publication of results. In the commercial context, the parties are able to agree to keep the results of the research confidential and to agree on how and when any results will be disclosed.

In these arrangements, due diligence on the part of the sponsor is also critically important, as often small biotech may have licensed in some of the IP that it proposes to license to the sponsor.

INDUSTRY–GOVERNMENT SPONSORED RESEARCH

The United States has an established policy, supported by laws and executive orders, to transfer government-developed technology to the private sector, including industry. For an overview of government policy, laws, and executive orders in this area, an excellent resource is the *Federal Technology Transfer Legislation and Policy* prepared by the Federal Laboratory Consortium for Technology Transfer (*www.federallabs.org*).

One way that industry can access federal government technology is by sponsoring collaborative research at a federal agency or department. In the life sciences field, the National Institutes of Health (NIH) and the National Science Foundation research centers are probably the prime agencies.

Sponsored research with the government is generally conducted under a Collaborative Research and Development Agreement (CRADA). While each agency has its own form, they are generally substantively the same.

With a couple of exceptions, the substantive provisions of a CRADA are similar to those of an industry-university SRA, as discussed. Two significant exceptions are the grant of rights to the government in the sponsor's intellectual property that is developed in the course of the CRADA and the right of the government to grant third-party licenses if the sponsor is not fulfilling its commercialization obligations.

As suggested in the context of industry-university sponsored research, if a party is considering collaborative research with a government agency, it should review the agency's Web site, which should include policies and forms. A suite of NIH forms are available at *www.nih.gov*.

University and Government License Agreements.   The mission of a university and of the U.S. government is to make its research and knowledge available for the benefit of the general public. Stated differently, a university or the government does not want the subject invention of a license to "sit on the shelf" of a licensee.

Therefore, a university or the government often will require that a detailed development and commercialization schedule be built into the license agreement. If the licensee fails to meet the schedule, it will be in default under the license and risk termination of the license, loss of exclusivity, or some other penalty.

Typical development benchmarks for a pharmaceutical product, the achievement of which generally triggers a milestone payment to the licensor, are some or all of these:

- Identification of lead candidate for development
- Filing of IND or equivalent
- Completion of Phase I clinical trials
- Completion of Phase II clinical trials
- Completion of Phase III clinical trials
- Filing of NDA or equivalent
- Approval of NDA or equivalent

The development schedule requires the sponsor to achieve each milestone within a specified period of time (except for the first benchmark, measured from the date of achieving the prior benchmark). Given the unpredictable nature of the pharmaceutical development process and the severity of the penalty for failing to achieve a development benchmark (e.g., loss of the license), these time frames are the subject of extensive negotiation.

In pharmaceutical licenses, the three phases of the clinical trial process often are used as development benchmarks and/or triggers for milestone payments. The license agreement should be clear whether these are achieved by "completion" or "satisfactory completion." The licensee would prefer the latter, as it would indicate that the development is progressing satisfactorily. The licensor, however, would obviously prefer the former because it will be paid the milestone payment even if the licensee is not satisfied with the results of the clinical trial. In order to avoid the possibility of disagreement over what constitutes "satisfactory completion," sometimes the agreement provides that commencement of the next phase of the clinical trials is deemed to evidence satisfactory completion of the preceding phase (e.g., commencement of Phase II clinical trials means that Phase I clinical trials have been successfully completed).

You should try to be creative in crafting penalties that are less severe than termination of the license for failure to meet development benchmarks, particularly in the later stages of the development process. You want to avoid losing a license agreement in its entirety for failing to achieve by a week a benchmark with a long performance time (a year or more is not uncommon for pharmaceutical development benchmarks) even though the licensee had diligently tried to achieve the benchmark throughout the entire period.

Clinical Trial Agreements.   Clinical trial agreements (CTAs) govern the conduct of the clinical (human) trials that are a prerequisite to regulatory approval of a new pharmaceutical product or medical device. The terms of these agreements often are dictated by the site at which the clinical trial is being conducted, especially if the site is a prominent teaching hospital. However, if the study is to be conducted at multiple sites, it is advisable to have a template agreement for use at all sites in order to achieve some degree of uniformity. In this situation, it is advisable to craft a template agreement that is likely to be generally acceptable to the most exacting (in terms of agreements) of the prospective sites. If you are considering entering into a clinical trial agreement, you should consult the hospital's Web site or call the clinical trial oversight office to see if the institution has a model agreement. A brief discussion of a few key terms common to CTAs follows.

PUBLICATION OF RESULTS

A hospital's mission regarding publication of results is similar to that of a university: It wants to publish the results of its work. This issue is generally dealt with in the same manner as it is in an industry-university SRA. In a multisite study, publication of results by an individual site/PI is delayed, usually for up to 18 months after completion of the study by all sites, to permit a joint multisite publication.

WHO OWNS WHAT

The data from a clinical trial are collected at the site by the PI on case report forms (CRFs) approved by the sponsor. Generally, the sponsor owns the completed CRFs and all of the data from the study (which can have real value). The hospital owns the patient medical records, the PI's research notebooks and related documentation, and all IP resulting from the study, usually subject to an option to the sponsor to take a license of the IP.

INDEMNIFICATION; INSURANCE

The sponsor generally must indemnify the PI, the hospital and its trustees, directors, officers, employees, and the like from all loss or damage incurred as a result of their undertaking the clinical study, except for loss or damage directly caused by their negligence, reckless misconduct or intentional misconduct, or their failure to adhere to the terms of the protocol for the clinical trial or to the terms of the CTA. The sponsor also will undertake to cover the cost of care and treatment of any injury or side effect to any patient participating in the clinical trial (usually with offset for any health insurance recovery). The sponsor will be required to carry a specified amount of liability insurance specifically covering clinical trial activity of the sponsor.

MATERIAL TRANSFER AGREEMENTS.   A material transfer agreement (MTA) is an agreement that establishes the terms under which one entity or scientist will transfer unique biologic materials to another person for purposes of research and testing.[4] This section describes the origin of MTAs and of the widely used form developed by the National Institutes of Health (NIH), known as the "Uniform Biological Material Transfer Agreement," and summarize the most important issues that must be covered by MTAs, including scope of use, ownership and IP rights, redistribution, liability, publication, compliance with law, term, applicable costs, payment terms, and publication issues.

What Are Material Transfer Agreements and Why Are They Needed?
MTAs are agreements that establish the terms under which one entity or scientist will transfer to another entity or scientist unique biologic materials for purposes of research, testing, and perhaps distribution for further research and testing. The terms of transfer may differ depending on the players. That is, since nonprofit institutions and the government have somewhat different needs and expectations from private industry, the terms of transfer between nonprofit and governmental entities often differ from the terms of transfer from nonprofits to industry and from industry to nonprofits.

MTAs can be used for other purposes, including the transfer of other types of materials (e.g., specially developed inorganic compounds

---

4.   This information is taken from materials written by Howard G. Zaharoff of Morse, Barnes-Brown & Pendleton, Waltham, Massachusetts.

or computer software) and granting rights of commercialization. However, the most common types of MTAs involve the transfer of biologic materials for research. When commercialization is intended, a more standard commercial license agreement is generally used.

As indicated, virtually any type of entity may use an MTA to transfer unique materials, including "federal laboratories, industrial research laboratories, and laboratories in universities, hospitals, or independent research institutes."[5] Thus, even industry can use MTAs, for example, to make certain unique materials available to universities for pro bono research or in connection with ongoing or potential sponsored research, or to obtain university material for its own research and development.

Why is it important to use an MTA when transferring biological materials?

> MTAs are important because they require the recipient to exercise care in the handling of the materials, to maintain control over the distribution of the materials, to acknowledge the provider in publications, and to follow relevant PHS [Public Health Service] guidelines relating to recombinant DNA, protection of human subjects in research, and the use of animals.[6]

"When scientists began warning that the progress of research was increasingly hampered by lengthy MTA negotiations, universities and the National Institutes of Health (NIH) took action by joining to develop a standard material transfer process for transfers between academic entities."[7] The result was the Uniform Biological Material Transfer Agreement, discussed next.

Uniform Biological Material Transfer Agreement.   Following years of discussion, in 1995 the National Institutes of Health issued three documents,

> the final version of the Uniform Biological Materials Transfer Agreement (UBMTA), to be used by public and nonprofit organizations; an implementing letter to memorialize individual exchanges

---

5. Council on Governmental Relations, "Materials Transfer in Academia" (1997), *www.cogr.edu* (hereafter COGR Brochure).
6. "Uniform Biological Material Transfer Agreement: Discussion of Public Comments Received," *Federal Register*, March 8, 1995.
7. COGR Brochure.

under the UBMTA; and a simple letter agreement for transferring nonproprietary biological materials among public and nonprofit organizations.[8]

Appendix 3B contains a copy of the UBTMA.[9]

Once adopted by an institution, the UBMTA can be made to apply to any transfer transaction by proper execution of a simple letter agreement (a form for which was also issued by the NIH). It may not be appropriate for an adopter to use the UBMTA for all transactions, and it is often not used for materials exchanges with industry, since such exchanges often involve the question of commercial rights.

At least 233 institutions have adopted the UBMTA.[10]

Among the issues covered by the UBMTA—and most well-written MTAs—are permitted uses, further distribution, ownership, liability, publication, compliance with law, term and any applicable costs.

Most MTAs require certain technical definitions, including these terms:

- "Unmodified descendant from the Material, such as virus from virus, cell from cell, or organism from organism." UBMTA Section I.7. Thus, "progeny" are essentially unaltered copies of the original material.
- Unmodified derivatives. "Substances created by the Recipient which constitute an unmodified, functional subunit or product expressed by the Original Material. Some examples include: subclones of unmodified cell lines, purified or fractionated subsets of the Original Material, protein expressed by DNA/RNA supplied by the Provider, or monoclonal antibodies secreted by a hybridoma cell line." UBMTA Section I.8.
- Modifications. "Substances created by the Recipient which contain/incorporate the Material." UBMTA Section I.8.

---

8. *NIH Guide* 24, No. 14, April 14, 1995 (*http://grants.nih.gov/grants/guide/notice/not95-116a.html*).

9. Copies of the UBMTA and associated documents and commentary can be found at the Web sites of the NIH (at *www.niehs.nih.gov/techxfer/ubmta.htm*) or the Association of University Technology Managers (AUTM) (at *www.autm.net*). AUTM serves as the official repository for signed UBMTAs of participating institutions.

10. See "Signatories to the March 8, 1995 Master UBMTA Agreement," published by Association of University Technology Managers, *www.autm.net/ubmta/signatories-list.cfm*. (This information has not been updated.)

Materials and Scope of Use   The MTA must clearly identify the materials to be transferred. Typically these are biological materials, such as bacteria, cell lines, cultures, nucleotides, plasmids, proteins, reagents, transgenic animals, vectors, and pharmaceuticals.

MTAs involving transfers to nonprofit institutions generally allow only noncommercial uses of the transferred material, typically research, testing, and teaching uses. Where the transfer is to industry or for-profit institutions, the typical MTA may not be adequate: Because commercial rights are generally sought, it is often more appropriate to work from a standard commercial development and license agreement.

Many MTAs prohibit further distribution of the original material, even for noncommercial research. UBMTA Section 4 requires the receiving scientist to refer requests for the material to the provider; the provider agrees that, to the extent it has sufficient supplies and is reimbursed for its costs, it will make the material available to other researchers who wish to replicate the recipient's research.

Many MTAs permit the recipient to distribute freely materials created by the recipient, generally provided that they are not progeny, unmodified derivatives, or modifications. See UBMTA Section 5(a).

Because materials provided to nonprofit recipients often are tested or further developed with federal funds, they are subject to the Bayh-Dole Act, which generally requires resulting inventions to be made available for commercialization. Thus, UBMTA Sections 5(c) and 7 permit the recipient to license its intellectual property in its modifications to industry; however, they do not require the provider to license its materials (including those incorporated in modifications) commercially.

Fees and Costs.   Most institutions do not charge license or similar fees for noncommercial use of their unique biological materials.

However, many biologic materials are costly to produce, package, and ship. Institutions generally will seek reimbursement for their costs of providing unique biologic materials to other researchers pursuant to an MTA.

If the material was developed with industry grants, the institution may be required to pass through certain fees, so that the industrial developer is reimbursed for some of its development costs by the transferee.

Intellectual Property and Ownership Rights.   Nonprofit institutions are increasingly sensitive to IP issues, especially as these may affect their ability to benefit financially from their unique creations and derivatives thereof. These concerns are less significant when the MTA permits only nonprofit research and teaching. However, often more is allowed, at least regarding derivatives that are not progeny, modifications, or unmodified derivatives.

Typically the provider of the original material will retain ownership and all IP rights in that material, in its progeny and unmodified derivatives, and perhaps in modifications as well. Generally the recipient will retain the IP rights in its own creations, provided they are neither progeny nor unmodified derivatives. This is a useful approach, particularly given that if the provider retains ownership of resulting modifications, this can make it difficult to secure outside funding to do further research on the modifications.

UBMTA Section 2 provides that the recipient retains ownership of all modifications, though not ownership of the original materials, progeny, or unmodified derivatives incorporated therein. Thus, the recipient may distribute modifications to nonprofit organizations for research and teaching, and may grant commercial licenses to its IP rights in the modifications; but it may not distribute modifications (which by definition contain original material) for commercial purposes without specific license from the provider, according to UBMTA Section 5.

Providers, especially industry providers, may seek licenses to use derivatives developed and owned by the recipient.

This is reasonable if the license is limited to noncommercial use. However, if the provider seeks use of the recipient's derivatives for commercial purposes, the recipient generally should seek compensation. Otherwise, in essence it may have just performed valuable commercial research—research it could have charged significant dollars for—for free. Providers—again, particularly industry—may request an option to acquire exclusive rights.

Confidentiality, Publication, and Attribution.   In those cases where providers treat their unique biological creations as confidential and proprietary (generally industrial providers rather than institutions), they will require confidential treatment of these materials, as well as their derivatives and progeny, by recipient organizations and individuals.

In those cases where the providers do not consider a particular material as confidential—because it is patented, described in published literature, or available from other sources—some form of transfer agreement is often advisable, for example, to deal with ownership of derivatives, reimbursement, and liability. The UBMTA was issued accompanied by a "Simple Letter Agreement for Transfer of Non-Proprietary Biological Material."

Most academics require the ability to publish their research findings. UBMTA Section 11 provides that it will not "prevent or delay publication of research findings resulting from the use of the Material or the Modifications." That section also requires that the scientist "provide appropriate acknowledgement of the source of the Material in all publications."

Liability   The provider obviously desires to minimize its potential liability for transferring and permitting use of its unique biological materials. Similarly, the recipient will not want full exposure for risks that in fairness should belong to the provider, for example, risks arising from any dangerous or toxic properties of the original materials, unless these risks are obvious or the recipient has been properly warned.

In most MTAs the provider gives no warranty for the materials it furnishes.

Providers also typically require recipients to use caution and take full responsibility for use of the provided material; disclaimers of liability are common.

UBMTA Section 10 provides that the provider is not liable for any loss, claim, or demand by the recipient, "except to the extent permitted by law when caused by the gross negligence or willful misconduct of the Provider."

Each party may desire some form of indemnity from the other. For example, a provider may desire indemnification from damages and third-party claims resulting from the recipient's use or misuse of the materials, or at least from the recipient's (gross) negligence and (willful) misconduct. Similarly, the recipient may desire indemnification from damages and third-party claims resulting from the provider's failure to use proper safety measures or provide notice of known hazards, or at least from the provider's (gross) negligence and (willful) misconduct. Bear in mind that many federal laboratories and state universities are prohibited from giving indemnities, or are limited in their authority to do so.

Term and Termination   The MTA must state how long the recipient may use the material. It should permit either party to terminate if the other party breaches or is guilty of misrepresentation. It may allow either party to terminate at will, with reasonable notice (typically 30 days to the other). This may be unfair to the recipient, particularly if it is building a research project around the use of the material. UBMTA Section 13 states that if the provider terminates for reasons other than the recipient's breach or other cause (e.g., health risk or patent infringement), upon request the provider will defer termination for up to a year to permit completion of research in progress.

Compliance with Law   Many laws will apply to both the provider's transfer, and the recipient's use, of the materials. MTAs should obligate the recipient to comply with these laws. Consider the next examples.

Many laws apply to hazardous materials, including occupational health and safety laws and laws governing the storage, transport, use, and disposal of hazardous materials. Ideally, the provider will inform the recipient of those relevant environmental laws and regulations familiar to the provider. Of course, the provider also should give the recipient sufficient information about the material for the recipient to determine on its own what laws apply. However, providing this information should not absolve the recipient from the obligation to learn and comply on its own.

Federal and state privacy laws may apply, for example, to the handling and use of personal data and human genetic materials.

Certain rules may apply when importing materials into the United States: "Importation of many biological materials to the U.S. requires USDA permits.[11]

Another set of laws concerns export of materials. Although U.S. export control laws will allow most materials to leave the United States without a special license, special licenses may be required for materials that could be used in chemical or biological weapons, including, for example, human pathogens and toxins.[12]

---

11.   COGR Brochure, Q17.
12.   COGR Brochure, Q20

UBMTA Section 12 requires that the recipient use the material "in compliance with all applicable statutes and regulations, including ... those relating to research involving the use of animals or recombinant DNA."

LIMITING LIABILITY WHEN LICENSING AND DISTRIBUTING TECHNOLOGY PRODUCTS.   There is tremendous potential liability in distributing technology products, such as computer software.[13] The two main types of liability arise from performance failures and infringements of third-party intellectual property rights.

Performance Problems.   Potential failures, defects, or problems in technology products pose special risks. This is particularly true of widely distributed technology products, such as home and small business computer software because such products serve many businesses and consumers with whom the licensor has no direct relationship, often in circumstances where failure can cause significant loss or damage.

- Wide distribution increases the likelihood of problems arising and the difficulty of managing problems that do arise.
- Use by businesses and consumers means that the licensor must take into account both commercial rules and expectations and, where applicable, the special rights and protections offered by gederal and state consumer laws.
- Because the licensor does not have a direct relationship with the end user, the licensor cannot contract directly to disclaim warranties, establish exclusive remedies, or limit liabilities.
- Significant loss or damage can result from products used in high-risk fields, such as transportation, energy, and environmental applications, or in high-stakes fields, such as banking and insurance.

Intellectual Property Infringement.   The potential for third-party infringement claims should motivate licensors either to avoid liability if a third-party claimant appears or to manage the liability where avoidance is impossible.

---

13.   This information is taken from materials written by Howard G. Zaharoff of Morse, Barnes-Brown & Pendleton, Waltham, Massachusetts.

Liability for patent infringement poses unique problems: Although a person generally cannot be guilty of copyright infringement without copying or adapting a preexisting work, and cannot be guilty of trade secret misappropriation without wrongful acquisition (e.g., stealing the formula for Coca-Cola) or improper discovery (reverse engineering a product in breach of an enforceable contractual prohibition), people can infringe a patent in complete innocence, without any awareness or use of third-party knowledge or inventions. Indeed, the confidentiality inherent in the patent system often means that suppliers and licensors cannot learn about relevant pending patents for some period of time even if they conduct exhaustive patent searches.

Next we turn to practical measures and contractual techniques that licensors can use to control their liability when licensing and distributing technology products.

Practical Measures for Containing Performance-Based Liabilities.
A technology provider should never underestimate the extent to which reasonable conduct can reduce its exposure. Reasonable measures are discussed next.

CARE

Most important is the use of proper care and diligence in the creation, manufacture, and distribution of the technology and its by-products.

NOTICE

The technology supplier should consider the full scope of risks, provide due notice to customers, and recommend or require precautionary measures.

- **Scope of use.** One important technique is to specify the uses which customers may—and may not—make of the technology. For example, a supplier may prohibit deployment of the product in nuclear, mass transportation, and energy-related applications.
- **Training.** The supplier may require that only trained and qualified personnel be permitted to use the technology. The supplier may include such training (for a fee) as part of the package of products and services it contracts to provide.
- **Guidelines.** The supplier may recommend, or require, that the licensee adopt specific error-detection, backup, and security procedures. (Alternatively, the supplier may merely recite the danger of failing to adopt reasonable procedures and obtain the

licensee's agreement to do so, without specifying the procedures.)

PROPER COLLATERAL

The supplier must also use care and precision in preparing its sales
literature and product documentation.

- **Clear instructions.** The supplier must provide clear product
  specifications and instructions on proper use.
- **Trained and restrained sales force.** The supplier must be sure
  that its sales force understands the product, sticks to "the script,"
  and does not oversell. Major, avoidable problems often arise
  when products perform substantially beneath the sales pitch.
- **No side agreements.** Similarly, sales personnel must be restrained from offering special guaranties and promises, unless
  these have been approved by a knowledgeable superior and ideally embodied in an accurate writing, so there can be no later
  dispute as to what was promised.

POSTTRANSFER SUPPORT (AND CONTROL)

Suppliers should consider offering ongoing support services to licensees, including opportunities for continuous training and consultation,
at a reasonable charge. This will give the supplier additional opportunities to discover and correct problems, and may shift some blame
onto licensees who refuse support, where problems would have been
avoided or mitigated had they purchased support. Posttransfer support
might include:

- **Reporting.** Customers should be encouraged or required to report problems discovered in the licensed materials, including
  problems in the user documentation.
- **Correction.** Support should include the correction of discovered defects in a manner that is reasonable in both cost and
  timing. Indeed, it may be prudent for suppliers who discover
  a major problem to contact and offer a reasonable fix even for
  customers who did not purchase support. Although establishing
  a custom of contacting customers, whether they have bought
  support or not, may create an expectation and even an implied
  obligation to do so, contacting customers generally outweighs

the risk of allowing a customer to continue using a product with known problems, especially problems that could cause major damage if uncorrected.

- **Control.** Suppliers should consider whether the nature of the application, or special aspects of its deployment, make it desirable to deploy a facilities management approach, or at least offer it as an option.

SHIFT RISKS TO THIRD PARTIES
Never underestimate the value of shifting risks to, or at least sharing them with, third parties (including the customer/licensee, as discussed later).

- **Insurance.** Obviously in most cases suppliers should have their own insurance policies to cover the most obvious and insurable risks. However, in certain circumstances it is reasonable for suppliers to require their resellers and customers to carry insurance and even name the supplier as an additional insured.
- **Indemnities.** Because a technology's deployment may be beyond the supplier's control, it is often appropriate to require the licensee to defend and indemnify the supplier for third-party claims or injuries arising from the licensee's uses (except to the extent attributable to the supplier's fault). Because indemnities are no better than the solvency of the indemnitor, financial factors must be considered and may suggest the need for additional protections, including advances, pools, bonds, or insurance.
- **Warranties.** Well-designed warranty policies protect the supplier by carefully defining its commitments and specifying the remedies available when products do not perform as promised.

Practical Measures for Containing Infringement-Related Liabilities.
A technology provider should use reasonable measures to minimize the likelihood of an infringement claim arising. Some of these measures are discussed next.

COPYRIGHTS
Technically, infringements of third-party copyrights can occur only if someone has copied or adapted a preexisting work. Therefore, technology developers must instruct their employees not to borrow any copyrightable expression (e.g., words, images, software code, etc.) from

outside sources, unless the borrowing has been vetted and blessed by knowledgeable superiors (who are either legally trained or are advised by legal professionals).

TRADE SECRETS

The greatest risk here is often new employees who use trade secrets that are the property of their prior employers. Thus, developers must instruct their employees that such "generosity" with ex-employers' ideas and know-how is not welcome and that, in general, they should not "borrow" third-party ideas, information, know-how, and so forth unless these have been properly obtained (e.g., legitimately reverse engineered—which in most cases should be determined by a lawyer).

TRADEMARKS

Suppliers must be sure that their sales and marketing staff understand the importance of proper trademark selection, clearance, and use. Adopting generic or descriptive terms as marks may minimize the risk of infringement but leave a company with an unenforceable mark. Using marks without legal clearance may cause a company to invest in packaging, collateral, signage, and other materials that will need to be corrected or destroyed if a conflicting, preexisting mark is later discovered.

PATENTS

Technical staff should learn to document their inventions (regular lab reports and notebook entries should be required or encouraged); employees should again be reminded to avoid using inventions learned at a prior employer; executives should be instructed not to ignore reports or claims of patent infringement, but to report these immediately to minimize the risk of committing "willful" infringement (which may entitle the patentee to recover treble damages). The company should engage competent patent counsel, who can advise when technologies or products should be subjected to patent clearance or patent prosecution.

Contract Techniques for Containing Performance Liabilities. A technology provider should do business under comprehensive contracts containing protective clauses that disclaim warranties, cap damages, and otherwise reduce liabilities.

EXPRESS WARRANTIES

The license/distribution agreement should state expressly what warranties are given and the duration of the warranty (typically 30 to 90 days after installation or acceptance for performance-based warranties). If warranties are made by incorporating other materials, review those materials carefully. Try to avoid wholesale incorporation of a response to a request for proposal, as these tend to be sales-focused documents and may promise more than intended. Carefully review schedules and supplementary documents (such as purchase orders): These are often prepared by lower-level sales or technical personnel and receive only cursory legal review, yet they may contain significant commitments. Indeed, review all sales literature and advertisements to avoid promises that cannot be kept; courts generally will hold companies to their express written promises, despite general disclaimers in their sales contracts.

DISCLAIMER OF WARRANTIES

The agreement should disclaim express warranties, except those stated in the document and any implied warranties, including warranties of merchantability, of fitness for a particular purpose, and against infringement. Disclaimer language should be clear and *conspicuous*.

EXCLUSIVE REMEDIES

To avoid being subject to broad remedy and damage claims, the contract should identify the reasonable "exclusive" remedies available if any warranty is breached. For performance issues, these typically include replacements, repairs, and refunds.

LIMIT LIABILITY

There are two typical liability limitations: (1) no consequential or other indirect damages (except perhaps for breaches of confidentiality or other IP violations), and (2) no liability for damages in excess of the fees received (often except for IP indemnification and sometimes other indemnifications, such as claims of personal injury caused by the breach or negligence of the licensor).

LICENSEE/RESELLER INDEMNIFICATION

It is often appropriate for the licensor to seek indemnification from the licensee for third-party claims directed at the licensor that are attributable to acts or omissions of the licensee, particularly the licensee's negligence or its use of the technology beyond the permitted scope.

CONTROL FEATURES

As suggested, the licensor can reduce its risks by imposing controls on the licensee, such as requiring the licensee to use specific precautions and trained and qualified personnel and obligating it to incorporate specific liability waivers and caps in its own sublicense and sales contracts.

PRIVATE STATUTES OF LIMITATIONS

Ideally the sales/license agreement will require all claims to be brought within one (or two) years after the claim arises.

ALTERNATIVE DISPUTE RESOLUTION

Depending on the circumstances, liability may be reduced by providing for specific dispute resolution procedures, which may include face-to-face meetings, mediation, arbitration, and other options. The processes of structured negotiation and mediation often prompt settlement, and arbitrators are less likely to award outrageous damage sums than U.S. juries. Further, a properly drafted clause can ensure that the matter is heard by a knowledgeable arbiter, minimize the risk of punitive damages, and avoid class action suits.

Containing Intellectual Property Liabilities: The Indemnification Clause.   In most cases technology providers should include comprehensive, well-crafted, reasonably protective IP indemnity provisions in their license and sales contracts. Although some licensors resist this, licensors generally should include these provisions. Most licensees will insist on indemnification; if serious IP problems arise, the licensor will be pressured by licensees to provide a solution and licensors will probably need to do so to keep their business and reputation intact. Assuming, therefore, that licensors will likely be forced to respond to IP claims, it makes sense for them to accept this responsibility from the outset and manage their liability by appropriate IP indemnity clauses. The main features of such clauses follow.

INDEMNIFY AND HOLD HARMLESS

The centerpiece is the licensor's commitment to indemnify, hold harmless, and (generally) defend the licensee (and perhaps its customers) against IP claims. The debate usually concerns the IP covered. Licensors generally accept responsibility for copyrights and trade secrets but may refuse liability for patents or limit the patents for which they are liable to: U.S. patents, patents of which they knew (or should have known), patents issued or published at the time of the agreement, and/or patents that their technology actually infringes (in contrast to patents that are asserted but not actually infringed). Licensors may also seek specific caps (e.g., $1 million) or liability sharing (e.g., 50/50) for patent infringements.

EXCLUSIONS

The licensor should exclude liability for infringements caused by: following the licensee's designs or instructions, any contributions or modifications by the licensee, use of the licensed technology outside the scope of the license, or using the licensed technology in combination with third-party materials not furnished or authorized by the licensor (where the infringement would not have occurred but for such combination).

NOTICE AND DEFENSE

Typically, licensors require, as a condition of indemnification, that licensees: provide prompt notice of any claims; tender defense of the claim to the licensor; and cooperate with the licensor's efforts to defend and settle the claim. Licensees usually are allowed to participate in the defense with their own lawyer at their own expense. Licensees may demand the right to assume the defense, at the licensor's expense, if the licensor refuses to do so or does so negligently. Licensors typically are prohibited from agreeing to a settlement that encumbers or otherwise impairs the licensee without the licensee's consent (not to be unreasonably withheld).

CONTROL

If the licensor will be liable for infringement, it should insist that, in the event of a covered claim, or if it has reason to suspect that infringement has occurred or that a claim of infringement is likely, it should seek a right to attempt to resolve the matter by obtaining a license from the

IP owner, modifying the technology to avoid infringement (without diminishing the important features of the technology) or, if neither of these is feasible, terminating the license and refunding a reasonable (often prorated) portion of any license fees paid.

INDEMNITIES

Often the parties disagree over whom the licensor must indemnify. Licensees often seek broad indemnification, not only of the licensed entity and its officers, directors, employees, and agents, but of all affiliated entities and their officers, directors, employees, and agents. Licensors generally resist such potentially unlimited exposure.

SECURITY

In a transaction where the licensee is required to make ongoing payments to the licensor (e.g., a royalty based on sales), the licensee may seek the right to suspend and withhold payments until the IP claim is resolved (or it receives reasonable assurances of indemnification).

INSURANCE

Recognizing that the cost of indemnification could exceed the licensor's ability to pay, licensees sometimes demand that the licensor obtain insurance to cover a significant part of any likely exposure. Although protection for copyright and trademark claims is relatively affordable, the cost of patent infringement indemnification insurance can be prohibitive and generally is not a cost of doing business that licensors build into their price structure.

APPENDICES

These appendices are located on the Web site that accompanies this book. For information on the Web site, see the "About the Web Site" section.

Appendix 3A: Software License Agreement: Licensor Draft/Licensee Comments
Appendix 3B: Uniform Biological Materials Transfer Agreement

CHAPTER 4

PRIVATE PLACEMENTS, INITIAL PUBLIC OFFERINGS, AND PUBLIC COMPANY REGULATION

BASICS OF SECURITIES REGULATION FOR PRIVATE COMPANIES

Federal and state securities laws apply to every issuance of stock or other securities by private and public companies, no matter how big or small they are or their stage of development. It is important to comply with the securities laws from start-up through initial public offering (IPO) and beyond. Litigation over securities laws violations is almost nonexistent in the world of private technology companies, but compliance still is extremely important because sloppiness here may interfere with the company's ability to get venture financing, do an IPO, or be acquired. Securities laws violations create a right of rescission in the purchasers of the securities, and investors are leery of investing in companies with that contingent liability. The same goes for the underwriters in an IPO and the potential acquiror in a merger and acquisition (M&A) transaction, particularly in the latter case if the purchase price per share in the acquisition is less than what all or certain stockholders paid in acquiring their stock.

The basic rule is that all sales of securities (i.e., in this context, founders' stock or preferred stock sold to venture capitalists [VCs]) must either be registered with the Securities and Exchange Commission (SEC) or exempt from registration. As the next section explains, registration with the SEC, other than in connection with an IPO, is completely impractical for a private company and ill-advised as well. So, for every issuance of stock by the private company, care must be taken to be sure that an exemption from SEC registration is available and is properly documented.

In addition to being registered or exempt from registration, any sales of securities must also comply with the antifraud provisions of federal and state securities laws. At the federal level, the principal provisions are Section 10(b) of the Securities Exchange Act of 1934 and the implementing rule, Rule 10b-5. These provisions make illegal any untrue statement of a material fact or any omission to state a material fact necessary in order to make the statements made not misleading. There are no exemptions from the antifraud rules, regardless of the size or circumstances of the offers and sales. As a practical matter, however, it is hard to imagine how sales of cheap stock to founders could violate these provisions. However, compliance with these rules is critical where the sales of securities are for "real money."

Over the lifecycle of a private technology company, securities are sold in three typical contexts: to the founders; to employees and consultants who work for the company; and to angel, venture capital, and other investors. We discuss separately the practical aspects of compliance with the securities laws in sales to founders, employees, and investors, but first we discuss the regulatory scheme and the underlying principles of investor protection behind it.

OVERVIEW OF SECURITIES LAWS EXEMPTIONS. There are a number of federal securities statutes, but the principal one applicable to private companies is the Securities Act of 1933 ('33 Act or the Securities Act). The other principal statute is the Securities Exchange Act of 1934 ('34 Act or the Exchange Act). The Exchange Act contains Section 10(b), the antifraud statute, and contains extensive provisions regulating public companies. The Securities Act contains Section 5, which is the basic provision requiring registration of securities with the SEC unless an exemption from registration is available. The principal exemptions are contained in Section 4 of the '33 Act and the rules adopted under Section 4. There are additional exemptions of various types of securities in Section 3, but these exemptions are not generally applicable in our context.

The principal exemption applicable to offers and sales of securities by private companies is Section 4(2), which exempts securities issued in a transaction not involving a public offering. The SEC has adopted a safe harbor implementing various statutory provisions in the form of Regulation D (Reg. D). In a nutshell, the way it works is that a private company should attempt to comply with Reg. D for all offers and sales of securities. Where compliance with Reg. D is not possible as a practical matter, some lawyers may be comfortable with relying on the exemption contained in Section 4(2) itself where the transaction fits within the case law defining the underlying principles of investor protection.

SECTION 4(2).   Section 4(2) exempts from registration transactions by an issuer not involving a public offering. Whether offers and sales amount to a public offering depends on a number of factors, particularly the identity of the offerees/purchasers and the manner in which the offering is conducted. The offering must be conducted in a manner to make the offering private rather than public—otherwise known as a private placement. Case law has defined the parameters of what constitutes a private placement. These parameters are:

- **Access to material information.** Offerees have access to the same kind of information about the company that a prospectus would provide.
- **Investors are sophisticated.** Offerees have such "knowledge and experience in business and financial matters" ("sophistication") to be able to evaluate the merits and risks of the investment.
- **No general solicitation or advertising.** There is no general solicitation of investors or advertising in connection with the offering. This means, among other things, that the company cannot make mass mailings of offering materials, place ads in the media or on the Internet, or hold public meetings about the offering. In addition, it means that issuers should limit the number of offers because making a large number of offers could be deemed to involve a general solicitation.
- **No purchaser intent to resell.** Investors must purchase the stock "for investment" (i.e., they must intend to hold on to it for an indefinite period and not resell it without an exemption for the resale). Customary practice dictates that they must represent to that effect in one of the subscription documents.

REGULATION D: SAFE HARBOR.   SEC Regulation D provides a safe harbor for the Section 4(2) nonpublic offering exemption (Rule 506), and exemptions for offerings not exceeding $5 million under '33 Act Section 3(b) (Rules 504 and 505). Reg. D consists of Rules 501 through 508. Rule 501 provides definitions of terms used in Reg. D. Rule 502 contains general conditions applicable in each of the exemptions provided by Rules 504, 505, and 506. Rule 503 contains a filing requirement with the SEC (Form D). Rule 504 provides an exemption for offerings not exceeding $1 million. Rule 505 provides an exemption for offerings not exceeding $5 million. Rule 506 provides an exemption for offerings without regard to the dollar amount of the offering. Some additional details are:

- **Rule 501/Definition of "accredited investor."** The key definition in Rule 501 is "accredited investor." Offers and sales to accredited investors are not subject to the informational and certain transactional restrictions of Reg. D. For this reason, it is prudent to try to limit "real-money" offerings solely to accredited investors. Accredited investors include:
  - Any individual with a net worth, or joint net worth with spouse, at the time of purchase exceeding $1 million.
  - Any individual with an income in excess of $200,000 in each of the two most recent years or joint income with spouse in excess of $300,000 in each of those years and who has a reasonable expectation of reaching the same income level in the current year.
  - Any director, executive officer, or general partner of the issuer of the securities being offered or sold.
  - Any trust, with total assets in excess of $5 million, not formed for the specific purpose of acquiring the securities offered, whose purchase is directed by a sophisticated person, as defined.
  - Corporations and various other entities (provided that they have not been formed for the specific purpose of acquiring the securities offered) with total assets in excess of $5 million.
  - Banks, broker-dealers, insurance companies, and various other institutional investors.
  - Any entity in which all of the equity owners are accredited investors.

The SEC revises these provisions from time to time, and care must be taken to determine the current provisions.

- **Rule 502/General Conditions**
  - **No integration.** This term means that certain offerings will be combined for purposes of establishing an exemption if the offerings, although technically separate, are really part of the same offering.
  - **Information requirements.** Special information must be furnished to nonaccredited investors in offerings under Rule 505 and 506 but not Rule 504. These information requirements are quite onerous and require in most cases IPO prospectus-level disclosure and in some cases audited financial statements. As we discuss later, as a practical matter, these requirements are nearly impossible for private technology companies to meet in all respects.
  - **Access.** Mimicking the case law under Section 4(2), the issuer must make available to each prospective purchaser the opportunity to ask questions of the issuer concerning the terms and conditions of the offering and to obtain any additional information that the issuer possesses or can acquire without unreasonable effort or expense to verify information provided to the investor.
  - **No general solicitation or advertising.** The offerees must be restricted to a reasonably limited number of persons with a prior relationship to the issuer in some manner. Note that under Reg. D, there is no other requirement relating to the identity of the offerees—that is, there is no restriction on the sophistication of the offerees or the number of offerees per se (other than if there is a general solicitation); compliance is measured by the sophistication and number of actual purchasers in the offering.
  - **Limitations on resale.** The issuer must exercise reasonable care to assure that purchasers do not resell securities in a nonexempt transaction, including: reasonable inquiry regarding the purchaser's investment intent; written disclosure to the investor prior to sale that the securities have not been registered and cannot be resold unless registered or exempt from registration; and placement of a restrictive legend on the certificate evidencing the security.

- **Rule 503/Form D filing requirement.** SEC Form D must be filed no later than 15 days after the first sale of securities (which occurs whenever the issuer takes money or has investors sign subscription agreements even if the closing has not occurred).
- **Rule 504/Small offering exemption.** The aggregate offering price for offerings under Rule 504 must not exceed $1 million. Under Rule 504, no special information must be disclosed to unaccredited investors.
- **Rule 505/Exemption for offerings of $5 million or less.** There must be a maximum of 35 unaccredited purchasers, plus the informational and other transactional requirements of Reg. D must be satisfied.
- **Rule 506/Exemption for offerings of any size.** Same as Rule 505, but each unaccredited investor either alone or with his or her "purchaser representative(s)" must have "such knowledge and experience in financial and business matters to be capable of evaluating the merits and risks of the prospective investment"—mimicking the investor sophistication requirements of the Section 4(2) case law.

SEC RULE 701/EMPLOYEE BENEFIT EXEMPTION.   Rule 701 exempts with specified dollar limits, securities issued by private companies under written compensatory employee benefit plans or written compensation agreements.

STATE SECURITIES OR "BLUE SKY" LAWS.   Burdensome though it may be, all offerings and sales of securities must also be exempt from registration under the securities (or so-called blue sky) laws of the states. Most states have adopted a limited offering exemption patterned after Section 4(2) of the '33 Act. A federal law, the National Securities Markets Improvement Act of 1976 (NSMIA), preempted state registration/exemption provisions for transactions qualifying under Rule 506— another reason to try to limit private placements to solely accredited investors. Each state usually has other limited offering exemptions based on the number of purchasers in the state or based on the investors being "institutional investors" as defined in the applicable state regulations. Important traps for the unwary in complying with blue sky laws are often present where a non-Rule 506 offering involves the payment of commissions on sales (and particularly where the commissions are paid to an unregistered broker-dealer) or where the offering is to persons in states such as New Hampshire, which has its own unique view of securities laws. In those cases, it is important to check the state law requirements for such compliance items as a required filing that must be made before offers or sales are made. Compliance with the blue sky laws often requires filing a copy of the SEC Form D and payment of a filing fee—even for all-accredited-investor offerings exempted under NSMIA.

PRACTICALITIES OF SALES OF SECURITIES TO FOUNDERS, EMPLOYEES, AND INVESTORS

Founders.   When the founders start a business, technically what happens is that a new company is formed and the new company sells stock to the founders. These sales in theory must comply with the securities laws. These sales are normally of no concern from a securities law perspective, however, because no one would argue that the sale is not a private placement, and if founders want to get their pennies back and return the stock in a rescission action, the company would be more than happy to accommodate them. Therefore, not much thought or effort has to go into securities law compliance for sales of founders stock for nominal consideration; the share certificates should contain a Securities Act restrictive legend, and many lawyers also have the founders sign a simple investment letter or subscription agreement that contains representations to the effect that the founders had access to material information and know that the stock is restricted and cannot be resold freely. You should also look at the state securities or blue sky laws where the founders reside for compliance with the state regulatory scheme.

Employees.   Similarly, sales of stock to employees, including on the exercise of options, are noncontroversial. The same reasons apply: If stock is actually sold, the amount of money involved is generally relatively insignificant, at least in the early stages, so a rescission claim is not a big threat. Second, usually without much effort the sale falls under Section 4(2), Reg. D, or SEC Rule 701. The principal exemption relied on is Rule 701, which is discussed next. Nevertheless, because the number of employees and the dollar amounts involved can get larger in a successful start-up over time, securities law compliance for employee stock issuances is an area that should be carefully monitored. In issuing stock or options to employees, Rule 701 should be examined and periodically reexamined. Compliance is relatively easy, but care must be taken to ensure that the dollar limits of the rule are not violated.

RULE 701 BASICS.   Rule 701 covers issuances of securities only in compensatory circumstances. The awards must be a component of compensation, rather than capital raising. The principal provisions of the rule follow.

- It covers sales pursuant to awards made prior to the issuer's IPO. The exercise of options may occur before or after the IPO.
- Disclosure about the issuer, including risk factors and financials, must be provided only if the issuer makes more than $5 million in awards in any 12-month period. This is rare, but the limit must be watched.
- No federal filing is necessary to perfect the exemption; state filings may be necessary.
- Beginning 90 days after the issuer becomes a public company, the securities may be resold by complying with the applicable provisions of SEC Rule 144.

Awards of stock or options under Rule 701 must be made under a written compensatory benefit plan or written compensation contract. These persons are eligible to receive awards: employees; officers and directors; general partners; and consultants and advisors, provided that they are natural persons (this is actually a bit more complicated), they provide bona fide services to the issuer, and the services are not in connection with capital raising.

There are limits on the number/amount of securities that a company can sell in reliance on Rule 701. If those limits are exceeded, you must find an alternate exemption from registration. An issuer can, in any 12-month period, "sell" (which means "grant" in the case of an option) the greatest of:

- $1 million.
- 15 percent of assets (measured as of the issuer's most recent balance sheet date, if no older than the last fiscal year end).
- 15 percent of outstanding shares (measured as the most recent balance sheet, if no older than the last fiscal year-end).

In addition, with respect to option exercises, it is prudent to file a Form D with the SEC in case there is some flaw in the Rule 701 analysis. Filings may also be required under the blue sky laws of the state where the option holder resides.

Once the company becomes public, the rule is not available and new compensatory issuances are almost always registered on SEC Form S-8.

There are other infrequent problematic issues to keep an eye on. If the number of option holders in the private company grows to exceed 500, the company may, under certain circumstances, have to register as a public company under Section 12(g) of the Exchange Act. The reason is because an issuer must register under the Exchange Act (and become a public company even if it has not had an IPO) if it has more than 500 holders of a class of securities and $10 million in assets (Rule 12g-1) or its stock is listed on a national securities exchange (now including Nasdaq) (Section 12(b)) or is quoted on an automated interdealer quotation system (e.g., the OTC Bulletin Board) (Section 12(g)). Having a large number of "unaccredited" employee stockholders may jeopardize the ability of an acquiror to acquire the company in a private placement for stock; this issue is dealt with in Chapter 5.

The rule does not exempt issuers from the antifraud provisions of the '33 Act nor does it obviate the need for compliance with state blue sky laws, although nearly every state has some form of exemption for employee benefit plans. Some states regulate the grant of an option as well as the exercise of the option. California has substantive requirements.

SALES TO VENTURE CAPITAL AND OTHER INVESTORS. As discussed, the two principal exemptions for sales of stock by private companies in financing transactions are the private placement provisions: SEC Regulation D and Section 4(2) of the Securities Act.

Regulation D is a safe harbor, and the principal task of securities law compliance by private companies is trying to come within the provisions of this regulation. If compliance with Reg. D is impractical, then the offering must be examined under Section 4(2). Analysis for compliance under Section 4(2) is as much risk analysis as technical analysis.

Sometimes rigid technical compliance with Reg. D is simply impractical. For example, take the situation where a company is doing a private placement to several top-tier venture capital investors (i.e., as accredited as you can get) but also wants to make the offer available to a handful of existing stockholders who want to maintain their percentage interest in the company. The irony here is that you can have an all-accredited investor, no disclosure document, Reg. D offering if the stockholders are all accredited dolts who are trust jockeys or who just inherited $1 million, but you cannot sell the same securities without a disclosure document under Reg. D if just one of the stockholders is a genius who just completed her MBA and is now working for a large investment bank. So much for bright-line tests. This is where Section 4(2) comes in. Most practitioners would advise their clients not to bother to do a prospectus-like disclosure document because they consider the offering exempt under Section 4(2) as having the look and feel of a private placement—it is made to a limited number of investors all of whom are accredited or sophisticated. Even where there is one stockholder who may not be sophisticated in the previous example but for whom the company has a good reason to sell some stock, most practitioners would likewise consider the offering exempt under Section 4(2) because the risk of challenge to the exemption is extremely low. This risk is low because generally, under these circumstances, the supposedly unsophisticated investor is one whom you can argue really is sophisticated and is not likely to complain later; and you give that investor access to the company's management to ask questions about the company at, for example, an information session for all prospective investors. In addition, this investor is required to sign extensive subscription documentation to the effect that he or she really is sophisticated, had full access to all "material information," and was able to bear the risk of loss of the investment. In order to claim later that the offering was not a valid Section 4(2), the purchaser would have to assert that he or she really is stupid, was not listening at the information session, and was lying when he or she signed the requisite subscription agreement. In other words, the availability of the Section 4(2) exemption is as much art as science, particularly where you have made a reasonable effort to educate and protect the supposedly unsophisticated investors. Experience and judgment are essential here. But in any event, file a Form D anyway.

Offerings under Reg. D where there are real "outside" unaccredited investors may be very risky because of the disclosure requirements applicable under Reg. D to offerings with those sorts of investors. If things go wrong later, it is fairly easy to find fault with the disclosure documents. As a practical matter, it is very difficult for private companies to comply with the Reg. D disclosure requirements since most do not have the requisite information (particularly audited financial statements) to comply with the prospectus-like disclosure requirements, plus there is often not enough time (or money for legal and accounting fees) to prepare the full-blown disclosure documents. A sample offering memorandum is included as Appendix 4A.

We again come back to the statutory exemption, Section 4(2). As we have seen, the requirements are somewhat nebulous, and the degree of risk varies with the type of client, the nature/number of the investors, and the dollar amounts raised from unaccredited investors. If you have too many unaccredited investors in a Reg. D offering, and if they are all "sophisticated," you can qualify for a Section 4(2) exemption if the offering is to a reasonably small number of qualified people. Here again is where the necessity for judgment comes in; sophistication is in the eye of the beholder to some extent, and lawyers are more prone to find sophistication in an investor who is less risky, as was suggested already. If the newly minted MBA is the college roommate of one of the founders, it is an easy call. The same is true for the kindly brother-in-law. If the newly minted MBA is known as a litigious jerk, it is in everybody's interest not to let her into the deal. This is what really happens: You structure the private placement to comply with as many Reg. D requirements as you can and you eliminate the truly unsophisticated or risky investors.

Once you conclude in good conscience that you have a valid private placement, the next task is properly documenting it. This is always critical, particularly where there are unaccredited investors. Documentation includes a subscription agreement or an investment letter where the purchaser agrees that he or she is sophisticated, is purchasing "for investment" and is not purchasing with a view to resale, along with other representations, such as an acknowledgment that that he or she can bear the economic risk of the investment and understands that there will be no opportunity to resell the securities until well into the future. A sample subscription agreement is included as Appendix 4B.

The other critical document is the investor questionnaire, which is really needed only for unaccredited investors. In the questionnaire, you elicit from prospective investors a representation that they are in fact sophisticated even if they do not look like it. You hope that they are at least sophisticated enough to give the right answers.

You also have to remember to make sure that there is a blue sky law exemption for the unaccredited investor deal because the blue sky law exemption requirements may not be preempted in that case. Particular care should be paid to determine if there are any pre-offer or presale state filing requirements. Even in all-accredited-investor offerings, there are usually state filing requirements; these requirements are not preempted by NSMIA.

Another issue to consider is the impact of using a broker or finder for the private placement. Federal laws require persons deemed to be in the business of effecting transactions in securities to register unless exempt from registration. States have similar provisions. A company planning to compensate, directly or indirectly, any unregistered person or placement agent for soliciting investors must consult state broker-dealer laws and regulations to determine if an exemption from broker-dealer registration is available. In most jurisdictions, direct or indirect remuneration may not be paid to persons who are not registered. Failure to comply with applicable broker-dealer registration requirements possibly can be grounds for rescinding the transaction and can give rise to civil or criminal liability. Form D requires the client to disclose their names to the SEC and state regulators, so you cannot hide them.

HOW TO APPROACH A PRIVATE PLACEMENT.   Now that you have a good feel for the regulatory background and the approach experienced professionals take in private placements, how do you actually go about one? Here are the suggested steps that companies and their lawyers should take.

Step 1. Discuss the business parameters of the proposed transaction.

   ○ Determine the maximum and minimum (if any) number of shares or other securities the company wants to sell and the expected dollar size of transaction.

- ○ Determine who will be approached. What is the basis for approaching potential investors (i.e., is there prior professional contact)?
- ○ Determine the target number and identity of the actual buyers.
- ○ Determine if all of the prospective buyers will be accredited investors.
- ○ Determine if there is an investment banker or placement agent involved in the process.

Step 2. Discuss the basic legal parameters of a private placement.
Discuss the prohibition against a general solicitation and the costs and risks of different structures. If at all possible, limit the private placement solely to accredited investors; this is by far the least risky and costly alternative. Note the significant reduction in time, expense, and risk if the offering is limited to accredited investors.

Step 3. If the offering is limited to accredited investors, technically no disclosure materials need to be given to investors. Determine what materials the company and the banker want to use for marketing, not legal, purposes. If there are to be written materials, the materials cannot be misleading. In one sense, it is better not to use any written materials, but that is rarely practical. As soon as you say one thing (and you will), you have to think about what else must be said. Therefore, an analysis must be done to determine what legal disclosures must be made to ensure that the offering materials are not misleading. (One advantage to written materials is that investors can be asked to represent that they have relied only on those materials and not on any oral statements.)

If the offering is not limited to accredited investors, for the offering documents to comply with Reg. D, they must be (nearly) as comprehensive as an IPO prospectus. Review the disclosure requirements of Reg. D and allocate responsibility for drafting the private placement memo.

- ○ Is the company willing to spend the time and the money to prepare the necessary disclosure document?
- ○ Is it even feasible to do a prospectus-like document? For example, what financial statements are available; are they audited? In reality, as discussed, preparing a private placement memo that fully complies with Reg. D is a daunting task for a private company.

Note that Reg. D says, in effect, that the prospectus-like information must be given to the extent material to an understanding of the client's business. With a very early stage company with little or no assets and limited operations, you might convince yourself that audited financial statements are not material and that not all that much other information is material either. However, it may be hard to argue that information specifically required to be included in a prospectus is not material—especially in hindsight when something has gone wrong.

○ If the offering is not limited to accredited investors, determine the Reg. D exemption to be relied on, and follow the additional requirements of the exemption you are relying on (e.g., appointment of an "offeree representative").

Step 4. If there must be unaccredited investors, and if preparation of the technically necessary disclosure documents is impractical, what do you do?

○ You must make a determination as to whether the offering can be structured under Section 4(2) of the Securities Act.

○ You assess the risks involved in doing a Section 4(2) private placement. As we have seen, the requirements are somewhat nebulous, and the degree of risk varies with the type of issuer the nature/number of the investors, and the dollar amounts raised from unaccredited investors.

○ If the investors are all "sophisticated" and can afford to lose their investment and there is no general solicitation, a Section 4(2) private placement is technically feasible. But, in reality, are there really sophisticated investors who are not accredited? Were they just unlucky in their financial life?

○ Conversely, if there are unaccredited unsophisticated investors and no IPO-equivalent private placement memo, a legal private placement is not possible.

Here is some additional practical advice on how to do a private placement where there are unaccredited investors:

• Prepare a disclosure document as close to a prospectus as is possible. Look on the web (*www.sec.gov*) for an IPO prospectus as close to the business of the issuer as possible and draft a private placement memo that is reasonable under the circumstances.

- Appoint a sophisticated offeree representative for the unaccredited/potentially unsophisticated investors (e.g., could be an officer of the company).
- Be as conservative as possible in the other documentation for the private placement.
- Use a detailed investor questionnaire.
- Get a written agreement from the marginal offerees to use the offeree representative.
- Keep the dollar investments as low as possible for the unaccredited/unsophisticated investors.
- Remember blue sky law requirements and filings; the Form D filing with SEC and the states.
- Do a long-form investor questionnaire and subscription agreement.
- Legend the stock certificates.

INITIAL PUBLIC OFFERINGS

IPO PROCESS, PLAYERS, AND MECHANICS.   What is an IPO? An IPO is a sale by a private company of its common stock to the public after the registration of the stock with the SEC pursuant to the Securities Act. As part of this process, the company also registers its securities under the Exchange Act. The stock is also registered (or listed) for trading on a securities exchange, such as the New York Stock Exchange or, for almost all technology companies, on one of the Nasdaq trading markets. In addition to the company selling shares, the private company's stockholders may sell a portion of their shares in the IPO; regardless, after the IPO, they will own publicly traded stock that they can sell at any time (subject to certain restrictions to be discussed). Many entrepreneurs have become rich through this process, sometimes with a staggering paper net worth. The venture capital investors do not become rich because they were rich already. Paper net worth does not always translate into real net worth since many newly public companies go into the tank (i.e., suffer a drastic price decline) before the entrepreneurs have an opportunity to sell their stock.

IPOs are happy times for all of the participants. This is payoff time for the company founders and for the venture capital investors. It is also payoff time for the company's lawyers and for the investment bankers who manage the IPO. The legal and accounting bills for an

IPO are always very hefty and have escalated greatly over the last few years (for no apparent reason); frequently they amount to $1 million or more. So with an IPO, everybody is happy, everyone is nice to one another, and everyone compliments one another, particularly at the closing dinner. An IPO is a cooperative, not an adversarial, effort.

It is not really possible to describe how to do an IPO. It is not rocket science, and the applicable law is relatively straightforward. To reduce it to its simplest form, you fill out a prescribed form and file it with the SEC. But that truly is a gross oversimplification. To be an effective IPO lawyer, you must have a lot of experience doing IPOs. The really tough calls relating to what needs to be disclosed and the proper disclosure, and what does not need to be disclosed, are often difficult judgment calls. All that we will try to accomplish here is to explain how the process works and what the legal basics are. In addition, we provide some pointers for how to prepare a company for an IPO.

Perhaps the best way to get to know the process is to know who the players are and their respective roles. The principal players and buzzwords follow.

The issuer or the registrant is the company that is going public. An IPO is simply the issuance by the issuer of additional common stock to the public in a public offering. After the public offering, the company's stock is owned by the new public investors and by the stockholders who owned the company pre-IPO. In order to sell the stock to a wide audience and have the stock not be subject to the restrictions on transfer required in a private placement, the new stock has to be registered with the SEC. Hence the term "registrant."

"Registration" is the process by which the securities to be sold to the public are registered with the SEC. This involves preparing and filing a registration statement (generally on Form S-1) with the SEC. The registration statement contains the prospectus, which is the document that is actually circulated to the prospective investors. The prospectus is printed by the financial printer, which is a company that specializes in high-pressure, short-deadline printing of documents for companies that are going public and public companies that are doing subsequent securities offerings. Electronic delivery is now permitted by the SEC, but printers are still engaged to print smaller quantities of the prospectus and to arrange for the filing of the registration statement electronically with the SEC on its electronic data gathering and retrieval (EDGAR) filing system. Substantially all documents filed with the SEC must be filed electronically, and the SEC and private firms maintain searchable online databases containing all SEC electronic filings. The SEC's Web site is at *www.sec.gov*. One of the first tricks you learn when drafting a registration statement or any other SEC document is to obtain models of the registration statements of competitive companies or models of similar transactions. These documents are not copyrighted, and much of the material in a registration statement is likely borrowed from another document already on file.

As you will see from a review of Form S-1, extensive information is required. Form S-1, as you might imagine, is actually a form to be filled out, and it can be found on the SEC's Web site. The goal of the form and the related disclosure rules is to tell the public everything that is relevant to making an investment decision whether to buy the IPO stock. The form requires, among other things:

- An extensive description of the registrant's business, including a description of the industry in which the company competes, its products, its strategy, its marketing plan, its intellectual property protection, any relevant regulations to which it is subject, competition, and the like.
- Audited financial statements for the last three years.
- A discussion of what is really going on in the business and the financials, called MD&A (Management's Discussion and Analysis of Financial Condition and Results of Operations).
- Management biographies.
- All the factors that make an investment in an IPO company risky (which it almost always is), or risk factors.
- Multiple technical disclosure sections.

The preparation of the registration statement is a joint, time-consuming, and extremely tedious effort. The first formal step is an organizational meeting (org meeting), at which all of the principal participants in process meet to discuss the steps that all parties need to take to complete the IPO and set out a timetable for completion of the steps. The most time-consuming task is drafting the registration statement. It takes many days of sitting in a conference room to draft the registration statement in meetings with representatives of the company, company counsel, the underwriters and underwriters' counsel.

The standard of writing is extremely high, even though it is drafting by committee.

The completed registration statement is filed with the SEC. The SEC takes about a month to review it, then sends the registrant a letter describing all of the things that the SEC thinks the registrant should have done and all the things that the registrant could have done better. The SEC comments are prepared by a junior SEC staff member and are reviewed by more senior lawyers before the letter goes out. Some comments are just annoyances—they did not get the point—and some make you scratch your head as to why you did not think of that. Worst of all are comments that point out a legal flaw in the prospectus. Regardless of which SEC comments you get and how many, the SEC controls the process. Although sometimes you can get the SEC to withdraw a comment or soften it, your main job is to get the registration statement cleared (or "declared effective") as soon as possible. A lot of money is at stake.

Unfortunately, once the company actually goes public, although the founders may have large or even staggering paper net worths, the money still is only on paper. In a strong IPO market, the founders and the VCs are allowed to sell some of their stock (selling stockholders) in the IPO, but usually not a significant percentage of their holdings. They are also subject to *lock-up* agreements that contractually prevent them from selling into the public market, typically for six months. Even when the contractual restrictions are lifted or expire, insiders who are considered affiliates of the issuer (officers, directors, and principal stockholders) are limited to how much they can sell under SEC Rule 144, which currently has volume and manner of sale limitations. The really fortunate may also be allowed to participate in a follow-on offering within a few months of the IPO, which is another public offering where all or most of the stock sold is outstanding stock owned by the founders and VCs.

Once a private company completes its public offering, it becomes a public company subject to a maze of SEC regulations under the Exchange Act governing public companies. These rules are described in the section called "Public Company Regulation." Having its stock publicly traded makes the public company vulnerable to securities class action claims filed by "strike suit lawyers."

Other players in this process are the investment bankers or underwriters and their lawyers, counsel for the underwriters. Technically, the underwriters buy the stock from the issuer pursuant to an underwriting agreement, which is essentially just a stock purchase agreement tailored to the IPO process. Multiple underwriters in an *underwriting syndicate* sell the stock in an IPO, but their involvement in the process varies widely. The underwriters who run the show are called the lead underwriters, and the first among equals is the book-running manager. The book-running manager retains most of the power over the process, including the ability to allocate the stock among the syndicate members and the institutional buyers. This is a really big deal in IPOs, and underwriters fight in their negotiation with the company as to which firm is the book-runner. The names of the lead underwriters appear in large font type at the bottom of the cover of the IPO prospectus; the names of other underwriters who are mere participants in the underwriting syndicate appear in small print at the back of the prospectus, or book. The book-running manager's name is always on the left side of the cover of the prospectus, and this announces to the investment community who really won the deal. The underwriting syndicate is formed to help the lead underwriters sell the deal and share the risk of the underwriting. Risk is created because these underwritings are almost always "firm commitment" underwritings (rather than "best efforts" underwritings). In a firm commitment underwriting, the underwriters buy the stock at a negotiated discounted price from the company and then turn around and sell it to the public at the fixed price to the public to make their profit. Buyers are lined up beforehand to minimize risk, but things can go wrong and the underwriters can get stuck with a portion of the stock—a sticky deal.

The roles of the respective underwriters can best be explained by an overview of syndicate economics. The underwriters make their money on the spread or the underwriting discount on the shares of stock sold. The IPO underwriters almost always buy the stock at approximately a 7 percent discount from the price the stock is initially sold to the public or the price to the public set forth in a table on the front cover of the prospectus. The spread is divided up three ways: a portion goes to the lead managers for their role in managing the offering; a portion goes to the underwriting syndicate, which is the large group of underwriters who sign the underwriting agreement and commit to taking the investment risk of buying the stock from the issuer—this portion is usually almost nothing because the underwriters' legal and marketing expenses are deducted from this portion; and the last, and largest, piece of the spread, is the selling concession that is paid to the underwriters based on how many shares they actually sell. At this point, syndicate politics and economics get more complicated than we can explain here, but basically the book-running manager tells each of the syndicate members how much they can sell. Because all of the underwriters are talking to the same large institutional buyers, there are mechanisms to determine who gets the credit for the sale. These methods include a pot split or a jump ball or a combination of the two. The final major player is the "underwriters' counsel" (or counsel for the underwriters), which is the law firm representing the underwriters, chosen by the book-running manager, that does due diligence on the issuer and participates in the drafting of the registration statement. This firm also handles the necessary filings by the underwriters with the National Association of Securities Dealers (NASD), which regulates underwriting commissions and practices. All of the bankers are members of the NASD. The NASD is a self-regulatory organization (SRO) that has its own rules governing underwriters and brokers. The NASD has a specific rule that sets out what it considers to be fair underwriting compensation. Counsel for the underwriters makes filings with the NASD disclosing underwriting compensation. The NASD must clear the underwriting arrangements before the deal can be sold. The NASD filing process, as well as the Nasdaq listing process, goes on in parallel with the SEC filing process, but is much simpler and less controversial. As for legal fees, the industry rule of thumb for the fee for underwriters' counsel is half of what issuer's counsel gets.

At the closing dinner, hosted by the book-running manager, the company and the bankers toast all of the players, and the underwriters pass out the deal cubes (little Lucite blocks that each contain a miniature prospectus inside).

PREPARING FOR AN IPO.   Because the public markets are fickle, a private company contemplating an IPO should begin its preparation at least a year prior to the expected SEC filing date. In fact, many pre-IPO steps and practices should be kept in mind from the founding of the company. Most early-stage mistakes can be fixed, but some cannot.

Among the preparatory steps that a private company should take before the IPO are these 12:

Step 1. Corporate housekeeping. The company's lawyers should do a comprehensive review of the legal affairs of the company to make sure everything is in perfect order. The investment bankers will advise whether the company needs to do a forward or reverse stock split (to bring the price per share in the IPO into the customary range: $10 to $15, more or less). The company will also adopt, contingent on the success of the IPO, a new public company charter and public company bylaws that, among other things, authorize sufficient shares to do the IPO, additional public offerings, and future acquisitions and allow room to do a future stock split if the stock price significantly rises. Public company charters also authorize so-called blank check preferred stock that can be issued by the board without further stockholder authorization, usually in connection with the later adoption of a poison pill. Further, public company charter documents contain customary antitakeover provisions, such as a staggered board, prohibition on stockholder written consents, advance notice of stockholder proposals, and the like. Prior to the IPO, many companies adopt new stock incentive plans or add additional shares to existing plans; also, public company plans contain provisions, such as those permitting cashless exercises, that may not be contained in the company's existing stock plan. The company also needs to consider the adoption of other types of equity plans, such as a tax-qualified employee stock purchase plan.

Step 2. Management of public relations. Well before the IPO, the company must take care not to make overly optimistic, or puffing, statements to the press or to analysts. If an article about the company, particularly one that talks about financial matters or mentions the prospective IPO, is published shortly before or during the offering, especially in the general press, the SEC often will suspend the offering for a period of time to allow the impact of the article from this *gun-jumping* activity to diminish. Similar rules apply to the content of the company's Web site. Ordinary course of business product announcements are permitted, as are appearances at industry conferences where the presentation is limited to product or scientific material. There is a risk to the latter, however, since the general press may be in attendance and an offending article may appear at exactly the wrong time.

Step 3. Underwriters' due diligence. As mentioned, both the underwriters and their counsel do a due diligence investigation of the company's business and legal affairs. Underwriters' counsel prepares a lengthy due diligence checklist of all of the legal documents that they need to review. Since these lists are largely all the same, the company and its lawyers can begin to assemble beforehand the documents that are likely to be on the list. In order to make the process a smooth one, these documents should be uploaded to an online data room.

Step 4. Management team. To the extent there are weaknesses in the company's management team, additional managers need to be hired well prior to the IPO. Part of the assessment that underwriters make in determining whether the company is ready for an IPO is the quality and depth of the management team. Frequently, the existing chief financial officer CFO is replaced if he or she does not have public company/IPO experience. Usually the CFO manages the IPO process on behalf of the company. The CFO must also prepare financial projections for the investment bankers to review; the bankers need to have a significant degree of comfort into the company's earnings visibility, particular in the fiscal quarters immediately following the IPO. Earnings disappointments can cause a severe drop in the company's stock price and expose the company and the underwriters to legal liability and investor wrath.

Step 5. Accounting systems. As discussed in detail under "Public Company Regulation," the Sarbanes-Oxley Act imposed rigid and extensive new accounting requirements on public companies and companies that are going public. Some take effect after the completion of the IPO, but a compliance plan needs to be in place beforehand. The most onerous of these requirements are new accounting standards for "internal control over financial reporting." Complex bookkeeping systems need to be implemented that satisfy the internal control requirements. Also, the company will need an auditing firm that meets stringent independence requirements and that has public company/IPO experience that will satisfy the underwriters. Private companies often skimp on accounting costs and hire lower-tier accounting firms. The underwriters may insist that the company's accounting firm be replaced with a more experienced firm, which, because of the consolidation in the accounting industry, need not necessarily be limited to the "Big X." The process of selection and the new accountants getting up to speed is time consuming and must be planned for well in advance of the IPO.

Step 6. Financial statements. The company needs to be certain very early in the IPO process that it will have available financial statements that comply not only with generally accepted accounting principles (GAAP) but also with the SEC's Regulation S-X. Three years of audited financial statements are required, and a frequent stumbling block is that the audited financial statements of acquired businesses must also be included, also GAAP and Regulation S-X-compliant. A possible cheap shot by the SEC over the issue of cheap stock (further discussed later) must also be considered and dealt with if necessary. Generally speaking, of all the pitfalls in the IPO process and public company status, inaccurate or otherwise noncompliant financial statements are by far the most common source of trouble and liability.

Step 7. Prospectus drafting. Optimally, the company and its counsel will have prepared a draft of the sections of the prospectus that describe the business and its risk factors. Nothing makes the IPO process go more smoothly than having a polished first draft of these sections available at the IPO organizational meeting. The typical process for the drafting of these sections is for the company to do a rough first draft of the description of the business after the company's lawyers advise on necessary content. The company's lawyers then polish the draft and redraft the language to make it prospectus-like. Before beginning the drafting process, the company and its counsel should attempt to identify IPO prospectuses or other SEC filings of companies that are competitors. All of this documentation can be obtained online. Reviewing competitors' SEC filings can give the company a good sense of the scope and quality of the "Business" section. The company's counsel also uses these models to do the first draft of the "Risk Factors" section. Many of the risk factors are boilerplate, but care must be taken to identify the real risks of the business and candidly describe them. The SEC closely scrutinizes these sections.

Another section to prepare that would also expedite the IPO process is MD&A. The section contains a year-to-year comparison of the principal line items in the company's income statement and the reasons behind the year-to-year increases or decreases. The section is also required to disclose "known trends and uncertainties" regarding the company's prospective financial performance. Although the company technically is not required to furnish projections, this somewhat nebulous standard is meant to elicit disclosure that will eliminate surprises in the company's future operating results. This is another section that is closely scrutinized by the SEC.

Step 8. Restructure the board of directors and board committees. One of the principal features of the Sarbanes-Oxley Act and related SRO requirements was to require stringent new corporate governance standards for public companies and companies that file to go public. Compliance with certain of these requirements can be delayed, but the company nevertheless must be aware of these requirements and have a plan in place for compliance. These requirements are discussed in detail in the "Public Company Regulation" section, but among the principal requirements are:

○ The board of directors must have a majority of members who are "independent" under applicable SEC/Nasdaq/stock exchange rules.

○ The board must have an independent audit committee of the board of directors. As a practical matter, one of the members should be a so-called financial expert—someone like a CFO of a public company, who has had responsibility for public company financial reporting.

○ The board should also have an independent compensation committee and a nominating committee. There are detailed requirements for disclosure of executive compensation in the IPO prospectus as well as a report of the compensation committee and a description of the company's compensation processes. Recently, the SEC also required a new compensation discussion and analysis section that describes the company's philosophy and procedures in determining executive compensation.

Step 9. Scrutinize stock option plans and practices. One issue that both the accountants and the SEC focus on is whether the company has issued cheap stock in the year or two prior to the filing of the registration statement. A significant disparity between the exercise price of stock options and the IPO price per share invites inquiries as to whether the company granted the options at the required fair market value, failing which an increased charge to earnings must be taken. Companies are frequently challenged to demonstrate that they have priced options at fair market value. Almost always, common stock options are priced below the last round of preferred stock because of the preferred stock's superior rights. The question is how much below. In the Internet craze, the SEC began to challenge the discounts more seriously because companies were going public quickly and in connection with an IPO, the preferred stock converts to common stock. It became difficult to convince the SEC that common stock options granted at a 90 percent discount to the IPO price within a few months of the IPO were really granted at fair market value. It then became common practice not to fight the cheap stock fight any longer. After the Internet stock crash in 2000, after which the liquidation preference of preferred stock became only too real, companies nevertheless gave up the cheap stock fight in advance. Also, for these reasons and because of new tax regulations that also require fair market value pricing, companies contemplating an IPO took the valuation process more seriously, including retaining valuation consultants.

The other side of the equation is that once the company becomes public, stock options must be granted at the trading price of the stock; companies should consider additional option grants while the company still has some flexibility in pricing options because of its private status. As stated, the company must amend its equity compensation plans or adopt new ones to ensure that they are public company–compliant. The pool of stock option reserved shares is almost always increased because increases after the IPO are subject to stockholder approval regulated by the SEC's proxy rules and SRO rules and the hostility of a number of institutional investors to equity compensation that they consider excessive.

Cheap stock principles have also been applied by the SEC to shares issued to inside investors prior to the IPO and to companies with which the company has a commercial relationship, such as suppliers and customers.

Step 10. Consider settling troublesome litigation. Because the IPO will generate significant cash for the company, the company will find it more difficult to settle litigation after the IPO because of its deeper pockets. Also, announcement of a pending IPO often brings "vulture" claims forward. To the extent prudent, the company should try to dispose of these claims.

Step 11. Pay off insider loans. Loans to insiders are no longer permitted for public companies, and a quirk of the SEC rules requires that insider loans be repaid before the *filing* of the IPO registration statement, even though the deal may not proceed to pricing and closing.

Step 12. Analyze the company's financing needs. Companies can conduct private placements prior to an IPO and even, in certain extremely limited circumstances, concurrently with the IPO. But there are significant limitations on the company's ability to do so. The company's financing plans and needs must be shared with its advisors to make sure that they are not inconsistent with the IPO rules.

PUBLIC COMPANY REGULATION

The decision to go public has far-reaching ramifications affecting the company's relationship with its stockholders, the timing and content of the public disclosure of financial and other information about the company, corporate governance, and the applicability of insider trading laws. The Securities Act contains the rules applicable to the company's IPO of its common stock and subsequent securities offerings by the public company. The Exchange Act regulates the company's continued existence as a public company. Public companies are also regulated by the stock exchange or other trading market on which their stock trades. The Sarbanes-Oxley Act of 2002 impacts almost all aspects of the regulation of public companies and is implemented largely through exchange regulations. The new Sarbanes-Oxley regulatory framework impacts public companies (as well as companies considering going public), their officers and directors, outside auditors, and counsel in an attempt to address many of the corporate governance and financial reporting abuses that came to light in the wake of the Enron and World-Com bankruptcies. Sarbanes-Oxley has a lesser impact on companies traded on the Over-the-Counter Bulletin Board or on the "Pink Sheets" since they technically are not regulated by a securities exchange.

WHY GO PUBLIC?   There are a number of reasons for companies to go public:

- Being public gives its stockholders the opportunity to sell their stock in the public markets. Thus, there is a liquidity path for insiders, investors, and employees.

- A public company can access the public capital markets. Larger amounts of money can be raised and can be raised more quickly.
- A public company can do more and larger acquisitions because it can use its publicly traded stock as currency to acquire other businesses.
- Going public gives the insiders bragging rights.

Being a public company is also a significant burden. For one, being an officer of a public company is akin to living in a fishbowl—the trading markets scrutinize every move, and there is a lot of pressure to perform and keep the stockholder base happy. Lots of people have their money riding on company insiders (and company insiders have a lot of money riding on their own performance), so the pressure to constantly produce better revenues and earnings is relentless. This pressure causes many smart people to do incredibly stupid things, such as manufacturing financial results and hiding the facts from the company's accountants. There have been innumerable revenue recognition and similar scandals. Apart from the legal and moral issues, it is staggering that otherwise smart people think that they can get away with these scams beyond the short term.

Being public brings out the greed in people. Frequently people simply cannot stand seeing their fortune and glory go down the tubes, and so sell on adverse inside information before it becomes public. Conversely, many cannot resist the quick buck that can be made by buying on favorable inside information.

Last, even for the good guys, there are liabilities at every turn. Strike suit lawyers see fraud behind any stock decline, particularly a precipitous one. Some think that people who volunteer to be directors of public companies have a death wish. These pressures have been exacerbated by increasingly stringent laws directed at improving corporate governance. This kind of draconian approach may play well with the public, but the incentives not to become or remain a public company director are continually increasing.

OVERVIEW OF PUBLIC COMPANY REGULATION.   Generally, the obligations of the company and its insiders fall into three categories:

1. Disclosure obligations of the company, including financial and other reports required to be filed with the SEC, as well as proxy statements and annual stockholder reports; general disclosure of

corporate information to the marketplace; and reports and filings related to the listing of the company's common stock on the stock exchanges, now including Nasdaq. We discuss only requirements imposed by Nasdaq and not the other exchanges. Their regulations are closely similar. There is also a separate, somewhat less stringent, set of regulations for companies that qualify as small business issuers, which we also do not discuss separately; these rules are also quite similar to the rules applicable to larger companies.

2. Corporate governance obligations of the company, including Sarbanes-Oxley–mandated and SRO-mandated requirements relating to board of directors and board committee formation and independence and certifications by principal officers relating to the company's compliance with its disclosure and financial reporting obligations.

3. Disclosure requirements and trading prohibitions for insiders, including general insider trading restrictions relating to company information and personal securities transactions, short-swing profits and beneficial ownership reporting to the SEC of transactions in company securities, and rules (e.g., Rule 144) relating to sales of restricted securities.

   Some short memoranda on various securities law–related topic can be found in Appendices 4E and 4F. Note that the exact requirements in these forms and the following information can quickly become dated as a result of SEC rule changes.

PERIODIC SEC REPORTING REQUIREMENTS

Form 10-K, Form 10-Q, and Form 8-K.   Once a company goes public, it becomes subject to the periodic reporting requirements contained in Section 13(a) of the Exchange Act. These include the annual report on Form 10-K, quarterly reports on Form 10-Q, and current reports on Form 8-K. In addition, for each shareholder meeting, the Exchange Act requires companies to provide a proxy statement (or an information statement if proxies are not solicited for the meeting). The principal purpose of various SEC filings required of the public company is to provide information about the company on a continuing basis to ensure that buyers and sellers of the company's securities in the public markets have all the information needed to make informed investment decisions. Some of these forms are also intended to give existing stockholders information needed for voting on various corporate matters as well as information about certain trading activities by insiders and potential acquirors. These forms can be accessed by the public on the SEC's Web site, and proper corporate governance also requires them to be accessible on the company's Web site.

Whenever reference is made to a filing date or due date, it refers to the date that the filing must actually be *received* by the SEC. Generally, if the due date of an SEC report is not a business day, the report is due on the next succeeding business day. SEC filings generally are required to be filed electronically using the SEC's EDGAR system, which is discussed in further detail later. Companies need to determine if they will make their own EDGAR filings directly or rely on a third party, such as a financial printer, to do so. Procedures must be put in place in advance of the due date of the first filing.

The annual and quarterly reports include prescribed financial information and financial analysis. Management's Discussion and Analysis of Financial Condition and Results of Operations initially prepared and included in the IPO prospectus must be prepared each quarter and included in the company's periodic reports. In addition to financial information, the 10-K includes information about the company and its various business segments, including competition, customers, prospects, intellectual property, properties, employees, recent developments, and litigation, as well as information on executive compensation, related party transactions, and accounting fees that can be incorporated by reference from the company's proxy statement. While the SEC does not review in advance the company's periodic reports as it does with the registration statement for the IPO, it does review registrants' 10-Ks and other reports on a periodic basis. This review process often focuses on the company's financial statements and MD&A. Technically, the required information need not include projections. Nevertheless, the MD&A requires disclosure of known "present trends and uncertainties"—essentially a schizophrenic attempt to require, but not really require, forward-looking information.

The current report on Form 8-K is used to report late-breaking news on a current basis. Sometimes the filing of an 8-K is optional, but for specified significant matters, discussed in detail later, it is required. In the wake of the Enron debacle, the SEC has amended the 8-K rules to broaden substantially the types of information required to be disclosed currently on a Form 8-K and to decrease the time between the event and the filing of an 8-K.

FORM 10-K: ANNUAL REPORT

Form 10-K must be filed with the SEC after the end of each fiscal year. For so-called accelerated filers, Form 10-K is due within 75 days after the fiscal year; for large accelerated filers, this deadline is 60 days. For all other issuers, the report is due in 90 days. The term "accelerated filer" means an issuer after it first meets these conditions as of the end of its fiscal year:

- The aggregate market value of the voting and nonvoting common equity held by nonaffiliates of the issuer as of the end of its second fiscal quarter is $75 million or more (for "large accelerated filers" the threshold amount is $700 million).
- The issuer has been subject to the requirements of Sections 13(a) or 15(d) of the Exchange Act for a period of at least 12 calendar months.
- The issuer has filed at least one annual report (e.g., Form 10-K) pursuant to Section 13(a) or 15(d) of the Exchange Act.
- The issuer is not eligible to use Forms 10-KSB and 10-QSB (small business forms) for its annual and quarterly reports.

Form 10-K calls for information much like that in a public offering prospectus. The information prescribed by the form includes:

- Description of the company's business
- Discussion of risk factors impacting the company's business
- Description of properties used in the company's business
- Description of legal proceedings in which the company is involved and certain tax penalties, if any
- Matters submitted to a vote of security holders
- Market for the company's common stock, related stockholder matters, and any company purchases of its equity securities
- Selected financial data for the last five fiscal years
- Management's Discussion and Analysis of Financial Condition and Results of Operations for the last two fiscal years (Both by rule and current practice, MD&A disclosures are significantly more complete and candid than they have been historically, and,

although financial projections are not technically required, disclosure of "known trends and uncertainties" is required.)

- Any unresolved SEC staff comments
- Quantitative and qualitative disclosures about market risks
- Audited financial statements and supplementary data (two years of balance sheets and three years of income statements)
- Changes in and disagreements with accountants on accounting and financial disclosure, if any
- Management's report on controls and procedures and an audit report on internal control over financial reporting (for which compliance dates vary)
- Information on directors and executive officers of the company, including compensation
- Security ownership of certain beneficial owners and management as of a current date
- Availability of the company's code of ethics
- Principal accounting fees and services
- A description of the audit committee's functions and the identity of the audit committee's "financial expert" or the absence of one
- Certain relationships and related insider transactions in which the company and its officers, directors, and 10 percent stockholders participate
- Exhibits and financial statement schedules

There are rules permitting the incorporation of information by reference into Form 10-K from the company's proxy statement (discussed later) and its annual report to stockholders and permitting a deferred filing of certain financial schedules. It is important to note that the Form 10-K must be signed by the company's "principal executive officer," "principal financial officer," and "principal accounting officer," as well as by a *majority* of the company's board of directors. A copy of Form 10-K and the related instructions can be found at *www.sec.gov/about/forms/secforms.htm*.

FORM 10-Q: QUARTERLY REPORT

Form 10-Q reports must be filed with the SEC after each of the company's first three fiscal quarters. For accelerated and large accelerated filers, the report is due 40 days after quarter-end. For all other issuers, the report is due in 45 days. Form 10-Q must include this information:

- Condensed, unaudited comparative balance sheets, statements of income and statements of cash flows
- Management's Discussion and Analysis of Financial Condition and Results of Operations and a discussion relating to certain accounting changes and other data
- Qualitative and quantitative disclosures about market risk
- Management's report on controls and procedures
- Information with respect to changes in legal proceedings, changes in risk factors, unregistered sales of equity securities, use of proceeds and issuer repurchases, defaults in senior indebtedness, results of votes by security holders, and certain other information
- Periodic update regarding the use of proceeds derived from the company's initial public offering

A copy of Form 10-Q and the related instructions can be found at *www.sec.gov/about/forms/secforms.htm*.

FORM 8-K: REPORT OF MATERIAL EVENTS

Form 8-K must be filed with the SEC within four business days after the occurrence of any of the specified events. This form has been revised to include far more reportable events than had been required for many years, and issuers must be constantly on guard to inform their legal advisors of the occurrence (or prospective occurrence) of these events. The events can be simply summarized as including virtually any material event relating to the company. This list of reportable events includes:

- Entry into a material definitive agreement. Requires the disclosure of material definitive agreements entered into by the company that are not made in the ordinary course of business and material amendments.
- Termination of a material definitive agreement. Exemptions include expiration of an agreement on a stated termination date and completion of the obligations by all parties to an agreement.
- Bankruptcy or receivership.
- Completion of acquisition or disposition of assets. Although the disclosure concerning a completed acquisition is required to be filed in the Form 8-K within 4 business days, the pro forma

financial information and financial statements for a completed acquisition (but not disposition) are permitted to be filed by amendment up to 71 days later.

- Results of operations and financial condition. Requires information with respect to public announcements or releases of material nonpublic information regarding a company's results of operations or financial condition for a completed fiscal period (e.g., an earnings press release), except where an earnings release is published before an analyst call and the release gives notice of how to attend the call.
- Creation of a direct financial obligation or an obligation under an off-balance sheet arrangement. Requires disclosure if a company becomes obligated under a direct financial obligation, such as a material loan agreement.
- Events that accelerate or increase a direct financial obligation or an obligation under an off-balance sheet arrangement.
- Costs associated with exit or disposal activities.
- Material impairments. Requires disclosure when a board or an authorized officer concludes that a material charge for impairment to one or more of the company's assets, including an impairment of securities or goodwill, is required under GAAP.
- Notice of delisting or failure to satisfy a continued listing rule or standard; transfer of listing.
- Unregistered sales of equity securities.
- Material modification to rights of security holders.
- Changes in registrant's certifying accountant.
- Nonreliance on previously issued financial statements or a related report or completed interim review.
- Changes in control of the registrant.
- Departure of directors or principal officers; election of directors; appointment of principal officers, and entry into compensation agreements or other arrangements with these individuals.
- Amendments to corporate charter or bylaws; change in fiscal year.
- Temporary suspension of trading under registrant's employee benefit plans.
- Amendments to code of ethics; waiver of a provision of the code of ethics.

- Regulation FD disclosure. Permits information to be furnished pursuant to and within the time periods mandated by Regulation FD (discussed later). The accelerated four-business-day filing deadline does not apply to disclosures under this item, but if used as the primary Regulation FD compliance vehicle, an even shorter deadline may apply.
- Other events. Permits disclosure of information that a company deems of importance to security holders, including information required to be filed pursuant to Regulation FD. The accelerated four-business-day filing deadline does not apply to disclosures under this item.
- Financial statements and exhibits (generally related to acquisitions).

A copy of Form 8-K and related instructions can be found at *www.sec.gov/about/forms/secforms.htm*.

General Issues Relating to Filing Requirements.   All Exchange Act filings must be carefully prepared and filed in a timely manner to ensure full compliance by the company with the Exchange Act. It is also important to note that the company's reports under the Exchange Act are likely to be incorporated by reference (a) in any number of presently unanticipated agreements or documents (e.g., merger or acquisition agreements), and (b) in current and future registration statements of the company, whether filed on behalf of itself or on behalf of selling security holders. Therefore, the uses and, in particular, the liabilities that can attach to these reports can go beyond those associated strictly with Exchange Act compliance.

Compliance with the reporting requirements of the Exchange Act is also a precondition to the availability of the exemption from the registration requirements of the Securities Act afforded by Rule 144 (described later). For that reason, Rule 144 is of special importance to all of the company's stockholders who bought their common stock prior to the company's IPO and who wish to sell that "restricted stock" publicly. The company's affiliates (officers, directors, and major stockholders) must also use Rule 144 to sell their stock. In addition, SEC Form S-8, which is a simplified form for registering option plan shares. will be unavailable if the company is not up to date in its Exchange Act reporting. Finally, future use by the company of a short-form registration statement on Form S-3, which facilitates and expedites certain offerings by more seasoned companies, is conditioned on 12 months of timely filing of Exchange Act reports.

In making public disclosures, the company should also be mindful if it intends to include financial measures not calculated in accordance with generally accepted accounting principles. A common example is the use of earnings before interest, taxes, depreciation and amortization (EBITDA) in a press release. While not prohibited, Regulation G and related rules require certain reconciliations and disclosures regarding the usefulness of such measures. Counsel should be consulted prior to including non-GAAP financial measures in any filing, press release, Web site section, presentation, or other public forum.

Controlling persons of the company can have liability with respect to any Exchange Act filings that are not in compliance with the rules and regulations of the SEC, unless the controlling person can show that he or she "acted in good faith and did not directly or indirectly induce the act or acts constituting the violation or cause of action." Accordingly, internal procedures should be established by the company to assure timely, accurate, and complete reporting as required under the Exchange Act.

All exhibits to EDGAR filings must be filed in computer-readable form. Accordingly, the company should retain in computer-readable form copies of all material contracts, organizational documents, and other documents that may be needed as exhibits.

As this discussion of Exchange Act reports reflects, there are a number of interrelated processes that recur on an annual cycle in connection with the company's SEC reporting. In order for a company to prepare its SEC filings, each year it must circulate questionnaires to all directors, officers, and 5 percent stockholders as a means of generating the required information. A specific schedule will have to be established to ensure timely SEC reporting and proper organization of the annual meeting and related matters. Close coordination is required among the company, counsel, auditors, printers, and anyone else participating in the preparation of the annual report to stockholders (to be described). To allow a comfortable timetable:

- Questionnaires should be circulated to directors, officers, and 5 percent stockholders in ample time to consider replies in preparing proxy material.

- Preliminary proxy materials (if required) should be filed with the SEC at least 20 days prior to the expected date of delivery to stockholders.
- Definitive proxy materials and the annual report to stockholders should be mailed (or, if SEC rules allow, posted electronically) to stockholders, the SEC, and Nasdaq at least four weeks prior to the annual meeting date.
- A record date should be established in consultation with the transfer agent prior to the mailing or electronic delivery date.
- Inquiries must be made by the transfer agent of brokers and others concerning the number of sets of materials they will require for persons whose stock is held in street names.
- Inquiries must be made by the transfer agent of clearing agency nominees concerning the brokerage firms and other institutions that hold the company's stock on the clearing agencies' books, to get names of clearing agency members who hold the stock.
- Nonroutine agenda items for the annual meeting need to be identified.
- Board resolutions should be adopted dealing with formalities relating to the annual meeting (e.g., setting meeting and record dates, specifying purposes of the meeting, designating proxies, authorizing preparation and distribution of proxy material).
- Signatures of a majority of the board of directors must be obtained on the Form 10-K.

Other Company Disclosure and Filing Obligations

RULE 10B-17 REPORT

Under Rule 10b-17 of the Exchange Act, the company must give notice to Nasdaq at least 10 days prior to the record date of a dividend or other distribution in cash or in kind, including a dividend or distribution of any security; a stock split or reverse split; or a rights or other subscription offering. Nasdaq has developed a short form for reporting cash dividends, with all other reportable actions requiring a long form. These forms are available at *www.nasdaq.com*.

REGISTRATION STATEMENT ON FORM S-8

A registration statement on Form S-8 provides a short-form registration statement on which the company can register shares for offer and sale pursuant to certain employee benefit plans (including certain compensatory contracts), so that certain employees may receive publicly tradable securities under such plans. Form S-8 registration statements become effective immediately upon filing and are updated continuously and automatically when the issuer files its reports required under the Exchange Act. Instead of delivery of a formal prospectus, the company is required to deliver its annual report to stockholders (or until preparation of its first annual report, the IPO prospectus), together with a document containing other specified information with respect to the benefit plan, to participants in the plan. The company is required to maintain, in a separate file, copies of the Form S-8 registration statement, its most recent annual report (or IPO prospectus), and the legal documents containing information regarding the plan. In addition, the company is required to deliver to all employees participating in the plan (including all holders of outstanding options) copies of all reports, proxy statements, and other communications sent generally to stockholders at the same time as they are sent to the stockholders. Directors and officers acquire registered shares upon exercise of a stock option covered by a Form S-8 registration statement; nevertheless, they will have to resell those shares either pursuant to Rule 144 or pursuant to a separate resale prospectus. (See "Procedures for Sales of Unregistered Stock and Stock Held by Affiliates" regarding Rule 144 restrictions if no resale prospectus is on file.)

SEC's Electronic Data Gathering and Retrieval System.   Most SEC documents, including Forms 10-K and 10-Q and proxy statements, must be filed with the SEC electronically using the SEC's EDGAR system. A brief discussion regarding the broad implications of the EDGAR rules for the company and the steps needed for compliance with the EDGAR rules follows.

EDGAR-MANDATED FILINGS
Every EDGAR-mandated filing by a public company must be made in electronic form. EDGAR-mandated filings include Forms 10-K; Form 10-Q; Form 8-K; proxy statements; Forms 3, 4, and 5; Schedules 13D and 13G; all registration statements; and most other SEC filings. At present, these filings do not need to be made via EDGAR: Form 144 and the annual reports to stockholders.

How to Use EDGAR

Documents are filed with the EDGAR system electronically. The company must obtain (via a short electronic application) specific identifying codes and passwords that will allow it to make filings via EDGAR. These numbers can be obtained, usually within one or two days, by electronically filing a short application called a Form ID (see *www.sec.gov/about/forms/formid.pdf*) followed up by a notarized fax of the application. For questions about obtaining EDGAR identification numbers, contact company counsel or go to the SEC's EDGAR filer management Web site at *www.filermanagement.edgarfiling.sec.gov*. The document and all exhibits must be provided to the SEC in computer-readable form. Moreover, the EDGAR system contains a complex system of rules regarding the format of the electronic submissions. A substantial amount of work may be required to prepare a document for filing once it is in its final substantive form. Specifically, since all exhibits must also be filed electronically, it is important to obtain computer-readable forms of all requisite material agreements (e.g., leases and bank loan agreements) that have been prepared by firms other than the company or counsel preparing the EDGAR filing. This can be accomplished either by requesting an electronic version or by scanning the paper copy delivered at the closing to create a new electronic document.

Implementing Methodology to Comply with EDGAR

Public companies have taken one of two approaches to addressing the EDGAR requirement. A large number of companies have charged their own accounting staff with the task of setting up a suitable computer facility and making the required filings in-house. A second group of companies use their financial printer or outside counsel to make their filings. A manually executed hard copy of every EDGAR filing must be retained for at least five years. All signatures must be also be typed into the exhibits.

COMPANY DISCLOSURE OBLIGATIONS OTHER THAN PURSUANT TO SEC REPORTS.   In addition to the formal disclosure requirements imposed by the SEC forms just discussed, a public company is also subject to new obligations relating to informal communications, such as press releases and communications with analysts and the news media. These obligations are governed by antifraud principles developed by the courts and by the rules of the SEC. These rules are intended to keep the securities markets and stockholders informed of material developments, both favorable and unfavorable, concerning the company's affairs without favoring any special person or group. The company should establish and follow a general practice of prompt and complete disclosure of material developments. Care must be taken to avoid inaccurate, incomplete, or misleading disclosure. In particular, the company should exercise great care in the preparation of press releases and in disclosures to analysts and news reporters.

As a strictly technical matter, absent a specific statutory or regulatory requirement to disclose, such as the filing of current and periodic reports with the SEC, there is no general duty to disclose. But this is a technical view that is not universally shared and is not practical. For one thing, a practical element severely penalizes companies for nondisclosure. The breadth and depth of the trading market for a company's stock (and hence its stock price) is partly dependent on the extent to which the company is followed by investment analysts who publish research on the company. In addition, institutional investors, which tend to dominate the trading markets, are leery of maintaining positions in companies that "surprise" their stockholders. If a company is in possession of bad news, there is a strong human tendency to want to hide it until disclosure becomes mandatory in the legal sense. But if the company permits the market to continue to trade unaware of the bad news, when the news subsequently comes out, the company will have lost significant credibility and goodwill in the investment community. This credibility and goodwill are very difficult to recover. Nevertheless, while it is a bad idea to withhold bad news, companies continue to do it. Frequently they try to justify their actions because they believe (or, more likely, try to convince themselves) that the bad news will have been offset by good news before disclosure becomes mandatory. Unfortunately, this is rarely the case.

Another consideration is that the stock exchanges have their own rules about prompt disclosure of material information. The company agrees to comply with these rules when it lists its common stock at the time of the IPO. These self-regulatory organizations watch for unusual trading patterns. If there are big swings in trading activity or stock price, representatives may pressure management for a statement to explain the activity. Failure to disclose could result in a suspension of trading and, in extreme cases, delisting. Companies are not required, however, to jeopardize business deals and the like by premature disclosure. In those circumstances, the exchanges may temporarily suspend trading in the company's stock to avoid public harm because of the acute inequality of information.

There are some circumstances where immediate disclosure may not be wise. Occasionally, however, circumstances arise in which the company may temporarily refrain from publicly disclosing material information, provided that complete confidentiality is maintained. The circumstances where disclosure may be withheld are limited and constitute an infrequent exception to the normal requirement of immediate public disclosure.

One such circumstance often presents itself in the M&A context. It would be disastrous to disclose merger discussions prematurely. The Supreme Court has set a standard to the effect that the materiality of merger discussions depends on the significance of the transaction and its likely occurrence. Companies are loath to disclose merger discussions because of the potential for drastic swings in stock price based on guesswork as to what is really going on. Thus companies try to hide behind the probability prong of the Supreme Court test. Because there is not, even in this context, clear law requiring any disclosure (other than if there is insider trading, an SEC reporting obligation, or a duty to correct a prior statement), companies frequently defer announcing these deals until they are signed up—unless a company suspects leaks or other extenuating circumstances.

Another exception is when disclosure of uncertain developments may be premature when facts are in a state of flux. Matters that are or may develop into material corporate events also frequently require discussion and study by company officials before final decisions can be made. Such premature disclosure could risk liability for misleading investors if an anticipated event does not occur. Also, successive announcements concerning the same subject but based on changing facts may confuse or mislead, rather than enlighten, the public. Consequently, if the situation is about to stabilize or resolve itself in the imminent future, it may be proper to withhold public announcement until a firm and complete announcement can be made, provided that the confidentiality of the matter can be maintained. Premature public announcement may properly be avoided only where it is possible to confine formal or informal discussions to a small group of the senior officers and their individual confidential advisors, but extreme care should be used to keep the information confidential.

Immediate public disclosure of material information should be made if the company learns that insider trading has taken or is taking place while such material information is being temporarily withheld. The company should be prepared to make an immediate public announcement if unusual market activity occurs or when there has been a leak, or selective disclosure of such information to outsiders. Whenever material information is being temporarily withheld, market activity in the company's securities should be closely watched, since unusual market activity frequently signifies that a leak may have occurred.

Where the company has made a previous public announcement that is still reasonably current and on which security holders could reasonably rely, but which is no longer accurate because of subsequent developments, or which was found to have been erroneous at the time of initial disclosure, or where there is a rumor or a market report circulating for which company personnel had some responsibility, the company may also be required to make corrective disclosure.

Responding to Inquiries.   The company may occasionally receive inquiries from the press, financial analysts, or Nasdaq seeking comment on rumors or unusual market activity, or an inquiry as to matters as to which the company has determined disclosure is premature or otherwise inappropriate, as just discussed. There is *no* general legal duty to deny, correct, or verify rumors (unless the rumor is attributable to the company or its employees). Accordingly, as a general matter, the company should consistently respond to such inquiries with a "no comment" response, unless there is otherwise a duty to disclose, as discussed. The company should use those two words—"no comment"—and say nothing else except that it is the company's policy (assuming that to be the case) not to comment on rumors and similar matters. Further responses to those inquiries raise several risks, including triggering a duty to update and commenting incorrectly because of lack of complete information. Also, commenting on the accuracy of some rumors may give rise to an obligation to comment on all rumors, which could put the company in a position of continuously having to make premature disclosure of material developments. A deceptive response should never be given in response to these inquiries.

Disclosure Procedures.   The normal method of publication of important corporate data is by means of a press release. Any release of information that could reasonably be expected to have an impact on the market for the company's securities should be given to the wire services and the press "FOR IMMEDIATE RELEASE." News that ought to be the subject of immediate publicity must be released by the fastest available means.

Similarly, release of such news exclusively to the local press would not be sufficient for adequate and prompt disclosure to the investing public. To ensure adequate coverage, releases requiring immediate publicity should be given to Dow Jones & Company, Inc. and to other national newswire services: Associated Press, Reuters Economic Service, and so forth. These releases should also be given simultaneously to at least several newspapers of general circulation in New York City that regularly publish financial news, including the *Wall Street Journal* and the *New York Times*. Nasdaq and the other exchanges also requires advance notice of significant press releases.

These guidelines for distribution of releases should be regarded as minimum standards. Many companies may wish to give even broader prompt distribution to their releases. The company should include media in its major business locations as well as trade publications. Some of these media may refuse to publish information given by telephone until it has been confirmed in writing, or may require written confirmation after its publication.

Annual and quarterly earnings, dividend announcements, acquisitions, mergers, tender offers, stock splits, and major management changes are examples of news items that should be handled on an immediate release basis. News of major contract awards, expansion plans, and discoveries fall into the same category. Unfavorable news should be reported as promptly and candidly as favorable news. Reluctance or unwillingness to release a negative story or an attempt to disguise unfavorable news endangers management's reputation for integrity. (Any changes in accounting methods to mask such occurrences can have a similar long-term impact.) These guidelines for overseeing the preparation of press releases and other public announcements should help to ensure that the content of such announcements will meet requirements:

- Every press release and other public announcement should be either prepared or reviewed both by an official of the company having familiarity with the matter about which disclosure is to be made and by the company's disclosure committee or other designated officers. An exception to this procedure might apply to routine personnel announcements.
- Review by outside legal counsel of press releases and other public announcements is usually necessary, depending on the importance and complexity of the announcement.
- The company should coordinate statements issued by marketing, public relations, and investor relations personnel and agents to ensure consistency and accuracy of the release.

In view of the importance of confidentiality and nondisclosure and the potential difficulties involved, a periodic review should be made of the manner in which confidential information is being handled within the company. A periodic reminder notice of the company's policy to those in sensitive areas might also be helpful.

Whenever the company plans to issue a press release, counsel should be consulted beforehand as to whether the press release should be furnished to the SEC on Form 8-K. As discussed, the scope of developments that are required to be reported on Form 8-K is expansive. Even where a Form 8-K is not technically required, good corporate practice may nevertheless dictate a filing.

Discussions with Analysts and Other Outside Persons by Management.   The regulatory environment regarding a company's relationship with financial analysts (the people who cover the company at the large investment banks, also called sell-side analysts), has flipflopped over the years. This is particularly true regarding the desirability of a company making projections about its future performance. For a long time, projections were regarded as evil and were discouraged where possible by the SEC. There was a similar schizophrenic attitude toward financial analysts; they performed a service by disseminating material information to the trading markets (a good thing), but companies were not supposed to cross a somewhat nebulous line and give analysts inside information. The intricacies with which commentators tried to analyze these circumstances resembled early astronomers trying to describe how the sun revolved around the earth.

The problem was that the markets are essentially trading on what they expect companies to do in the future. Companies tiptoed through this minefield by playing a game much like charades. What has always been evil is the outright selective disclosure of material inside information to analysts (or to anyone else, for that matter). Companies would never outright leak projections to analysts because that would be selective disclosure, but they would let analysts tell them the analysts' own projection for the company and then indicate whether the analysts were close or not. Bizarrely, for years companies and their lawyers convinced themselves that this was not selective disclosure. Companies could hide their heads in the sand and not cozy up to analysts, but avoiding analysts merely discouraged them from following the company to the detriment of its stock price. Necessity, as the mother of invention, invented the game of charades to deal with this problem.

As a general matter, the SEC and the exchanges encourage corporations to seek formal and informal contacts with analysts and others and generally to maintain an open-door policy. However, potential liability may arise from these communications in several ways. First, selective disclosure of internal information to one or more persons that is not provided to the market generally may be deemed a tip, exposing the company and the recipient to potential liability to investors who did not immediately receive the benefits of such information. Second, the information disclosed may, in hindsight, be deemed premature, false, or misleading. Finally, the information disclosed may trigger a duty to make further public disclosure.

The basic rule for company officers when dealing with the press, financial analysts, and other members of the investment community is that no item of previously undisclosed material corporate information should be divulged or discussed unless and until it has been disclosed formally to the public by a general press release. Typically, in addition, a public access conference call is announced and scheduled with respect to such information and a Form 8-K is furnished to the SEC. The company should carefully review and monitor statements made at both group meetings and one-on-one sessions to ensure that no selective disclosure of material inside information is made. Private "guidance" to a limited group of analysts is not permissible. In the event of an inadvertent disclosure, immediate public disclosure must be made.

Estimates of future earnings or revenues are particularly sensitive. Estimates should be phrased in ranges or in nonspecific terms. The assumptions underlying such estimates should be discussed. If a company forecast is disclosed, it will often be advisable to update the forecast if and when it determines either that it will likely not be met, or that it will likely be exceeded.

Although selective disclosure has always been illegal, the adoption by the SEC in 2000 of its Regulation FD nevertheless radically changed the relationship between public companies and analysts and the extent and timing of disclosure by public companies. Formerly, a cat-and-mouse game was played between the company and its analyst such that the company would hint about purportedly inside information without actually disclosing it. That practice has ended, and the corollary is that in order to feed the market's appetite for information, companies now disclose far more information than they once did, particularly forward-looking information. When they disclose this information, they take care to make sure it is simultaneously disclosed in a broad and concurrent manner. A number of techniques have evolved to make sure the playing field is level. For example, the practice of openly webcasting a company's quarterly earnings teleconferences has developed, accompanied by posting on the company's Web site financial and other information likely to be discussed during the teleconference and the publication of a press release containing all material information along with the furnishing of a Form 8-K.

Whenever any forward-looking statement such as an estimate of future earnings is made, whether written or oral, additional technical requirements should be followed to protect the company. Such statements should (i) be identified as a forward-looking statement and (ii) be accompanied by meaningful cautionary statements identifying important factors that could cause actual results to differ materially from those in the forward-looking statement. As an alternative to clause (ii), an oral forward-looking statement may be accompanied by a statement that (a) actual results might differ materially from those projected in the forward-looking statement and (b) additional information concerning factors that could cause actual results to materially differ from those in such forward-looking statement is contained in a readily available written document, or portion thereof, such document or portions thereof being identified, and (c) such document or portions thereof actually satisfy the requirements of clause (ii). Although awkward and odd, this litany should be recited before all conference calls or other public presentations.

Financial analysts frequently ask the company's management to comment on estimates made by such analysts with respect to a future period or periods. Practice has changed in this regard, and such comments should not be made.

Corrections may be made to nonfinancial factual assumptions or other statements proposed to be made by analysts to the extent that such corrections do not involve any new material undisclosed information. However, if a company reaffirms financial information or projections that have previously been given, this is considered nonpublic information because of the lapse of time. In other words, the fact that projections have been achieved is different information from the projections themselves.

The authority to deal with the investment community in general should rest solely with one or more designated officers. Similarly, those designated officers should bear the responsibility, along with the disclosure committee, for reviewing texts or outlines of speeches in advance to ensure, among other things, that they are not misleading and do not contain any material undisclosed information. Formal procedures should be established by the company to ensure that its employees are aware of the need to preserve confidentiality for "Company Confidential" information. Generally, there should be limitations on the number and type of persons within the company who are entitled to receive nonpublic material information.

A short memorandum of each meeting or conversation with financial analysts or other members of the investment community, stating the names of the persons involved, the date of the meeting or conversation, and the items discussed, should be prepared and retained for at least one year.

The requirement that disclosure be accurate and complete applies not only to press releases and statements to financial analysts but to all company statements that can reasonably be expected to reach investors. Such statements often include speeches and statements touting new facilities and programs, even if the intended primary audience is not the securities markets.

COMPANY'S RELATIONSHIP WITH SHAREHOLDERS: PROXY SOLIC-ITATION PROCESS. Corporations are creatures of state law, and it is principally state law that regulates the election of directors and officers, the calling of annual meetings, and the votes required to adopt various corporate actions. Proxies are powers of attorney given to an attorney-in-fact to vote shares of stock held by someone else, and if a company's shares are broadly held, the corporation generally must solicit proxies from its shareholders in order to obtain the vote required to elect directors or accomplish other corporate actions that require shareholder approval.

Once a company has a class of securities registered under the Exchange Act, it becomes subject to the SEC's proxy rules. These rules prescribe the information the company must provide to shareholders when soliciting proxies as well as the mechanics for soliciting proxies from record and beneficial shareholders. The information required to be furnished to shareholders is contained in a proxy statement furnished to shareholders when proxies are solicited. The proxy statement furnished in connection with the annual meeting each year contains detailed information about significant shareholders of the company and about directors, board committees, and the executive officers (including compensation).

Proxy statements for a routine annual meeting (i.e., one at which the only matters to be acted on are the election of directors, approval of certain benefit plans, the ratification of accountants, and certain proposals by stockholders) must be filed with the SEC and the self-regulatory organizations not later than the date they are distributed to stockholders. Proxy statements for meetings at which nonroutine matters (such as an amendment to the company's corporate charter) are to be submitted to stockholders should be prefiled with the SEC a minimum of 10 calendar days before public distribution, although in most cases a period of up to 30 calendar days is appropriate. Each stock exchange has its own listing manual containing related, but separate, rules about disclosure, communicating with shareholders, and other matters regarding listed company status.

Normally, the company should plan on having its transfer agent mail the proxy statement to its stockholders at least five weeks to a month or so before the annual meeting. SEC regulations require inquiries of street and nominee name holders regarding the numbers of beneficial owners for whom shares are held, so that additional sets of materials can be supplied. These inquiries should be made by the company's transfer agent at least 20 business days before the record date of the meeting of stockholders, thus requiring adequate prior notice by the company to its transfer agent of such mailing date. The SEC has adopted rules that allow companies to deliver proxy statements and annual reports to shareholders (described later) by posting them on a company Web site and notifying shareholders by a postcard of their availability and Web site location, along with a notice of the meeting.

In addition to information about the meeting, required votes and prospectus-type information about management, related person transactions and stock ownership, the proxy statement must also contain specific disclosure concerning deliberations of the compensation committee of the board of directors as to the relation of corporate performance to executive compensation and as to the basis for all elements of executive officer compensation. In July 2006, the SEC approved extensive changes to the reporting of executive and director compensation, option grant practices, and related person transactions. These new rules require significant tabular and narrative information about all types of compensation and a "Compensation Discussion and Analysis" covering how executive compensation is determined and approved. The proxy statement must also describe committees of the board of directors, the determinations by the board of the independence of directors, the process for nominations and recommendations for nominations for board seats, beneficial ownership by directors and officers, minimum qualifications for directors, and potential payments upon a change of control, as well as fees paid to directors. Further, the proxy statement must disclose all of the fees paid to the company's accountants and any policy for preapproval of nonaudit services, as well as contain a report of the audit committee of the board.

If any other matters are submitted to stockholders for a vote, the proxy statement must contain disclosures with respect to these additional matters. If options are repriced, the proxy statement must also contain specific disclosures concerning such repricing. It is important to note that the proxy rules require specific disclosure if any director has attended fewer than 75 percent of the combined number of meetings of the full board plus any board committees on which such director serves, and also require a statement of the company's policy for directors' attendance at annual meetings of stockholders and how many directors attended the prior year's meeting. Additional SEC rules apply in the event of proxy contests and with respect to proposals furnished by stockholders. In addition, the company is required to disclose to the public in its proxy statement the name of any director, officer, or 10 percent stockholder who has not met the applicable Forms 3, 4, and/or 5 reporting obligations in a timely manner and note the existence of such disclosure on the cover page of its annual report on Form 10-K.

Under the SEC proxy rules, an annual report to stockholders must be distributed with or before the proxy statement furnished in connection with the annual election of directors. The annual report typically contains the president's letter to shareholders about developments in the business over the last year. Other than certain required financial information and a required graph illustrating company stock performance, there are only a limited number of specific SEC requirements as to content. The annual report is not required to be prefiled with or reviewed by the SEC, although it must be submitted to the SEC upon distribution to stockholders. The annual report to stockholders, like all other financial communications, can be a source of legal liability if it contains a material misstatement or omission.

DISCLOSURE RELATING TO CONTESTS FOR CONTROL.   The so-called Williams Act provisions of the Exchange Act (dealing with, among other things, the manner in which possible tender offers for the company's registered securities may be made and the ways in which management may resist a tender offer) and the rules relating to proxy contests for control of a company are very complex and are beyond our scope. Generally, persons making tender offers or owning beneficially more than 5 percent of the outstanding stock are required to file certain disclosure documents, as discussed later, and to comply with other substantive requirements.

MARKET REPURCHASES.   Repurchases by the company of its outstanding common stock and purchases of such stock on the open market by the officers and directors of the company are subject to a series of technical restrictions under Regulation M, Rule 102 and Rule 10b-18 under the Exchange Act as well as the "short-swing" profit provisions of the Exchange Act. In addition, if the purchaser possesses material nonpublic information concerning the company, such purchaser would violate the antifraud provisions of the Exchange Act. Finally, disclosures of repurchases by the company (including exercises of options paid for with company stock) are required in Forms 10-K and 10-Q. Accordingly, counsel should be consulted in advance of any purchase of outstanding common stock by the company, and internal clearance procedures should be followed in advance of any market purchase by any officer or director.

CORPORATE GOVERNANCE

Sarbanes-Oxley Act of 2002.   The justifiably much-maligned Sarbanes-Oxley Act of 2002 impacts almost all aspects of the regulation of public companies. The resulting regulatory framework impacts public companies (as well as companies considering going public), their officers and directors, and outside auditors and counsel in an attempt to address many of the corporate governance and financial reporting abuses that came to light in the wake of the Enron and WorldCom bankruptcies. As a result of Sarbanes-Oxley, the SEC has implemented numerous corporate governance rules, some of which have already been discussed. Additional requirements are discussed next. In addition to the new SEC governance requirements, the stock exchanges have also implemented new corporate governance rules.

Audit Committees and Prohibition on Loans to Executive Officers. Two significant changes in corporate governance standards are new SEC requirements for the composition, independence, and functioning of audit committees and a prohibition of personal loans to executive officers. As for the latter, the Exchange Act now provides that it shall unlawful for any issuer, directly or indirectly, including through any subsidiary, to extend or maintain credit, to arrange for the extension of credit, or to renew an extension of credit, in the form of a personal loan to or for any director or executive officer (or equivalent thereof) of that issuer. In an IPO, as discussed, loans by a private company must be repaid before the filing of the IPO registration statement. Audit committee requirements are discussed later.

Nasdaq Corporate Governance Rules.   The Nasdaq corporate governance rules are applicable to Nasdaq Global Select Market, Nasdaq

Global Market, and Nasdaq Capital Market companies. They do not apply to companies that are traded on the Over-the-Counter Bulletin Board or "Pink Sheets." The other stock exchanges have similar rules. We discuss only the Nasdaq rules. In summary form, these rules require that, among other things:

- A majority of directors be independent under new and tighter independence standards.
- Independent directors conduct separate regularly scheduled meetings, or "executive sessions," which are recommended to occur at least twice each year.
- The compensation of the CEO and other executive officers be determined (or recommended to the board of directors for determination) either by a majority of independent directors or a compensation committee comprised solely of independent directors.
- Director nominees be selected (or recommended for the board of directors' selection) either by a majority of the independent directors or a nomination committee comprised solely of independent directors.
- Audit committee members meet more stringent standards of independence and audit committees must assume increased powers and responsibilities.
- The audit committee or another independent body of the board of directors review all related person transactions.
- A code of conduct applicable to all directors, officers, and employees be adopted and disclosed.
- Shareholder approval be obtained of most equity compensation plans.

Some additional details regarding certain of these requirements are:

DIRECTOR INDEPENDENCE REQUIREMENTS

Nasdaq's rules require that a majority of the board of directors be comprised of "independent directors." The board of directors is required to make an affirmative determination that individuals serving as independent directors do not have a relationship with the company that would impair their independence, which determinations must be disclosed in the company's Exchange Act filings. The Nasdaq definition of "independent director" has become quite stringent; independence is considered inconsistent with the director or a family member having employment or specified compensation arrangements with the company, certain director/officer interlocks, association with the company's outside auditor, and other circumstances.

INDEPENDENT DIRECTORS MUST CONDUCT EXECUTIVE SESSIONS

Independent directors must have regularly scheduled meetings, or "executive sessions," at which only independent directors are present. These sessions, which Nasdaq contemplates will occur at least twice a year in conjunction with regularly scheduled board meetings, are designed to encourage and enhance communication among independent directors.

DETERMINATION OF EXECUTIVE COMPENSATION BY INDEPENDENT DIRECTORS

Nasdaq's rules require that the compensation of the CEO and all other executive officers of the company must be determined, or recommended to the board for determination, either by a majority of the independent directors or by a compensation committee comprised solely of independent directors.

NOMINATION OF DIRECTORS BY INDEPENDENT NOMINATIONS COMMITTEE

Nasdaq's rules require that director nominees must be selected or recommended for the board's selection either by a majority of the independent directors or by a nominations committee comprised solely of independent directors. Each issuer must certify that it has adopted a formal, written charter or board resolution, as applicable, addressing the nominations process.

HEIGHTENED INDEPENDENCE STANDARDS FOR AUDIT COMMITTEE MEMBERSHIP

The company is required by Nasdaq to certify that it has and will continue to have an audit committee of at least three members, each of whom must:

- In addition to meeting the general director independence requirements, satisfy the criteria for independence set forth in Exchange Act Rule 10A-3 (i.e., not accept any consulting, advisory, or other compensation from the issuer or be an "affiliated person" of the issuer or any subsidiary thereof) and not have participated in the preparation of financial statements of the company at any time during the past three years.

- Be able to read and understand financial statements at the time of appointment to the audit committee, including the balance sheet, income statement, and cash flow statement.

AUDIT COMMITTEE FINANCIAL EXPERT

Each issuer must certify to Nasdaq that it has, and will continue to have, at least one member of the audit committee who has past employment experience in finance or accounting, requisite professional certification in accounting, or any other comparable experience or background that results in the individual's financial sophistication, including being or having been a CEO, CFO, or other senior officer with financial oversight responsibilities. The SEC also requires that the name of any audit committee financial expert (using a somewhat narrower definition than Nasdaq) be disclosed in each Form 10-K. The SEC does not require that a company have an audit committee financial expert, but it must disclose if it does not. It is certainly good practice for there to be one member of the audit committee who qualifies not only under Nasdaq rules but under the SEC's definition.

DUTIES AND RESPONSIBILITIES OF AUDIT COMMITTEE

Sarbanes-Oxley, Exchange Act Rule 10A-3, and the Nasdaq governance rules prescribe certain duties and responsibilities of the audit committee. The audit committee:

- Is responsible for selecting, determining the compensation of and monitoring the performance of the outside auditors.
- Reviews the company's annual and quarterly financial statements and financial disclosures and discuss them with management and the outside auditor. The review must discuss:
  - The company's critical accounting policies.
  - Management judgments and accounting estimates.
  - Alternative GAAP treatments.
  - Off-balance sheet arrangements.
  - Material communications between the outside auditor, such as the management letter.

- Evaluates and oversees internal control over financial reporting and disclosure controls and procedures, and review management's and the outside auditor's reports on internal controls.
- Establishes complaint review procedures concerning accounting, internal accounting controls, and auditing matters and establish a mechanism for anonymous submissions by employees of accounting or auditing concerns.

Under SEC rules, the audit committee must preapprove any nonaudit service permitted to be provided by the outside auditor. There are also specified requirements for the audit committee charter and specified cure periods for audit committee composition requirements.

As noted, under Nasdaq rules and the Sarbanes-Oxley Act, the company's audit committee must establish certain complaint procedures, sometimes called "whistleblower procedures." It is good practice for these procedures to be recorded in a written document and distributed to employees or posted in common areas. Typical procedures often include toll-free anonymous telephone hotlines, intranet complaint mailboxes, and/or the opportunity to write to a designated recipient for complaints. The procedures usually provide for how complaints will be screened and investigated, retention of complaints, and how corrective action will be determined. The company may not retaliate against persons who make complaints in good faith.

APPROVAL OF RELATED PERSON TRANSACTIONS

The audit committee or another independent body of the board of directors must review all "related person transactions," as defined in SEC Regulation S-K, Item 404 (which broadly covers relationships between the company and any director, executive officer, 5 percent shareholder, or any of their immediate family members). Under SEC rules, the company's policies and procedures regarding approval of related person transactions must be disclosed in the annual proxy statement.

CODES OF CONDUCT MUST BE ADOPTED AND DISCLOSED

Each issuer must adopt a code of ethics for the CEO and senior financial officers (a Sarbanes-Oxley and SEC requirement) and a code of business conduct and ethics for all directors, officers, and employees (a Nasdaq requirement), which must be publicly available. Waivers to the code of conduct for executive officers or directors can be granted only by the issuer's board and must be disclosed, along with the reasons for the waiver, on Form 8-K, or, if announced in advance, on the company's Web site. The form of the code of ethics varies greatly from company to company.

SHAREHOLDER APPROVAL OF EQUITY COMPENSATION PLANS
Shareholder approval is required of most equity compensation plans, including plans in which insiders do not participate, as well as repricings (if not provided for in the original plan) and material amendments that increase benefits to participants.

Disclosure Controls and Procedures; Internal Control over Financial Reporting.   One of the requirements under Sarbanes-Oxley for the Form 10-K and the Form 10-Q are certifications by the company's CEO and CFO to the effect that they have reviewed the filing and believe that the filing does not contain any material misstatements or omissions and that the included financial statements and other financial information fairly present the company's financial condition. The certifications are also required to certify (if true) that the company's "disclosure controls and procedures" are adequate to ensure the timeliness, accuracy, and completeness of its periodic SEC reports. These disclosure controls and procedures are mandated by the Exchange Act and have to be reexamined by the CEO and CFO as of the end of each fiscal quarter and the results reported on. Among the procedures commonly implemented by reporting companies are the designation of a "disclosure committee" of key insiders that will assist in the evaluation process and review all Exchange Act filings and other public disclosures. Typically, the CEO and CFO have the most comprehensive and current information about the company that is relevant to disclosure compliance. These officers must be actively involved in the preparation of the company's disclosure documents.

Additionally, beginning with a company's second annual report, annual certifications are required that the company has in place internal control over financial reporting to provide reasonable assurance on the integrity of the financial statements and internal financial processes. The company's outside accountants must also provide an attestation report on internal controls. Management must base its assessment on a "recognized control framework." The so-called COSO (Committee of Sponsoring Organizations) framework is the most common framework of choice in the United States and is extremely complex. The SEC and the Public Company Accounting Oversight Board continue to try to modify the rules to make them more user-friendly, but to date they remain challenging to apply. As a result, although management's certifications are relatively simple in form, the underlying procedures and record-keeping requirements supporting the certifications have expanded exponentially the cost and complexity of Exchange Act compliance. The compliance dates for the internal control rules have been extended frequently and should be checked as necessary.

Other Nasdaq Required Reports and Filings
NOTICE REQUIREMENTS
In addition to the governance obligations just discussed, Nasdaq has certain notice requirements, including notices of: listing of additional shares; dividends; change in number of outstanding shares (5 percent or more); and change in auditors, transfer agent, or registrar.

DISCLOSURE PROVISIONS
Separate from the company's SEC disclosure obligations, Nasdaq requires listed companies to establish and follow the practice of prompt and complete disclosure of material developments that, if known, might reasonably be expected to influence the market price of the company's common stock.

Nasdaq requires Nasdaq-listed companies to disclose promptly to the public through the press any material information that may affect the value of their securities or influence investors' decisions. The company should notify Nasdaq, in accordance with specified procedures, before release of material news to the public through the press. Pending public disclosure of material information, Nasdaq may impose a trading halt on the company's securities. A trading halt normally lasts no longer than 30 minutes after the appearance of the news on wire services, but it may last longer if a determination is made that the news has not been adequately disseminated.

Continued Listing Standards.   In order to remain listed, a company must continue to maintain certain listing standards. These standards relate to stock price, market capitalization of total assets/revenues, public float, number of stockholders, number of market makers, and continued compliance with the governance requirements.

INSIDER REPORTING AND INSIDER TRADING. Because a public company's common stock is registered under the Exchange Act, the company's executive officers and directors are subject to their own set of filing and other requirements under the securities laws. The principal requirements are discussed next.

Disclosure Obligations of Insiders and Significant Shareholders
EXECUTIVE OFFICERS, DIRECTORS AND 10 PERCENT SHAREHOLDERS
Another underlying premise of the securities laws is that information about insiders' ownership and trading in their company's securities should be promptly disclosed to the public. Section 16(a) of the Exchange Act requires that within 10 days of an executive officer, director, or 10 percent shareholder becoming such, he or she must file a report of beneficial ownership of equity securities on Form 3 with the SEC. The report includes outright ownership as well as holdings of derivative securities, such as options and warrants to purchase equity securities. Shares held by immediate family members and through indirect holdings, such as partnerships or trusts, are included as indirectly owned by the insider. Thereafter, insiders must report to the SEC on Form 4 changes in beneficial ownership of securities or derivative securities, including transactions by family members (purchases, sales, exercise of options) within two business days of executing the trade.

Copies of these forms can be found at *www.sec.gov/about/forms/secforms*. There are no filing fees for these forms.

Generally:

- Most transactions, such as sales of stock or exercise of an option, must be reported on Form 4 within two business days after the date of the transaction on which such person's ownership of the Company's securities changes.
- A few other reportable transactions, such as gifts of stock, must be reported on Form 5 within 45 days after the end of the fiscal year if not voluntarily reported earlier on Form 4 during the year.

Forms 3, 4, and 5 must be filed electronically with the SEC. Because these are not company filings, each executive officer, director, and 10 percent stockholder required to make a filing must obtain a separate EDGAR identification number. The company is required to post or link to the reports on its Web site.

To ensure filing compliance, any executive officer or director who proposes to dispose of or acquire shares (or options or other derivative securities) of the company's common stock or any rights to acquire such shares should immediately report such proposed disposition or acquisition to the company's general counsel or other person designated to perform this function.

A discussion of the Section 16(b) six-month insider trading prohibitions to which Forms 3, 4 and 5 relate is set forth under "Prohibition against Short-Swing Trading by Insiders." Appendix 4E presents a more detailed explanation of the obligations of the company's executive officers, directors, and 10 percent stockholders under Section 16 of the Exchange Act, including Forms 3, 4, and 5.

5 PERCENT SHAREHOLDERS

Any person not eligible to file a Schedule 13G (to be described) who makes an acquisition of an issuer's stock that results in beneficial ownership of more than 5 percent of the class of securities must file a Schedule 13D with the SEC within 10 days of such acquisition. Beneficial ownership of stock for this purpose is based on the sole or shared power to vote or to dispose of the stock, even if the beneficial owner has no economic interest in the stock. The underlying purpose of Schedule 13D is for the investors to disclose their plans or intentions regarding the control, business purpose, and structure of a public company. Any material change in information previously reported on Schedule 13D must be reported promptly on an amendment to that schedule. As a general rule, the acquisition or disposition of 1 percent or more of a registered class of securities is considered material. Schedule 13D requires disclosure relating to the issuer, the security, the stockholder's identity and background, the source and amount of funds or other consideration, the purpose of the transaction, the stockholder's total equity interest in the issuer, and other information. A copy of the Schedule 13D or 13G must also be sent to the company by registered or certified mail.

The short-form Schedule 13G, which requires much less detail about the background of the acquisition of the stock and the beneficial owner, applies to certain qualified institutional investors where securities have been acquired in the ordinary course of business without the intent of affecting the control of the company. Some examples of such qualified institutional investors include banks, insurance companies, and the like. In 1998 the SEC expanded the provisions of Section 13(d) by allowing all investors beneficially owning less than 20 percent of the outstanding class of securities to report their holdings on the short-form Schedule 13G, provided such investors have not acquired or held the securities to influence control of the issuer. The rationale behind the short-form Schedule 13G is that such "passive" investors do not intend to affect the control of the issuer. Any such Schedule 13G-eligible person who owns, directly or indirectly, more than 5 percent of a class of equity securities of the company as of the effective date of the company's registration statement under the Exchange Act or as of December 31 of each year is required to make a filing with the SEC on Schedule 13G by February 14 of the following year. Each person or group of persons who owns (and/or holds presently exercisable options for) more than 5 percent of the company's common stock and who has filed a Schedule 13G must file amendments to that schedule by February 14 of the year following the year in which certain changes in their equity ownership occur.

No fee is required for a Schedule 13D or 13G or for a 13D or 13G amendment.

A copy of Schedules 13G and 13D and the related instructions can be found at *www.sec.gov/about/forms/secforms.htm*.

Prohibition against Short-Swing Trading by Insiders.   There are special provisions regarding so-called short-swing profits that apply to every director and executive officer of the company as well as any beneficial owner of more than 10 percent of the outstanding common stock (an insider). Subject to certain exceptions, Section 16(b) of the Exchange Act provides that any profit realized on a purchase and sale of stock beneficially owned by an insider within a six-month period is recoverable by the company. Although it is the individual director or officer's responsibility to avoid short-swing profit recapture, because mistakes are so calamitous, most companies establish internal clearance procedures for stock traders to minimize the chance of mistakes.

For this purpose, it does not matter whether the purchase or the sale occurs first. It is not necessary for the same shares to be involved in each of the matched transactions. Losses cannot be offset against gains. Transactions are generally paired so as to match the lowest purchase price and the highest sale price within a six-month period.

Good faith on the part of the insider is no defense. If the company itself does not press a claim, a claim for recovery of the profit may be asserted by any stockholder for the benefit of the company. Section 16 short-swing profit recapture is enforced by a group of securities lawyers who make their living by discovering and prosecuting short-swing trading violations.

Many types of transactions constitute a purchase or a sale for this purpose in addition to transactions, such as those on the open market, that are commonly thought to involve purchases or sales of securities. Transactions in derivatives may be deemed to involve purchases and sales of the underlying security. Changes to certain terms of a security may be considered to be purchases or repurchases of the security. Corporate reorganizations and acquisitions may be deemed to involve purchases or sales. Even the receipt of a stock option from the company may be deemed a purchase unless it is approved in the proper manner in accordance with SEC rules.

Section 16(b) has produced a number of unfair penalties over the years, and there are periodic calls for its repeal. The SEC has responded with a number of rules under Section 16 that relax the requirements, particularly in the area of stock options and employee benefit plans. The principle here is that many matching trades in the stock option context do not merit a presumption or wrongdoing. If an employee exercises an option at $10 per share and then immediately sells the stock at its then-trading price of $50 per share, odds are he or she is merely trying to capture the gain accumulated over many years. SEC Rule 16b-3 exempts from the short-swing profits rules the grant of options that meet certain requirements (such as they have been granted by the board of directors or an independent committee under a benefit plan). The exercise of options is treated as a nonevent, on the theory that the insider is merely monetizing gain that is already built in.

"Beneficial" ownership for this purpose may include indirect ownership of stock through partnerships, corporations, trusts, or estates. In some circumstances, stock held by close relatives of a person may be considered to be owned beneficially by such person, and a purchase (or sale) by one individual may be matchable with a sale (or purchase) by his or her close relative to produce a recoverable profit. The provisions also apply to stock registered in a street name.

The short-swing profit recapture provisions require a great deal of advance planning. In addition, the rules are complex, may vary in their impact on different individuals, and often change. Insiders should always check with counsel before engaging in transactions in the company's securities. (See the previous discussion of Forms 3, 4, and 5.)

The Exchange Act also prohibits the company's directors, officers, and 10 percent stockholders from making "short sales" of any equity security of the company (regardless of whether that class is itself registered). "Short sales" are sales of securities that the seller does not own at the time or, if owned, securities that will not be delivered currently.

Prohibition against Trading in the Company's Stock by Insiders on the Basis of Undisclosed Inside Information. Section 10(b) of the Exchange Act (which is applicable to all purchases and sales of securities) prohibits trading by insiders of a company in that company's securities on the basis of undisclosed material information. For this purpose, "insiders" include the company's employees, officers, directors, controlling stockholders, attorneys, accountants, investment bankers, public relations and advertising firms, other consultants, and immediate family members of such persons. For example, if an insider who was aware of the fact that the company was about to receive a major order that would have a material effect on the financial position of the company were to purchase securities of the company before that information had been publicly disseminated, he or she would be in violation of this rule and would be subject to criminal prosecution as well as civil liability for any profits gained or deemed gains on the basis of that inside information.

Similarly, if such person were aware of adverse information concerning the company (such as the loss of a large customer) that had not been made public, he or she would be precluded from selling securities of the company until such information had been disseminated to the public. Around the time that material corporate developments are unfolding, insiders must be careful about the timing of their trades in the company's stock.

Trading before the information is released may constitute fraud if it can be proven that the insider had an unfair informational advantage or made the transaction on the basis of the inside information. How soon after the release of material information insiders may begin to trade depends on how quickly and thoroughly the information is published by the news-wire services and the press.

In addition, insiders should refrain from trading even after dissemination of sensitive information until the public has had an opportunity to evaluate the information thoroughly. Where the impact of the information on investment decisions is readily understandable, as in the case of an earnings report, a 48-hour waiting period should be observed. A longer period should be observed if the information does not receive wide distribution or is complex in nature.

This prohibition on trading in securities of the company applies not only to officers, directors, and employees but to any person who engages in any such trading on the basis of information that officers, directors, employees, or other insiders have provided (these persons are called tippees). Not only may a tippee be found to have violated the law, but the person giving the tip may be held personally liable for any profits realized by his or her tippee, even though he or she realized no personal profit. Accordingly, no transaction involving the company's securities should be initiated by any person, whether a company employee or not, who is in possession of inside material information, favorable or unfavorable.

A suggested Policy Regarding Insider Trading as well as Black-Out Period Procedures are attached as Attachment A and Attachment B, respectively, to Appendix 4F.

Because the restrictions on insider trading are so stringent, and because potential liability is often asserted with the benefit of hindsight, the SEC in 2000 adopted its Rule 10b5-1. This rule creates a safe harbor for insider trading under specified circumstances. It provides an affirmative defense to insider trading charges for trades if they were made pursuant to a preexisting plan, contract, or instruction adopted while the person was not aware of material nonpublic information—a so-called 10b5-1 plan. These plans usually are implemented through an insider's brokerage firm, but the company should be involved in the process and kept up to date with respect to sales and prospective sales under the plan. Note that 10b5-1 plans do not relieve an insider of his or her duty to file Form 4s or Form 144s or potential liability for short-swing profits. Rule 10b5-1 plans are increasingly being scrutinized by the SEC. Insiders must make sure to enter into these plans in good faith and while not in possession of material inside information.

Insider Trading and Securities Fraud Enforcement Act of 1988. In addition to the penalties imposed on persons who commit insider trading, insiders or "controlling persons" who fail to take adequate steps to prevent insider trading by those whom they control may be liable for harsh civil penalties under the Insider Trading and Securities Fraud Enforcement Act. Even where the controlling person does not participate in the trading violation or profit from it, he or she may be liable for criminal fines of up to $1 million and civil fines of three times the amount of the profit gained or loss avoided as a result of the controlled person's violation.

The term "controlling person" in the insider trading context is not limited to employers, but includes any person with power to influence or control the direction or the management, policies, or activities of another person. For example, an officer or director of the company may be considered a control person and thus become liable for insider trading committed by a person under his or her control.

Liability may occur if the controlling person:

- Fails to take appropriate action once aware of the fact, or recklessly disregards circumstances indicating a likelihood that a controlled person was engaged in or was about to engage in an ongoing insider trading violation, or
- Fails to take appropriate action once aware of the fact, or recklessly disregards circumstances indicating a likelihood, that a control person was engaged in or was about to engage in a tipping violation.

To impose liability, the SEC must establish that a controlling person objectively disregarded a risk that a controlled person was engaged in violations of the insider trading laws. Such "reckless disregard" must constitute a gross deviation from a reasonable person standard of care.

PROCEDURES FOR SALES OF UNREGISTERED STOCK AND STOCK HELD BY AFFILIATES. Stock acquired in private transactions (i.e., all securities acquired by the company's stockholders prior to its IPO or in private placements since the IPO) are designated restricted securities under Rule 144 of the Securities Act. Securities acquired in the open market by controlling persons of the company (e.g., directors, executive officers, or 10 percent stockholders) (*control securities*) are also subject to restrictions. Restricted securities and control cannot be sold via the public market except pursuant to Rule 144, Rule 701, a registration statement under the Securities Act, or another exemption under the Securities Act.

Rule 144 is a safe harbor exemption. To utilize this safe harbor, a seller is prohibited from selling restricted securities until the 91st day following the effective date of the company's IPO and at least one year has elapsed since the specific shares were acquired from the company or an affiliate of the company and fully paid for. Such sales are subject to the quantitative and qualitative restrictions to be described. Restricted securities held by persons other than affiliates for longer than two years, however, may be freely sold without restrictions. Similarly, unrestricted securities (i.e., registered securities acquired in the public market or pursuant to a registration statement) held by noncontrolling persons may be sold without restriction. Conversely, securities held by affiliates, whether restricted or unrestricted, and even if acquired in the public market, must be sold pursuant to Rule 144 or another exemption from registration. These restrictions on insiders are in addition to the short-swing profit rules, insider trading rules, and company policies discussed earlier.

The qualitative restrictions generally require that the sale be handled as a routine open market brokerage transaction, although the seller also may deal directly with an over-the-counter market maker that deals as a principal for its own account rather than as a broker. Also, the company must be current in its reporting obligations to the SEC at the time of the sale (i.e., having filed its annual and quarterly reports).

The quantitative restrictions limit sales by the holder during each three-month period to an amount of securities equal to the greater of:

- One percent of the number of shares of common stock outstanding (based on the company's currently outstanding shares), or
- The average reported weekly trading volume during the four calendar weeks preceding the date placing the order to sell.

Thus, the amount of shares now permitted to be sold in any three-month period by each Rule 144 seller to whom the quantitative limitations apply would be at least 1 percent of the number of shares of common stock outstanding, but the amount that could be sold would be larger if the notice of sale is filed at a time when the weekly trading average during the preceding four calendar weeks exceeded that number.

Sales by closely related persons, such as spouses, parents, minor children and their trusts, donors and donees, and pledgors and pledgees, must be combined, as specifically provided by Rule 144, in applying the quantitative limitation, with sales made by the actual Rule 144 seller.

The person selling in reliance on Rule 144 (other than noncontrolling persons selling stock held for longer than two years) must file a notice with the SEC (with a copy sent to Nasdaq) on Form 144. A copy of Form 144 can be found at *www.sec.gov/about/forms/secforms.htm*. The Form 144 must be transmitted to the SEC concurrently with placing the order for sale; that is, the Form 144 can be mailed (or filed via EDGAR) to the SEC when the sell order is placed. There is an exemption from the filing requirement for transactions during any three-month period that do not exceed either 500 shares or an aggregate sale price of $10,000. If the sales are not completed within 90 days, a new Form 144 must be filed if additional sales are to be made. The filing of Form 144 is in addition to the requirement that officers, directors, and 10 percent stockholders also file the requisite Form 4 under Section 16(a) of the Exchange Act within two business days.

This discussion is an extremely simplified summary of very complex and detailed provisions that may have varying impacts on individual stockholders. Well in advance of any proposed sale, a controlling person or holder of restricted securities should seek specific advice relating to his or her individual circumstances before committing to make any public sale of the company's common stock. Also, these rules are under review by the SEC, and are likely to change.

This discussion relates solely to an exemption from the registration requirements of the Securities Act for unregistered shares acquired in private transactions and to any shares acquired in public transactions by affiliates or insiders (i.e., directors, officers, or 10 percent stockholders). Whether registration is required with respect to any given proposed sale, the antifraud provisions remain applicable. Thus, even if Rule 144 provides an exemption from Securities Act registration, no stockholder should make any public sale of any stock if he or she is then aware of material adverse information about the company that has not yet been publicly disclosed. In connection with Rule 144 sales, the seller normally has to furnish the broker with a completed questionnaire or representation letter. A broker's letter and a copy of the Form 144 intended to be used and some information from the selling stockholder must then be furnished to the company's counsel, who is required, in turn, to furnish the transfer agent with an opinion letter authorizing the transfer. Generally, when Rule 144 sales are proposed, the company's counsel is required to furnish any necessary assistance.

An exemption from the registration requirements under Rule 144 does not have any bearing on the exposure to short-swing profit recapture under Section 16(b) of the Exchange Act, as discussed. Thus, an exempt sale under Rule 144 may result in a short-swing profit recoverable by the company under Section 16(b) if the sale occurs within six months before or after the seller's purchase of any company stock at a lower price.

A registration statement on Form S-8 should be filed by the company to cover the offer and sale of the company's common stock pursuant to the company's stock option plan. Pursuant to Rule 701, however, shares held by noncontrolling persons that were acquired pursuant to stock options granted prior to the effective date of such registration statement on Form S-8 may generally be sold without restriction commencing on the 91st following the effective date of the company's IPO, subject to any applicable underwriters' lock-up agreements. The one-year holding period of Rule 144 does not apply to any shares sold under Rule 701.

SAMPLE MEMORANDA AND OTHER MATERIALS RELATING TO SEC COMPLIANCE. Included as appendices to this chapter are a number of checklists and memoranda that will assist companies and insiders in complying with the myriad of complicated SEC and Nasdaq regulations:

Appendix 4D: Summary SEC Compliance Checklist
Appendix 4E: Memorandum on Insider Reporting and Liability for Short-Swing Profits
Appendix 4F: Memorandum on Implementing Procedures Designed to Prevent Insider Trading

MOST PAINFUL MISTAKES BY PUBLIC COMPANIES AND THEIR OFFICERS. The breadth and complexity of the public securities laws and Nasdaq regulation, particularly after Sarbanes-Oxley, have made it extremely difficult for public company officers to keep in mind the myriad of requirements applicable to them. Counsel should be consulted in advance with respect to any significant activity or disclosure. Even though it is impossible to keep all of the rules in mind all of the time, these situations should always ring alarm bells:

- When selling or buying stock, or engaging in a transaction of any kind relating to the company's stock, make certain that there will be no short-swing violation.
- When selling or buying stock, make certain that counsel advises as to potential violations of the insider trading rules.
- Be circumspect at all times in talking about the company to friends, acquaintances, and, most important, investment professionals or the press.
- If you are contemplating an offering, make sure that no planned activities, such as scheduled press interviews or speeches, will implicate the "gun-jumping" rules.
- Be sure to check the company's SEC reporting calendar regularly to be sure deadlines and compliance requirements are met.
- Assume that anything of importance that happens to the company and every material transaction may require immediate reporting under the new Form 8-K rules and/or a press release.

APPENDICES

These appendices are located on the Web site that accompanies this book. For information on the Web site, see the "About the Web Site" section.

Appendix 4A: Private Placement Memorandum

Appendix 4B: Subscription Agreement for a Private Placement

Appendix 4C: Investor Questionnaire for a Private Placement that includes Unaccredited Investors

Appendix 4D: Summary SEC Compliance Checklist

Appendix 4E: Memorandum on Insider Reporting and Liability for Short-Swing Profits

Appendix 4F: Memorandum on Implementing Procedures Designed to Prevent Insider Trading

CHAPTER 5

ACQUISITIONS

MERGERS AND ACQUISITIONS: STRUCTURING CONSIDERATIONS[1]

The technology company lawyer must be competent to handle mergers and acquisitions (M&A). Both public and private companies are active acquirers of other businesses. Business lawyers must be prepared to represent clients who become buyers or sellers. Unlike many other business transactions in the technology company arena, M&A work is adversarial—not in the sense of being nasty (usually), but in the sense that M&A is a zero-sum game. In an acquisition, what is good for one party is usually bad for the other. Generally, in other transactions, although the parties have different interests, in a sense they are ultimately on the same side. For example, in an initial public offering (IPO), both the issuer and the underwriters want the IPO to be a successful deal, with the IPO buyers ending up happy with their buy decision. Good disclosure in the IPO prospectus avoids liability for both the issuer and the underwriters. Not so in M&A. For that reason, acquisition practice is very demanding and may be the most difficult and complex test of a business lawyer's skills.

WHAT IS GOING ON: REASONS FOR ACQUISITIONS. Companies acquire other businesses for a number of reasons, including one or more of these:

- Extending a product line, where it is cheaper or faster (or both) for the buyer to purchase the product line and its underlying technology than develop it independently, or where the buyer

---

1. An extensive discussion of mergers and acquisitions is contained in the author's book, *Mergers and Acquisitions: A Step-by-Step Legal and Practical Guide* (Hoboken, NJ: John Wiley & Sons, Inc., 2008).

cannot develop it independently because it is blocked by the prospective target's patent portfolio.

- Enhancing a particular business function, for example, sales and marketing, where similar cost and speed considerations are present.
- Achieving economies of scale/cost savings. Similar businesses may join forces to achieve economies of scale; for example, two banks may combine and increase their customer base but eliminate costs, such as redundant branch offices in the same location.
- Enhancing financial performance, that is, increasing earnings per share (EPS). A business may acquire another for purely financial reasons, particularly where the acquirer has a higher price-to-earnings ratio (P/E ratio) than the target company. If the acquisition is for cash, then the incremental profits of the new business have to be measured against the loss of the income from the cash paid in order to determine whether EPS goes up. Where stock is involved, the measurement is the addition to net profits from acquiring the business against the number of additional shares of the acquiror's stock issued to pay for the acquisition.

In acquisitions for stock, there is often sophisticated financial engineering involved. Take this example: Two companies both have $1 million in annual earnings and 1 million shares outstanding. If the acquirer has a P/E ratio of twice that of the target, to acquire the target for a price that merely equals the current market price of the target, it must issue only half a million shares. It doubles its income but only has 50 percent more shares outstanding. Its EPS, therefore, goes up. Surprisingly, the stock market frequently maintains the old P/E ratio of the acquirer or something close to it, so the acquirer's stock price rises as a result of the acquisition. This also gives the target company some negotiating leverage; because the deal increases the acquirer's EPS, there is room to negotiate with the buyer to pay a premium to the market as the acquisition price. Doing a deal that prospectively raises EPS is called doing a nondilutive or accretive deal, even though there may be more shares outstanding in a deal where stock is the acquisition consideration.

Of course, acquisitions are done other than for purely short-term financial considerations. Even though a deal is not initially accretive, the acquirer still may want to acquire the business for its future economic potential—the acquisition ultimately will become accretive because of the growth of the acquired business or expected cost savings or other synergies over time.

BASIC ACQUISITION STRUCTURES.   There are three basic ways to structure an acquisition:

1. **Stock purchase.** In a stock purchase, the buyer purchases the outstanding stock of the target corporation directly from the target's shareholders. The purchase price can be cash, stock, notes (or a combination), or other property. A stock purchase is the simplest form of acquisition. Assuming that all of the outstanding stock is acquired, the target becomes a wholly owned subsidiary of the buyer, and the buyer, by operation of law, indirectly acquires all of the assets and indirectly assumes all of the liabilities of the target (now its wholly owned subsidiary). No change is made in the assets or liabilities of the acquired business as a direct consequence of the acquisition itself.

2. **Merger.** It is usually critical for a buyer to acquire all of the outstanding stock of the target. The reason is that the buyer usually does not want minority shareholders in the acquired business. Having minority shareholders subjects the buyer to claims of breach of fiduciary duty related to intercompany transactions. The buyer wants to be free to run the acquired business as it sees fit and be able to integrate the acquired business into its own without impediment. If there are too many shareholders to get everyone to sign the stock purchase agreement, or if there are dissidents, then the usual choice is a merger, which forces out the dissident. For targets that are public companies, a merger is always used because a public company has a large number of shareholders, and it is not feasible for all of the shareholders to sign a stock purchase agreement. An alternative is to acquire a majority of the stock from the shareholders, and then follow that up with a squeeze-out merger. This is what happens in public tender offers.

A merger is a transaction that is created by the relevant business corporation statute in the particular state of incorporation. These statutes differ in details, sometimes significantly, but the common theme is that the statute permits two corporations to merge one into the other so that all of the assets and liabilities of the corporation that disappears in the merger get added to the assets and liabilities of the surviving corporation by operation of law. Also by operation of law and as agreed in the merger agreement, the outstanding stock of the disappearing corporation is automatically converted into cash, stock, notes, or a combination thereof (or other property) of the buyer or the buyer's parent. This technique, therefore, is the vehicle for the buyer to acquire 100 percent ownership of the target corporation. In either a one-step merger or in a two-step merger involving a stock purchase followed by a squeeze-out merger, all of the stock held by each shareholder of the acquired corporation gets converted into the merger consideration, whether a particular shareholder voted for the merger or not. The one exception is so-called appraisal rights created by the merger statutes. Under certain circumstances, the shareholders of the target can object to the merger terms and seek an appraisal of their shares in a court proceeding. This rarely occurs in acquisitions of private companies because of the expense involved, but it is a threat that enters into structuring discussions. Mergers generally require a shareholder vote of the merging corporations and in most states a board of directors vote as well.

3. **Asset purchase.** In an asset purchase, the buyer acquires all or selected assets of the target and assumes all, a portion, or none of the liabilities of the target pursuant to an asset purchase agreement. Most state statutes require shareholder approval of a sale of "all or substantially all" of the assets of the target. As we will see, there are multiple reasons why a deal may be structured as an asset purchase, the most important of which is for tax benefits. In some cases, such as where the buyer is acquiring only one product line from an established business with multiple product lines and where only one legal entity owns the assets of all product lines, an asset purchase is the only way to accomplish this objective.

Let us now address the principal structuring parameters—tax and corporate law—that determine whether a stock purchase, merger, or asset purchase is the appropriate acquisition structure. In most cases, tax considerations are the primary structuring consideration, so it is important for business lawyers to understand the basic tax aspects of acquisitions.

TAX.   Acquisitions can be done on both a tax-free (meaning tax deferred) or taxable basis. Ordinarily a shareholder recognizes taxable gain or loss upon the sale of his or her stock, whether the consideration paid is cash, a note, other property, or some combination thereof. Congress acknowledged that, under certain circumstances, where a shareholder continues the investment through equity in another corporation, imposing a tax on the sale of a corporation or a merger of corporations could inhibit otherwise economically beneficial transactions. For example, shareholders owning Corporation A might be willing to sell their shares to Corporation B for cash in a taxable transaction, but not for B shares if a tax were due. Corporation B has insufficient cash. The A shareholders might not have sufficient cash to pay a tax if their only proceeds were illiquid B shares. Also, if Corporation B continues the business previously operated by Corporation A, it might be said that the A shareholders have simply continued their investment in another form and so should not be subject to tax.

A series of tax code sections permit the deferral (not elimination) of the tax realized by shareholders when corporations combine in transactions that meet certain requirements. These so-called reorganization (or tax-free reorg) provisions contain specific technical statutory requirements that are amplified by judicially imposed requirements designed to implement the congressional intent that tax be deferred only when a shareholder's investment and business continues in a new form.

In the most fundamental terms, in order to qualify as a tax-free reorganization, a significant portion of the acquisition consideration must be voting stock of the buyer corporation. The required percentage ranges up to 100 percent for certain reorganization structures. The percentage is lowest (some tax lawyers would say an absolute minimum is 40 to 45 percent) for an "A" reorg, which relates to nonsubsidiary mergers and forward subsidiary mergers (explained later) to 80 percent or more for reverse subsidiary mergers, stock-for-assets deals, and stock-for-stock exchanges. The portion of the acquisition consideration that is not stock is called boot and its receipt is taxable. Therefore, most reorganizations are only partially tax-free.

Unfortunately, the reorganization provisions do not permit tax-deferred combinations between partnerships (or limited liability companies [LLCs] taxed as partnerships) and corporations. These entities typically can convert to corporations on a tax-deferred basis (under an unrelated set of code provisions) but cannot convert to a corporation on a tax-deferred basis as part of a plan to combine with a corporation under the reorganization rules. This means that a partnership or an LLC taxed as a partnership must plan in advance for possible exit strategies, so that a conversion to a corporation, if desired, is done well before a plan to combine with a particular corporation is formulated.

Buyers and targets have different and conflicting tax objectives with respect to acquisitions. From the *target's* perspective, the shareholders of the target want the acquisition to be tax-free to them in a stock transaction, which is a practical necessity where the shares are illiquid and cannot be sold to pay the tax. If all or a portion of the consideration is not stock, then the shareholders of the target want to get long-term capital gains treatment. A tax-free deal allows the target shareholders to defer recognition of their gain until they sell the new shares. In the event of a shareholder's death, the cost basis of the assets of that shareholder can be stepped-up to their then fair market value, thus permanently avoiding income tax on that gain. The taxable gain is measured by the value of the consideration received over the basis in the shares or assets being sold (cost less depreciation, if any).

Shareholders want to avoid a deal that creates double tax—first at the corporate level and then at the shareholder level. In other words, a transaction is not tax efficient if the target corporation pays tax on its gain and the shareholders of that corporation pay tax on the after-tax proceeds distributed to them. Double tax happens in an asset purchase, with certain exceptions—the target corporation pays a tax on its gain from a sale of its assets, and, when the proceeds are distributed to the shareholders, another tax is due from the shareholders on their gain. This potential for double tax is the reason that asset purchases are relatively rare in the technology company arena. An asset purchase sometimes can be accomplished without double tax if there are sufficient tax-loss carryforwards available to shelter the selling corporation's gains or if the acquired entity is a flow-though entity, such as a partnership or LLC. This double-tax problem is why you should consider setting up the enterprise as a flow-through entity at the outset (including an S corporation), as we discussed in Chapter 1.

From the *buyer's* perspective, the principal tax concern relates to the tax basis that the buyer receives in the target's assets. The buyer wants what is known as a step-up in basis, since a higher tax basis in depreciable/amortizable assets allows greater depreciation deductions that will shelter other income going forward or will reduce the amount of gain when the assets are sold. The opposite of a step-up in basis is carryover basis, which means that the assets have the same tax basis in the hands of the buyer as they did in the hands of the target. In a tax-free deal, there is carryover basis. In a taxable asset purchase, there is a step-up in basis, but unless the target has loss carryforwards or is a flow-through entity, there is double tax. Taxable mergers can go either way depending on the form of the merger. You can see the points of contention between buyer and target developing already.

Let us approach it from another direction: the basic tax consequences of the three different structures. In a *stock* purchase, shareholders sell their stock directly to the buyer. The corporation itself is not selling anything, so the corporation pays no tax and therefore double tax is avoided. You can accomplish a stock-for-stock tax-free deal, but the requirements are strict, as noted. Stock deals are tax adverse for the buyer from the limited perspective that there is carryover basis, and not a step-up in basis, in the target's assets. There are some esoteric exceptions here for stock purchases of a corporation out of a consolidated tax group and for Subchapter S corporations using a so-called Section 338 election. The election effectively treats the stock purchase as an asset purchase for tax purposes.

As for *mergers*, there are taxable and tax-free mergers. A taxable merger can be structured to resemble a stock purchase or an asset purchase. We discuss different merger structures later.

In a taxable *asset* purchase, if the buyer acquires selected assets at a gain from the target, the target pays tax on the gain. If the proceeds are then distributed to the shareholders of the target, there is double tax if the transaction is followed by a liquidation (assuming that there is a gain on the liquidation of the stock). If the proceeds are distributed as a dividend and the corporation stays in business, a tax would be payable by the shareholders on the dividend, assuming there are corporate earnings and profits. From the buyer's tax perspective, taxable asset deals are good because there is a step-up in tax basis. (There are tax-free asset deals, but they are quite rare.)

CORPORATE LAW.   The corporate law parameters for an acquisition start with whether the buyer wants, or is forced, to acquire selected assets of the target and whether the buyer wants, or is forced, to avoid the assumption of certain or all liabilities of the target.

Selective acquisitions of assets or selective assumptions of liabilities generally have to be accomplished by an asset purchase structure because in a stock purchase or in a merger, all assets and liabilities are conveyed, directly or indirectly, as a matter of law.

Where the buyer wants to acquire the entire business, asset purchase structures are generally not used if there is double tax. They are also more complex mechanically.

As discussed, the next choice in this situation is a stock purchase. Buyers almost always want to acquire all, as opposed to a majority, of the outstanding stock of the target in a stock acquisition. That is because if minority shareholders remain, any transactions between the buyer and its new subsidiary are subject to attack on breach of fiduciary duty grounds by the minority shareholders— potential legal complications buyers generally (but not always) want to avoid. Also, funds flow is restricted from the subsidiary to the parent because if the subsidiary wants to pay a dividend to the parent, it must also pay it as well to the minority shareholders, which may not be desirable.

In order to acquire the entire business where the agreement of all shareholders cannot be obtained, there are two choices: a merger where the stock of the target is converted into stock of the buyer or cash or other property, or a two-step transaction where a stock purchase of a majority (preferably a large majority) of the stock is followed by a squeeze-out merger, as already discussed. If enough stock is acquired initially, a short-form merger can be effected by a board vote only, provided that the requisite amount of the target's stock is first acquired. Most state corporation statutes make a short-form merger available where the parent owns at least 90 percent of the stock of the target.

Another corporate law consideration in the choice of structure is the need to obtain consents from counterparties to contracts of the target and/or from government entities. Commercial contracts generally prohibit the contract from being assigned by a party without the consent of the other party. In an asset purchase, what is required is an assignment to the acquiring corporation of the contract rights of the target under the particular contract. The need to obtain these consents creates the possibility of delays and the possibility of a hold-up by the other contracting party to extract some monetary or other concession as the price for its consent.

One way to sometimes avoid the need for consents is by doing a stock purchase. In a stock purchase, because the contracting corporation is not really a party to the transaction, it generally is not considered to be assigning its contract rights for purposes of requiring consents from counterparties. To avoid this loophole, some contracts require consent for an assignment and also give the counterparty termination or other rights in a change in control transaction—in other words, an acquisition by stock purchase or any form of merger.

Similar to a stock purchase in this regard is what is known as a reverse triangular merger, which sounds sophisticated but is really quite simple. Most mergers are structured as subsidiary mergers; that is, the buyer forms a new corporate shell subsidiary that is the corporation that merges with the target. One reason for doing this is that the buyer may be able to avoid having to obtain approval of the merger from its shareholders. Literally, the merger statutes require approval by the shareholders of the *merging* corporations. In a subsidiary merger, the shareholder approval relating to the buyer can be that of the buyer itself, since it, not its shareholders, is the shareholder of the merging corporation. In a subsidiary merger, if the acquisition subsidiary (or acquisition sub) merges into the target, it is called a reverse triangular merger. If the target merges into the acquisition sub, it is called a forward triangular merger. Just as in a stock purchase, a reverse triangular merger is generally not considered as involving an assignment of the target's contracts; in a forward triangular merger, an assignment generally is considered to occur since it is a new corporation that is now a party to the contract. Forward mergers sometimes are required for tax reasons because the tax-free qualification requirements are less stringent than for reverse mergers.

Another significant structuring parameter is how buyers can protect themselves from misrepresentations by the target about its business. We explore that topic in more depth later, but two basic techniques are used: indemnification and escrows.

"Indemnification" means that the shareholders of the target agree to pay the buyer for any damages that the buyer sustains that relate to a misrepresentation or contractual breach by the target. An "escrow" means that a portion of the purchase price is set aside in a bank escrow account and is not payable immediately to the sellers. The escrow serves as a source of reimbursement of the buyer's damages from a misrepresentation. If not all shareholders sign the stock purchase agreement, how do you get all shareholders to pay their fair share of the damages? This is important from both the buyer's and target's perspectives—the buyer wants as many sources of reimbursement as it can get, and each shareholder of the target wants to bear only that shareholder's proportionate share of any liability. The simplest method by which recourse is obtained against all shareholders of the target is by a merger where a portion of the proceeds owing to all shareholders is put into escrow as part of the terms of the merger agreement. Post-closing protection for the buyer from all of the target's shareholders is another reason to do a merger over a stock purchase where all shareholders do not sign the acquisition agreement. In an asset purchase, the target is the seller, and the selling corporation may be the only source of indemnification. If the seller is selling all or substantially all of its assets, what is left as a source of reimbursement to the buyer for damages that the buyer sustains as a result of the target's misrepresentation or breach? In this situation, where the entire business is being sold and the proceeds are being distributed to the shareholders, well-advised buyers require the shareholders of the target corporation to sign indemnification agreements as a source of indemnification or provide for an escrow.

STRUCTURING CONSIDERATIONS

Regulatory Approvals. One issue that has to be analyzed at the outset is what, if any, regulatory approvals are required for the acquisition. The need for regulatory approvals affects the timing, certainty of completion, covenants, and closing conditions of the deal.

The need for regulatory approval can arise for two reasons.

1. One or both of the parties are in a regulated industry where acquisitions are scrutinized for compliance with applicable legal requirements—such as the acquisition of broadcasting assets.

2. The size of the parties and the size of the transaction may trigger filing requirements under the antitrust laws.

Although all deals are subject, in theory, to being overturned because of antitrust concerns, the principal antitrust hurdle in the acquisition arena is the Hart-Scott-Rodino Antitrust Improvements Act (or HSR or Hart-Scott). In acquisitions of a specified size ($50+ million or greater) and where the parties themselves exceed specified size hurdles ($100+ million in sales or assets for one, and $10+ million for the other), a filing with, and clearance by, the federal government is required. Some deals get scrapped because of antitrust review, but for most technology deals, an HSR filing requirement is merely an expensive nuisance and unwelcome delay.

Securities Law. The impact of the securities laws on acquisitions is discussed in detail below. In short, issuance by the buyer of its stock or other securities (or a vote by the target's shareholders to approve a deal where they are to receive stock or securities of the buyer in exchange for their target stock) is considered a purchase and sale of securities requiring either registration with the Securities and Exchange Commission (SEC) or an exemption from registration.

Accounting. In the relatively recent past, accounting considerations often were as important as tax considerations in structuring acquisitions. That is because there were two forms of accounting for acquisitions by the buyer with drastically different consequences. In purchase accounting, the buyer reset the fair market value of the acquired assets and any related goodwill had to be depreciated, sometimes over a relatively short period in technology deals. In the other form, a pooling of interests, there was no change in the book basis of the acquired assets and no amortization of goodwill. This was considered highly desirable, since it was difficult to do accretive acquisitions with goodwill amortization creating significant book expense going forward. The requirements for qualifying for a pooling were quite strict (e.g., the acquisition consideration had to be solely for voting stock). There were multiple other requirements as well. This all changed a number of years ago, and now there is only one form of accounting treatment for acquisitions: Postacquisition assets have a new book basis tied to fair market value, and goodwill is not written off unless it is, or becomes, impaired.

Summary.   The structure of acquisitions is dictated principally by tax considerations but also by considerations such as minimizing required approvals and providing a source of indemnification and escrows. Often these parameters are in conflict with one another, and the choice of structure will depend on the various parties' negotiating leverage.

OVERVIEW OF AN ACQUISITION AGREEMENT

Acquisition agreements—stock purchase agreements, merger agreements, and asset purchase agreements—are usually lengthy and complicated. As noted at the outset, they are also very important documents because M&A is a zero-sum game, and if one side gets something, inevitably the other party has an equivalent loss. Big money can turn on how particular representations or other provisions are drafted.

Nevertheless, there is wide overlap among the various forms of acquisition agreements: stock purchase agreement, merger agreement, and asset purchase agreement.

ECONOMIC TERMS.   The first sections of an acquisition agreement describe the economics and the mechanics of the deal: how much is being paid and the form of the consideration—cash, stock, both, other; whether there is an escrow; a listing of any ancillary contracts being executed in connection with the acquisition—employment agreements, registration rights agreements, noncompete agreements, shareholders agreements, and the like; if promissory notes constitute a portion of the purchase price, their terms—subordination, interest rate, maturity schedule, and so on. Sometimes there are purchase price adjustments—particularly if there is to be a deferred closing—based on changes in the seller's net worth or other financial measures between signing and closing. Purchase price adjustments are discussed later.

REPRESENTATIONS AND WARRANTIES.   The next major sections contain the representations and warranties, of both the target and the buyer. The target will make representations about its business over anywhere from 10 to 30 pages, covering such things as capitalization, pending or threatened litigation, required consents, no adverse change since the last published financial statements, no undisclosed material liabilities, environmental compliance, taxes, and on and on. The representations will make reference to a document known as the disclosure schedule, where the exceptions to the representations and warranties are disclosed and where various detailed information about the business is required to be listed. It is extremely important to get that document right because it serves as the basis for avoiding indemnification claims later, as will be discussed. Targets will always try to limit the representations by adding materiality and knowledge qualifiers (i.e., there are no *material* issues or problems or the target *does not know* of any particular issues or problems). Buyers resist these qualifications, particularly the knowledge qualifiers. Buyers argue that if there is a subsequent problem, it does not matter to them whether the seller knew about it or not because they still have suffered a loss. In other words, the representations make a risk allocation, and the buyer tries to shift the risk of an unknown problem to the target. The target tries to do the opposite.

The buyer will also make representations. If the deal is for cash, then the representations are minimal—just that the deal has been properly authorized and is valid and binding on the buyer. If, however, the buyer is issuing stock to the target shareholders, the representations and warranties of the buyer frequently are as extensive, or nearly as extensive, as those of the target. One buyer trick that usually fails is to circulate a draft of the merger agreement in a stock deal that requires the seller to make extensive representations and the buyer to make only minimal representations. There is merit to the argument that the buyer should make the same representations as the target because the sellers are in effect buying in part, or investing in, the buyer's business by taking the buyer's stock. The argument has less force where the buyer is a public company. In that case, there is a representation regarding the accuracy and completeness of the buyer's public filings under the Securities Exchange Act of 1934 (Exchange Act); in theory, that is all the target or its shareholders need to know since those filings are supposed to tell the market everything that is material about the buyer and its stock.

Sometimes the target's shareholders are required to join in to the target's representations. This is seen in stock purchase agreements since the target shareholders are already parties. In a merger agreement or asset purchase agreement, the principal purpose of target shareholder representations is to provide the buyer with direct indemnification claims against the target shareholders where they have liability beyond the escrow or are receiving the proceeds of an asset purchase. Having the shareholders sign also binds the shareholders directly to covenants like the no-shop clause that prohibits the company from trying to solicit other bidders. The target shareholders may also be required to make standard representations that they have duly executed the agreement and the like. The latter are not really necessary since they can be contained in the letter of transmittal or other document pursuant to which the target shareholders collect the acquisition consideration.

CONDITIONS TO CLOSING.   One big issue that arises is whether there is, or has to be, a deferred closing; that is, the parties sign the agreement but understand that they cannot close until certain external contingencies are resolved. For example, the contingencies could include the need to get antitrust regulatory clearance under HSR or approval of a disclosure document by the SEC, each of which requires filings with government agencies and a waiting period. Also, shareholder approval may be needed but cannot be obtained immediately, particularly where there are a large number of shareholders of the target. It is a lot simpler to do a simultaneous signing and closing than a deferred closing, not only in terms of the complexity of the agreement but in economic terms as well.

If there is to be a deferred closing, then the agreement must contain conditions to both parties' obligations to close. Typical conditions are the regulatory and shareholder conditions just discussed. But buyers also almost always insist that there be conditions that ensure that the target shareholders retain the risk of owning the business until the closing. Therefore, typical closing conditions include a bring-down of the target's representations and warranties, meaning that the buyer has to reaffirm those representations as of the closing date, including that there has been no material adverse change in the target's business. Sometimes the target has enough bargaining leverage to shift the risks of the business to the buyer upon signing, not closing. In that case, the bring-down of certain or all representations is not a condition to closing. The most important of those representations is that there has been no material adverse change (MAC) in the target's business since a reference point. A shift of this risk to the buyer is rare. Other conditions are the completion of various ancillary actions that are a part of the deal, such as the signing of the agreed-upon employment agreements, noncompete agreements, and the like.

COVENANTS.   If there is to be a deferred closing, there also is a section dealing with preclosing and postclosing covenants. Preclosing covenants limit what the target (and perhaps the buyer) can do between the signing and the closing—essentially that the business must be run in the ordinary course. This section contains the no-shop covenants, which are relatively standard. Postclosing covenants deal with such issues as how the target's employees and benefit plans are to be treated.

INDEMNIFICATION AND ESCROW.   As previously discussed, buyers require contractual protection in the event there is a misrepresentation in the acquisition agreement by the target or if the target violates any other provision of the agreement. The acquisition agreement therefore will say that the representations and warranties survive the closing and provide for indemnification of the buyer for a target breach. The only exception to this pattern is acquisitions of public companies; in this case, except in troubled situations, as a matter of commercial practice the representations and warranties do not survive the closing and there is no indemnification.

The language of indemnification provisions is basically the same across the various types of acquisition agreements: The indemnitors indemnify the indemnitees for all losses, expenses, damages, and liabilities arising out of a breach of a representation, warranty, agreement, or covenant in the acquisition agreement. That part is not controversial. Other related issues sometimes are quite hotly contested.

Although the inclusion of indemnification provisions in an agreement does not automatically require the creation of an escrow, buyers want to segregate funds so they are easier to reach if they have a valid claim and they can be assured that there will be a ready source of indemnification. Buyers also will argue that in a merger with multiple shareholders, the only practical source of protection is an escrow because you cannot sue everybody. Most acquisition agreements, at least where there are multiple target shareholders, provide for an escrow. Escrows sometimes are favorable, in a sense, from the point of view of the target shareholders because that is the only practical way to get all of them to come up with their fair share of the damages.

Once it is determined that an escrow will be part of the deal, additional questions arise, such as what percentage of the purchase price the escrow should be and how long it should last. Generally, the percentage ranges from 10 to 15 percent of the acquisition consideration, and the warranties survive for one to three years, with certain representations regarding capitalization and title to shares and tax and environmental representations occasionally surviving longer than the others. The target shareholders obviously would like to get their money sooner, and as a practical matter they probably have the better of the argument that new claims are highly unlikely to arise after a year or so.

In addition to the size and length of the escrow, the negotiations also will revolve around whether there will be exceptions and limits to the indemnification provisions. Sellers in a strong bargaining position try to limit the indemnification to the escrow, often even if it comes at the price of a larger escrow. This means that the escrow is the only source of indemnification for the buyer for misrepresentations (other than for fraud). For example, if there is a $10 million escrow and a $15 million problem, the buyer is out the $5 million. Target shareholders argue in support of limiting the indemnification to the escrow that they are selling the business and do not want to have to worry about it anymore and want the comfort that they can keep the money already received. Institutional investors, such as venture capital funds, will argue that they have to distribute to their investors the proceeds that they receive in the sale and so the money is gone as soon as they get it. Further, target shareholders will argue that the buyer should not be too worried because it did extensive due diligence on the business before signing the acquisition agreement and should know that it is a "clean" company. However, buyers will argue that the problems they are most worried about are the big ones and that limiting the indemnification to the escrow or otherwise will not cover them in any really big mess.

The other ploy target shareholders try is to limit the indemnification to a specified percentage of the proceeds above the escrow that is less than 100 percent of the proceeds. The arguments here are much the same.

Another provision that is almost always present is the so-called basket. A "basket" means that no claim for indemnification for a misrepresentation can be made by the buyer unless a certain dollar threshold of claims is reached and/or that each individual claim has to exceed a certain threshold before it can be asserted. Baskets should not cover covenant breaches, only misrepresentations. The rationale for them is that small mistakes are likely, and the parties should agree in advance that neither side needs to be bothered with the time and expense required to resolve small claims. The underlying assumption is that minor problems are an assumed part of the economics of the deal to the buyer. The dollar amount of the basket varies with the size of the deal, and a figure of 1 percent is mentioned frequently, although 1 percent can be a large number to cover small mistakes, particularly in large deals. There is also a distinction between a true basket or deductible, on one hand, and a threshold or disappearing basket, on the other hand. In the latter case, once the threshold of claims is reached, damages are to be reimbursed beginning at the first dollar. In the former, only the damages above the deductible are reimbursable.

One countertechnique used by some buyers is to say that because the basket is meant to cover immaterial mistakes, then, for purposes of indemnification only (and not the conditions to closing), all materiality qualifiers in the representations are to be ignored. The buyer wants to avoid having to deal with the issue of double materiality—first the buyer would have to prove that the misrepresentation was material because the representation at issue contains a materiality qualifier, then on top of that the target shareholders may argue that the only real damages are those that are above a materiality threshold. Target shareholders argue that you cannot ignore materiality qualifications for purposes of indemnification since the seller took those materiality qualifications into account in preparing the disclosure schedule. In effect, with no materiality qualifiers in the representations, the preparation of the disclosure schedule would be extremely onerous and difficult to get right. One technique used to solve this problem is for the agreement to provide that materiality qualifiers will be taken into account in determining whether a misrepresentation has occurred, but to make it explicit that materiality qualifiers are ignored for purposes of calculating damages arising from misrepresentations. Buyers will then counter that ignoring materiality qualifiers is appropriate for indemnification purposes since the purpose of the basket is to protect the seller against nonmaterial items. This discussion gets a bit mind numbing.

To see the implications of these variations, consider this example: $100,000 aggregate basket; a representation that there are no material undisclosed liabilities and no threatened litigation; after closing, the buyer determines that there are 20 undisclosed nonmaterial $10,000 liabilities and 1 undisclosed threatened material $200,000 lawsuit.

- **Threshold versus deductible.** There are a total of $200,000 in reimbursable damages, since each of the $10,000 claims is not material and therefore not reimbursable. If the basket is a deductible, then the buyer would get reimbursed for the $100,000 above the basket. If there is a threshold that resets to zero, then the buyer gets $200,000 because the $100,000 basket is exceeded.
- **Materiality qualifications ignored for indemnification purposes.** There is a $100,000 aggregate basket and there is a clause that the materiality qualifications are ignored for all purposes other than conditions to closing, including determining whether a representation has been breached and determining the amount of the reimbursable damages. So, there are $400,000 in damages—the $200,000 in undisclosed nonmaterial liabilities and the $200,000 undisclosed material lawsuit. If there is a $100,000 deductible, the buyer gets the $300,000 over the basket. If there is a dollar-one threshold, then the buyer gets the full $400,000.

Let us assume now that there is a $100,000 aggregate basket; a representation that there are no material undisclosed liabilities and no undisclosed threatened litigation of any type; after closing, the buyer determines that there are 20 undisclosed nonmaterial $10,000 liabilities and 1 undisclosed threatened arguably material $50,000 lawsuit.

- **Threshold versus deductible.** Each of the $10,000 claims is not material and therefore not reimbursable. With either a threshold or a deductible, the buyer would get back none of the $250,000 in aggregate damages because the $100,000 basket has not been reached, since the only misrepresentation that counts is the $50,000 lawsuit.

- **Material qualifications ignored for indemnification purposes.** If there is a clause that the materiality qualifications are ignored for purposes of indemnification, there are $250,000 in reimbursable damages, because all of the small claims are reimbursable. If there is a deductible, the buyer gets the $150,000 over the basket. If there is a resetting threshold, then the buyer gets the full $250,000, because the basket has been exceeded.

One additional issue to be aware of is how indemnification mechanics work in an asset purchase. Where you are buying selected assets from an established well-financed seller, there is no issue—you are adequately protected by indemnification from the seller. But if you are buying all assets and there is no escrow, and all of the proceeds are distributed to the seller's shareholders who did not sign the asset purchase agreement, there maybe no practical source of reimbursement. The solution here, obviously, is to get the seller's shareholders to sign the asset purchase agreement or separate indemnification agreements—or get an escrow—or both.

REPRESENTING SELLERS: A SUMMARY.   A list of issues that sellers and their counsel should consider in negotiating the detailed terms of acquisitions follows. Some of these points repeat the preceding material but may prove to be useful presented in one place. Whether some or all of these issues should be brought up at the letter of intent stage is discussed in the section on "Advanced Topics."

- **Purchase price adjustments.** Purchase price adjustments that tie to changes in net worth or balance sheet items may seem innocuous, but they invite claims that the target's books were not maintained in accordance with generally accepted accounting principles (GAAP) and also are an end run around the basket. These clauses are very tricky and should be reviewed by the target and its advisors carefully to make sure they work properly.
- **Liquidity issues.** Worry about liquidity. If it is a stock deal, is the market for the buyer's stock thinly traded? If the target shareholders are getting restricted stock in a public company, insist on a registration rights agreement with *shelf* registration rights. This means that the buyer automatically has to file a

resale registration statement for the shares issued to the target shareholders within a specified (short) period after the closing.

- **Ancillary agreements.** If there are to be noncompete agreements or employment agreements, have at least a term sheet describing what is to be in them at the outset.
- **Representations and warranties.** Add materiality and knowledge qualifiers wherever possible. If stock is part of the consideration, try to get buyer's representations as broad as the target's.
- **Conditions to closing.** Try to shift the risk of the business to the buyer by limiting the representations that have to be brought down or at least trying to avoid a bring-down of the material adverse change representation.
- **Indemnification**

  o Try to limit the amount of time that the representations survive to one year or less.

  o Try to limit the indemnification to the escrow, even at the price of a larger escrow—this may be the most important target provision of all.

  o If indemnification is not limited to the escrow, then try to obtain a dollar or percentage limit to indemnification claims.

  o If there is liability beyond the escrow, try to get a provision that the buyer can sue an individual seller only for its percentage of the overall damages. Even in that case, there should be a contribution agreement among the selling shareholders to reimburse each other if any shareholder pays more than its percentage share relative to the other shareholders (e.g., where only a few shareholders are sued).

  o Try to get a true basket or deductible, rather than a disappearing basket or threshold.

  o Try to get a provision that the buyer is not entitled to indemnification if it had actual knowledge of the condition or event that gave rise to the breach even though it was not disclosed in the target's disclosure schedule. Buyers usually strongly resist this provision since it invites sandbagging. What if the target, in a deferred closing transaction, discovers that it had inadvertently left out a particular claim in the disclosure schedule delivered at signing? Try to get a provision that the target is permitted to supplement the disclosure schedule before closing and that the buyer cannot seek reimbursement for items disclosed in the revised disclosure schedule—the buyer can still walk away if there was a material breach, but it cannot close and then sue the target shareholders a moment later. Buyers will advance a "sandbagging" argument against this provision as well.

- **Acquisitions for stock.** If the acquisition consideration is wholly or partly buyer stock, consider providing that indemnification claims can be paid back in buyer's stock valued at the time of the closing. Even better, insist that the target shareholders can at any time substitute cash for the shares in escrow valued at the fixed price or pay valid claims in cash. That way the target shareholders have the best of both worlds—if the buyer's stock goes up, they can keep it and pay the indemnification claim in cash; if the buyer's stock goes down, they can pay the indemnification claim in overvalued (for indemnification purposes) buyer stock. If the value of the buyer's stock is allowed to float for this purpose, try to get a floor on how low the stock can go for purposes of valuing it for reimbursement purposes.
- **Sole remedy.** Make sure that the agreement states that the negotiated terms of indemnification are the buyer's sole remedy for a breach of the agreement (i.e., that the buyer cannot sue outside the agreement under contract law).
- **Scope of damages.** Try to limit the type of reimbursable damages (i.e., try to exclude incidental, special, consequential, and punitive damages).
- **Damage measurement.** Try to include a provision that the buyer's damages are measured net of tax benefits from the loss and net of insurance recoveries. Try to exclude from the damages any that result from a change in target's tax allocations and positions prior to closing. Try to require the buyer to maintain insurance that will cover damages that are otherwise reimbursable.
- **Damage mitigation.** Try to require the buyer to use its best efforts to mitigate damages and to measure damages net of any recoveries that the buyer is entitled to (insurance, other indemnification sources, etc.), but that the buyer shall not be required

to consider or exercise any remedy against the corporate seller or any director, officer, or employee (whether current or former) of the seller.

ADVANCED TOPICS

SECURITIES LAWS ASPECTS OF ACQUISITIONS. An acquisition where the acquisition consideration consists, in whole or in part, of buyer's securities involves an offer and sale of securities that either has to be registered under the Securities Act of 1933 (Securities Act) or be exempt from registration. "Securities" for this purpose mean stock, notes, or other securities of the buyer. An earn-out, because the target shareholders are relying on the future performance of the business, may (or may not under SEC no-action guidelines) constitute a security.

What exactly is the offer in this context? SEC Rule 145 says in effect that an offer includes, so far as the security holders of a corporation are concerned, the submission to a vote of such security holders a merger or an asset sale where stock is issued as acquisition consideration. According to the introductory note to Rule 145, an offer occurs when there is submitted to security holders a vote where they must elect, in what is a new investment decision, to accept a new security. Technically, a stock-for-stock exchange does not fall under Rule 145, but that is because such a transaction is unambiguously a purchase and sale, as opposed to a merger or asset sale.

Where an acquisition is partly for stock or other securities of the buyer, the offer of that stock or those securities in any form of acquisition where the target shareholders have to make an investment decision involves first the offer and then the sale of securities. We generally discuss only stock in this section, although the rules apply equally to other securities.

If the transaction is an offer and sale of securities, there are two basic ways to achieve securities law compliance: Register the offered securities on a registration statement filed with the SEC, or structure the transaction to qualify under a private placement exemption. Buyers want to avoid going through the SEC filing process if at all possible because it is extremely expensive and involves significant delays. For acquisitions of public companies, registration with the

SEC is the only practical alternative since it would be impossible to find a private placement exemption where there are hundreds of public shareholders. In acquisitions of private companies, a private placement is possible, depending on the number and characteristics of the target shareholders.

Exemptions for issuances of securities in an acquisition involve the same exemptive scheme discussed in Chapter 4—sales can be made only to accredited investors, sales can otherwise be made in satisfaction of the other provisions of SEC Regulation D (Reg. D), or the offer and sale can be exempt under Section 4(2) of the Securities Act. If an offering is made to unaccredited investors, the informational requirements under Reg. D are nearly as strict as they are for a registration statement, although there is no SEC review of the private placement memorandum.

Acquisitions present unique structuring challenges because you cannot choose to whom you are going to offer the securities; you are stuck with offering them to the shareholders of the target, and in most private companies the shareholder base is sizable and is comprised of multiple shareholders who are neither accredited nor sophisticated (e.g., option holders who are lower-level employees who acquired the underlying stock under Rule 701). Even worse, option holders under the target's stock plan under certain circumstances may be required to make an investment decision and so must be counted as offerees/purchasers of securities.

If, for Reg. D purposes, you have more than 35 unaccredited shareholders of the target, what do you do? There are several tricks you can use that may solve the problem. The key to the solution involves using the Rule 145 concept that an investment decision is what constitutes the offer/sale in this context and then structuring the transaction so that the nonaccredited investor/shareholders of the target do not have to make an investment decision whether to take new securities or not.

One trick is to structure the deal so that unaccredited investors get all cash and no stock. Cash is not a security, so there is no investment decision to be made involving a new security. Delaware case law supports offering different consideration to different classes of shareholders in a merger, but only where there is a valid business purpose. Although law firms usually will not give an opinion that this structure complies with Delaware law (and/or that there is a valid private placement), because of the subjectivity involved. In the right circumstances, it seems reasonably clear that there are valid business reasons in using this structure and that the structure does not involve a Rule 145 investment decision. In short, the deal may not be cost-effective or otherwise practical if full-blow SEC registration is required. You must be careful, however, because the use of cash above a certain amount may disqualify an otherwise tax-free deal. Also, the buyer may not want to use its available cash for the deal.

Another technique that can be used where the use of cash is not desirable for business or tax reasons is to solicit votes approving the transaction by a written consent submitted only to shareholders who are accredited investors, assuming you can get the requisite shareholder approval just from them. There is some discomfort with this approach on the theory that even though the nonaccredited investors do not vote, they still have to make a decision as to whether to take the acquisition consideration or to exercise their state law appraisal rights. Some think that this is an investment decision that destroys the exemption. The better view is that even though a decision has to be made whether to seek a court appraisal or not, that decision is not an investment decision relating to taking a new security within the intent and language of the rule.

In summary, if the acquisition involves the issuance of stock or other securities by the buyer, you have to consider the securities law aspects as one of the structuring parameters.

PURCHASE PRICE ADJUSTMENTS.   Infrequently in technology company acquisitions, but quite commonly in acquisitions of companies with significant hard assets, the acquisition agreement contains purchase price adjustment provisions. These provisions appear more frequently in deals with a deferred closing, but do appear in others because of the gap between the signing/closing and the date of the most recent financials. Essentially, the purpose of these provisions is to keep the economic risks and rewards of the business with the target by retroactively adjusting the purchase price after the closing to reflect financial results between the latest target financial statements and the signing or closing.

Most commonly, a purchase price adjustment says that the purchase price is adjusted up or down retroactively based on the increase or decrease in the target's net worth in the applicable measurement period. Again, the base measurement date is the date of the most recent balance sheet prior to signing. Therefore, if the target has lost money, the purchase price will go down, and if the target has made money and not distributed it to its shareholders, the purchase price will go up. This is because the profit or loss is reflected in the target's net worth, assuming that there are no adjustments to net worth outside the income statement. In addition to the bona fide purpose of risk transfer, some aggressive buyers seek purchase price adjustments since the postclosing financial analysis to determine closing net worth gives them an opportunity to pick at the balance sheet the target supplied. If there are any problems in that balance sheet, then the buyer is entitled to an adjustment that is not subject to the basket discussed earlier.

Note that in a stock purchase, the business is effectively run for the account of the buyer if the target is not allowed to pay dividends between signing and closing. If the business deal is that the business is to be run for the target shareholders' account, however, then a purchase price adjustment is required.

Purchase price adjustment provisions are often complicated, and there are a number of common pitfalls. The most common mistake is to allow the purchase price adjustment to be based on only selected balance sheet items. The parties may say that they do not really care if there is any change, for example, in the value of fixed assets, but do care if there is a change in working capital. The logical conclusion is that the purchase price adjustment provisions only need to relate to working capital items. This might work, but the risks to this piecemeal approach to the balance sheet is that the target will manipulate the balance sheet by, for example, selling some capital equipment to increase working capital by the amount of cash received. That said, working capital adjustments, when combined with strict covenants to run the business in the ordinary course, simplify the calculation and often are used successfully. Another purchase price adjustment may be for an increase or decrease in long-term debt, but it does not make sense for the purchase price to change if the target merely pays down some debt with cash, or incurred debt and added an equivalent amount of cash to its balance sheet. For that reason, debt adjustments should be for net debt, or debt minus cash.

In an asset purchase, the risk of the piecemeal approach is exacerbated because in an asset deal where the buyer pays cash, cash is an asset that typically is excluded from the assets the buyer is buying—in other words, there is not any point to the buyer buying the target's cash with the buyer's cash. Therefore, cash is an excluded asset. Where cash is an excluded asset, you have to have a purchase price adjustment to take into account increases or decreases in the cash that the seller keeps because that differential is effectively an increase or decrease in the purchase price. Cash can change even if there is no change in the business (e.g., accounts receivable are collected and no new ones are generated). This would produce an anomalous result.

Exhibit 5.1 is an example of how purchase price adjustments work.

The point here is that mistakes are common in purchase price adjustment provisions, and businesspeople and investment bankers involved in the deal should be strongly encouraged to think through the details of these provisions.

EARN-OUTS.   An earn-out is an acquisition structure that is used to bridge the gap in price negotiations. The negotiations go something like this: The buyer says it will pay a certain (low) amount for the business because it does not really believe all of the fabulous things the target says will happen that justify a higher price. The target insists that all of these fabulous things really will happen in the future and that a higher price is justified. The parties cannot agree on the price because of their differing views of the business prospects. To bridge this gap, the parties sometimes agree that the buyer will pay the lower price at closing; if the fabulous things actually do happen, the buy will pay an additional amount later.

The additional amount to be paid by the buyer can either be a fixed or a formula amount tied to postclosing performance goals for the acquired business. Earn-outs generally are based on achievement of projected targets in income statement items, for example, at the top line (revenue), the bottom line (net income), or something in between, such as earnings before interest and taxes (EBIT). The earn-out also can be based on other operating targets, such as number of customers.

Earn-outs often are problematic, with the parties regretting that they used an earn-out rather than just compromising the difference in the purchase price. Earn-outs have a conceptual attraction, but they are difficult to implement. Disputes are common. The lower down the income statement that the earn-out target is, the more likely it is that there will be a dispute because many accounting judgments can happen

March 31 Balance Sheet

Cash	$1,000		Trade Payables	$1,000
Accounts Receivable	1,000		No other liabilities	
Inventory	1,000			
Fixed Assets	7,000		Net Worth	9,000
Total	$10,000		Total	$10,000

Assume

- The business operates at a 50% gross margin and sells $500 worth of inventory in April (i.e., sells $500 of inventroy for $1,000, creating a $1,000 receivable).
- The business collects $750 of accounts receivable in April adding that to cash. The only other expenses are general and administrative expenses of $250/month.
- Closing takes place on April 30.

April 30 Balance Sheet

Cash	$1,500		Trade Payables	$1,000
Accounts Receivable	1,250			
Inventory	500			
Fixed Assets	7,000		Net Worth	9,250
Total	$10,250		Total	$10,250

Purchase Price Adjustment Examples

Stock deal

- If there is no purchase price adjustment, the business is effectively "run for the account of" the buyer (i.e., the buyer gets the benefit of $250 in net profit in the month and the increase in net worth).
- If you change the example slightly, and general and administrative expenses are $750 rather than $250 as in our example, then there would be a decrease in net worth of $250 that the buyer would absorb.

Asset deal

Assume that the buyer is buying all assets but cash and is assuming all liabilities of the business, all for a fixed price. Assume that the business deal is that the target keeps interim income/loss.

- If the business did nothing but collect the accounts receivable (i.e., there were no revenues or expenses), then you would still need a purchase price adjustment to avoid an anomaly resulting from the increase in the excluded asset. The purchase price should be reduced for the increase in cash that the target keeps and the decrease in accounts receivable that the buyer purchases.
- If the business is run for the account of the buyer, then you would need to have a purchase price adjustment to reflect the increase in cash that the target keeps and the decrease in accounts receivable that the buyer purchases.

EXHIBIT 5.1   EXAMPLES OF A PURCHASE PRICE ADJUSTMENT

to items between the revenue line and the net income line. There is also an initial negotiating issue of who is going to run the business; if the target is to run it or have a significant hand in running it, the incentive is to run the business to maximize the particular income statement item that is the basis of the earn-out. That may not be what is best for the business. If the buyer runs it (as is normally the case), the business may be run based on what is best for the business (which may or may not coincide with the earn-out measure), or it may be run largely to minimize the earn-out adjustment that the buyer will have to pay (which may or may not coincide with what is best for the business).

The point is that what is best for the business may or may not be the same as the income statement item that forms the basis of the earn-out. Even if it is what the business needs, the decisions and methods used to achieve the performance goal may not be optimum.

For example, say that the earn-out goal is tied to net income. As is often the case, even if the buyer retains all rights to make decisions regarding the business, the managers of the business who previously worked for the business and had equity have a personal economic interest in the earn-out outcome. In order to maximize the earn-out amount, management will be tempted to take imprudent actions, such as deferring expenses that otherwise would not be deferred for business reasons, or pushing a product into the market that is not ready with attendant risk to the company's reputation, or pricing to maximize margins when lower margins may help to establish the product for the company's longer-term benefit.

In order to avoid these pitfalls and the potential accounting disputes that may arise from a bottom-line earn-out target, the parties may choose the simpler route of having the earn-out tie to top-line revenue. But that creates its own set of problems. What is best for the business, more often than not, is to maximize net income (in prudent and legitimate ways), not to maximize revenue. An extreme example would be to set pricing so low that the product flies off the shelf, but the company loses money on every sale. The obvious fix to that is to have both a revenue and a net income test.

If the earn-out route is chosen, the acquisition documents will set up complex rules and implementation procedures.

The target shareholders may assert that the earn-out payments should be accelerated under certain circumstances. These circumstances may include:

- Termination of members of management without cause.
- Sale of the business by the buyer, or the sale of the buyer itself.
- Breach by the buyer of any of its postclosing obligations.

Certain operating rules need to be established. For example:

- Is the buyer required to fund the business to a specified extent?
- Are the other business units of the buyer to be prohibited from competing with the acquired business?
- If the buyer's other business units sell products that cannibalize the products of the acquired business, are there to be any restrictions on those sales, or should those sales be hypothetically assumed to be part of the acquired business for earn-out purposes?
- What happens if the acquired business wants to acquire another business? How is it to be financed, and how are the financing expenses to be allocated? Should the acquired business have the first opportunity to purchase businesses that will have an impact on the earn-out calculation?

Accounting principles need to be specified. For example:

- It is normally specified that new items of expense allocated to the business from the write-up of assets for accounting purposes need to be excluded on a pro forma basis from the income statement of the business. That write-up creates additional depreciation expense that reduces net income and is, in target's view, not a consistent way to measure the performance of the business.
- If goodwill has to be written off or if acquisition reserves have to be created, those should be excluded as well.
- How is buyer overhead to be allocated to the business, if at all? A related question is if the buyer performs certain functions for the business that were formerly paid for by the business, such as finance or benefits administration, what adjustments need to be made to the net income of the business for the benefit of the buyer?

- Are the effect of "extraordinary items," such as the sale of capital assets, to be excluded?
- Who pays the cost of preparing the financial statements used to determine the earn-out amount?
- How are intercompany transactions priced, and do they require any special approvals?
- Are restructuring or severance expenses to be excluded?
- If the employees of the target receive different and more expensive benefits from the buyer, is the increase to be excluded?
- What happens if the buyer substantially changes the business plan of the acquired business?

Governance principles need to be included. Such principles might include:

- No commingling of the assets or business of the buyer and the target are permitted.
- The buyer will be obligated, in general terms, to not take any action that would have the effect of materially reducing the amount of the earn-out payment, other than in the ordinary course of business.
- Certain specified major actions require the consent of the former owners of the business, or a target shareholders' representative.
- The parameters of the ability of management to make operating decisions need to be specified, including compensation, pricing, hiring/firing, and the like.

A number of tax issues are involved in earn-outs. If earn-out payments are linked in any way to continued employment, then compensation income may need to be recognized. How is imputed interest handled? What are the implications relating to the installment method of tax reporting, and how is the tax basis allocated for purposes of calculating interim gain? How does the earn-out affect a tax-free reorganization, particularly if the earn-out is to be paid in cash?

CONFIDENTIALITY AGREEMENTS.   Other than the investment bank engagement letter (discussed in the next section), if there is one, the confidentiality agreement between the buyer and the target is the first document typically signed in an acquisition transaction.

In acquisitions of technology companies, the issue of confidentiality is extremely important and delicate. Two points must be considered.

1. In order to protect its intellectual property rights, the target always must get anyone, potential buyer or not, to sign a confidentiality agreement before revealing its confidential information.
2. The technology company target must realize that even the tightest confidentiality agreement is still just a piece of paper. If the agreement is violated by the potential buyer in a failed acquisition, that fact may not ever become apparent. Even if it is suspected, it will likely be extremely difficult and expensive to prove. Furthermore, the potential buyer may have far more resources than the target.

Because confidentiality agreements can never fully protect the target, the management of the flow of confidential information from the target to the potential buyer is equally important, regardless of what is in the confidentiality agreement. The conundrum presented is that the buyer will not be able to set a price for the business (or even decide to buy it) until it understands better the target's trade secrets and their value. However, the target will not want to disclose confidential information to a potential buyer until the target knows that it has a price that is acceptable, at least in principle.

How are these conflicting interest managed? If at all possible, the target must make a realistic assessment of what is truly sensitive information and what is not. After the confidentiality agreement is signed, the disclosure process always should start with the disclosure of the less sensitive material. The deep secrets should not be disclosed until the last possible moment—in some cases not until the closing or even after the closing. That may not be possible for obvious reasons. The procedure that should be followed, in general terms, is that as the transaction progresses, an appropriate level of disclosure should be made for the stage of the transaction. For example, the target may be able to disclose enough confidential information for the buyer to make an offer, but the deep secrets may be disclosed only after the definitive binding acquisition agreement is ready for signature (or immediately after). If the potential buyer is a competitor of the target, very strict limitations on the disclosure process are essential.

Confidentiality agreements themselves are (or should be) basically simple. Lawyers love to quibble over these agreements, but too much is made of them. A confidentiality agreement, in essence, says two things:

1. The recipient of the confidential information from the disclosing party agrees to keep the information confidential and agrees not to disclose it to anyone other than on a need-to-know basis and only to those who themselves have signed written confidentiality agreements that cover the confidential information to be received from the disclosing party or are otherwise legally obligated to keep the information confidential.
2. The recipient agrees not to use the confidential information for any purpose other than in connection with the proposed transaction at hand.

The description of what types of information are confidential is gloriously long, but exclusions from the definition of confidential information are largely standard:

- The information is or becomes part of the public domain, other than by misconduct of the recipient.
- The recipient can prove that it already knew it before disclosure.
- The recipient subsequently legitimately acquires the information from a third party or develops it independently without use of the confidential information (and can prove it).
- Information received by the recipient after it notifies the disclosing party that it no longer wishes to receive confidential information also is excluded.

The next discussion deals with some of the finer points. Confidential information may be defined to include only information that is in written form and is marked "confidential," or oral information that is subsequently reduced to writing memorializing its confidentiality. This definition is good for the recipient because it limits the scope of confidential information and may prevent a dispute later on as to what information is confidential, but it is not good for the disclosing party because it may inadvertently fail to comply with the procedure. In my view, this approach is reasonable, but technology companies should try to insert a clause that technical information (and/or information that a reasonable recipient should know is confidential) should be considered confidential, whether the procedure described is followed or not.

One very dangerous clause that sellers should strongly resist is the so-called residuals clause, which basically states that information that stays in the head of the recipient can be used for any purpose. Generally, only very large companies with a lot of leverage get away with including a residuals clause in a confidentiality agreement. Such companies make two arguments:

1. They are so big that it is simply impossible for them to identify and quarantine information that is not in tangible form (or people who receive it).
2. The lack of a residuals clause leaves them too vulnerable to claims that have no merit and are asserted because they have vast resources.

If a residuals clause winds up in the confidentiality agreement, the disclosing party should take great pains never to disclose the truly deep secrets.

Another very dangerous clause that is often overlooked is the term of the agreement. Many, if not most, confidentiality agreements contain a clause to the effect that after a specified period of years (three to five), the confidentiality obligations no longer apply. These clauses, although common, should never be agreed to if the value of keeping the information confidential may extend beyond the period specified.

Consideration should be given to including a nonsolicitation provision in the confidentiality agreement. In other words potential acquirers who got to know the target's management as part of the due diligence process are prohibited from soliciting them for employment if the deal doesn't go through.

LETTERS OF INTENT.   The use of letters of intent in acquisitions is not a universal practice. Some would argue that they are a waste of time—the letter of intent, because of its brevity, can never raise all of the contentious issues that appear in the definitive agreement, so the parties might as well go straight to the definitive agreements.

Letters of intent sometimes are not used where a public company is either the buyer or the target, particularly the target, because of the desire to avoid premature public disclosure. There used to be a bright-line test for the necessity of disclosure under the securities laws;

if the parties had agreed on price and structure, then the acquisition had to be disclosed if material. A letter of intent that memorialized agreement on price and terms created a paper trail for compliance purposes. Case law has eliminated the bright-line test and substituted what is essentially just a pure materiality test based on the probability and size of the acquisition. Under that test, the existence of a letter of intent to some degree makes it more difficult to assert that the deal was at an early stage and was still not probable. There is support for the idea that immediate disclosure is not legally required where it would damage the business or jeopardize the negotiations, but that is a murky area.

Instead, the practice in these deals is often to do a fairly comprehensive term sheet that is not signed by the parties and that leaves the price blank. The parties go straight to the definitive documents and then decide the price.

Many view letters of intent are useful in private transactions. Before the parties spend a lot of time and money, and before the target lets the buyer in on its corporate secrets, the parties want to be sure there is at least a meeting of the minds on the big points. Buyers also sometimes insist on a letter of intent because it contains a binding "no-shop" agreement, or an agreement by the target that it and its representatives will not seek, and will not enter into, discussions with another bidder for a specified period of time. Depending on the length of the no-shop, this usually is not an unreasonable request on the part of the buyer—all the target has to do is not shop the company for 30 or 60 days. If the target receives a better offer, or if it convinced that it can get one, all it has to do is to wait until the expiration of the no-shop. Conversely, because the clause is so easily avoided, it can be argued that the no-shop is not of great utility to the buyer. Also, because the clause is so easily avoided, no-shops in letters of intent should not implicate a board's fiduciary duty to get the best deal for the target shareholders.

Targets often resist signing a letter of intent for another important reason: Signing a letter of intent may increase the chance that information regarding the proposed transaction may leak out. Public disclosure of the deal before the parties are ready is often disastrous to a target because it greatly complicates its dealings with employees, customers, and suppliers. Employees may become extremely skittish and possibly even look for other jobs. Customers and suppliers may be afraid of a change in their relationship with the target. Competitors may use the instability of the situation to their competitive advantage.

These are real problems, but they may not really be problems with the letter of intent but with the process itself. With or without a letter of intent, the existence of the acquisition negotiations may leak out to the detriment of the target.

This leads to another issue. As discussed, the buyer will need to investigate the full range of the target's operations, including its relationship with customers, appropriateness and strength of its intellectual property, product development, and the like. This process must be managed carefully not only to protect trade secrets, but also to avoid disclosure of the existence of a possible transaction for as long as possible.

The key point in dealing with letters of intent is how much should be in them and in whose interest is more detail.

Targets generally should try to get as much detail into the letter of intent as possible. By detail, we mean all of the key economic points, including "legal points" that have significant potential economic impact. Because of all of the pitfalls of the acquisition process, often the maximum point of leverage in the deal for the target is at the outset. As discussed earlier in the overview of an acquisition agreement, definitive agreements contain provisions that are integral to the economics of the deal (e.g., the scope of indemnification, baskets, etc.). Therefore, before going very far down the acquisition path, it is in the target's interest to raise all of the hard issues at the outset, unpleasant though it may be.

Detail frequently is in the buyer's interest as well. Some buyers may want to save the hard issues until the deal has more momentum, given the frequently increasing of increasing weakness of the target's bargaining position. However, the target may not be so weak, and the buyer, like the target, does not want to spend a lot of time and effort on the deal only to find that the target has taken a hard line on a number of key economic issues in the definitive agreement.

A letter of intent does not have to be long. Some letters of intent mimic a short-form definitive agreement, with extensive pre–definitive agreement covenants on how the business will be run and the like. This approach usually is not necessary. What we mean by detail here, in addition to economic issues, are those issues that are likely to be contentious in the negotiations. Experienced deal makers and acquisition lawyers know that the boilerplate issues usually can be worked out. The economic and quasi-economic issues are the ones on which deals falter. These issues include price obviously, but also detail on purchase price adjustments and earn-outs if those elements are in the deal. Employment arrangements with key employees should be agreed to in principle; you do not want key employees holding up the deal. Another example would be some detail on the indemnification and escrow provisions.

Appendix 5B presents a sample short-form letter of intent.

INVESTMENT BANK ENGAGEMENT LETTERS.   Both targets and buyers frequently use the services of an investment bank in M&A transactions. Although targets are reluctant to pay the related fees, most experienced targets and their advisors believe that in transactions of any substantial size, an investment bank adds value in locating potential buyers, assisting in the pricing the transaction, assisting in negotiating the agreements, and bringing the transaction to a successful conclusion. The principles of supply and demand would suggest that generating interest results in better pricing. For public companies involved in a transaction where the board is making a recommendation to the shareholders, receipt of a fairness opinion from an investment bank is almost universal practice as a protective measure for the board. These opinions are relatively rare in private acquisitions and are obtained only if the transaction is controversial.

Selecting the investment banker is the first consideration. The normal reaction is that bigger or more famous is better. That is an oversimplification. Although the large investment banks generally do a highly professional job in M&A engagements, the attention they devote to any particular engagement varies. If the transaction is significant in size or prominence, or if they are not busy, the service is generally excellent. In the opposite case, the shepherding of the transaction may be delegated to more junior and inexperienced colleagues. Our experience is that the depth and quality of service at the midsize and regional banks is also extremely good. The client should explore the commitment of the bank and its senior staff to the transaction, as well as relevant industry expertise and contacts.

First on the list of matters to be negotiated in engaging the investment banker is the investment banker's fee and the appropriateness and size of a retainer. You should ask the banker for a list of fees charged in comparable recent transactions; this request is normally acceded to in a public transaction but not in a private one.

There are a number of widely known formulas for these fees. One example is the so-called Lehman formula, which is 5 percent of the first $1 million in consideration, 4 percent on the next $1 million, and scaling down to 1 percent. This formula is referred to often but is not used very frequently. Another variation is the modified Lehman formula: 2 percent of the first $10 million and a lesser percentage of the balance. Many would argue that the most sensible formula is one where the percentage of the consideration increases the higher the selling price, thereby providing a better incentive to maximize price and not take the easy deal. The breakpoint might be the price that the investment bank has indicated is a likely result—in other words, hoist the bank on its own petard. Investment banks, particularly larger ones, typically require a minimum fee for the engagement and always request a retainer. Retainers frequently can be eliminated or significantly reduced. If there is a retainer, the company should attempt to have it credited against the transaction fee in a successful deal. It also should be returned if the *banker* terminates the engagement. Expense reimbursements, which are typical, should be limited to those that are reasonable and properly documented. An overall cap should be considered on expenses, and preapproval by the target of expenditures above a certain amount also should be considered.

The engagement letter will provide a definition of the consideration that is in the fee base. Obviously, there is no debate that cash paid for stock or cash merger consideration is in the fee base. So is stock in a stock-for-stock deal or stock merger, valued at the trading price if public securities are at issue or by some means to determine fair market value if not. Frequently the company will request that if the merger consideration is other than cash, the bank take the same form of consideration, in whole or in part, in payment of its fee. A problem remains, however. For tax or accounting reasons (or worse), often a transaction is structured so that the real consideration is paid in part other than for the stock or assets of the target. For example, payments for a noncompete may be paid to all or a select group of shareholders, and above-market employment contracts may be entered into with senior management. To protect themselves from those occurrences, investment banks typically broadly define the consideration base to include those and similar items.

Another thorny issue is how to define the consideration so that each form of transaction results in the same payment to the banker. Buying stock or a merger essentially equates to the purchase of all assets and the assumption of all liabilities. Investment banks, however, frequently introduce the concept of enterprise value, where debt actually or implicitly assumed is considered separate consideration. This concept is a little hard to get a handle on from a conceptual and practical viewpoint. You would think that the only measure that makes sense is one that says that the banker only gets a piece of what the shareholders actually receive when they actually receive it, regardless of the form of the transaction. At minimum, if the enterprise value concept is employed, debt in that context is, or should be, limited to funded debt or debt for borrowed money, not trade debt and the like. This approach suggests anomalies. For example, the fee may differ if a company drew down on its credit line immediately prior to closing and added the money to its cash balance. These potential anomalies need to be analyzed carefully. One solution is to employ the concept of net debt, or debt minus cash, as the measuring point. Whether the enterprise value concept makes sense or not, it is quite common. The bank will argue that it used enterprise value in developing its fee proposal for the target.

Investment banks also usually seek to be paid at closing for the total deal value, even if a portion of the consideration is paid with notes, is put in escrow, or is contingent (e.g., an earn-out). Companies should argue that the bank should be paid only when the target or its shareholders actually receive cash or marketable securities. If there is other consideration, the banker should be paid on a deferred basis as well. These arguments are usually persuasive, except in the case of escrows. In those cases, the investment bank argues that it should not be penalized for company misrepresentations that are charged against the escrow.

Investment banks frequently seek to expand the nature of their engagement in the engagement letter. Their boilerplate forms typically provide that their engagement (i.e., the matters on which they get paid) includes not only a sale of the company, but also a private minority investment in the company or a strategic relationship. The scope of the engagement should be limited to what the target wants to use the bank for, but, in fairness, investment banks need to protect themselves in a situation where the nature of the transaction changes during the course of an engagement; for example, the company decides to accept a significant investment from a potential buyer introduced by the banker. In that case, it is hard to argue that the banker is not entitled to a fee.

If a fairness opinion is to be required, it is best for legal reasons that there be no additional consideration payable for a favorable opinion. A specific payment for a favorable fairness opinion is to be avoided because some court decisions look unfavorably on opinions that are "bought" because of the built-in incentive to render a favorable opinion. If separate consideration is to be paid, it should at least be creditable against the transaction fee. In that case, if the transaction does not close and the banker has not received a transaction fee (and therefore the opinion fee is incremental), there is no litigation risk because the transaction that was sanctioned never was consummated.

Next on the list of issues is whether there should be any exclusions from the fees. A related topic is exclusivity and "tail" clauses that require a fee payment under certain circumstances even if the agreement is terminated. Targets always should consider whether to request that certain prospects be excluded from the fee or that sales to those prospects carry a reduced fee. If the target has already identified and begun discussions with a potential buyer, then a reduced fee may be in order. Additionally, where an auction or limited solicitation is to take place and the target itself has identified certain prospects, a reduced fee may be in order.

First drafts of these letters from investment banks usually say that the engagement is to be exclusive and sometimes that the target itself is prohibited from discussing the transaction with potential buyers. All leads are to be referred to the investment bank. This is negotiable. In fact, the target should seek a different procedure where the bank first comes up with a list of potential targets and the target may prohibit certain potential buyers from being contacted, particularly competitors.

It certainly can be argued that exclusivity makes sense in order to ensure an orderly sale process. Nevertheless, exclusivity always should be tempered to some degree by a clause that says that the agreement is terminable by the target at will and with no consideration. The investment bank will rightly argue in that circumstance that it is unfair that it does not receive any compensation for a transaction on which it has worked hard; in an extreme case, the target could fire the banker immediately prior to the closing. The standard compromise in this situation is the so-called tail clause. This clause says that if an M&A transaction is concluded by the client within a specified period of time (e.g., six months or a year), then the banker is entitled to its full fee. The target should object to this because of the possibility of paying two full fees. Therefore, this clause can be further compromised by providing that the banker is entitled to the full fee only if the client is acquired under these circumstances:

- An acquisition by a potential buyer identified by the banker as opposed to identified by the target (and set forth on the initial list of contacts, as amended),
- The target is acquired by an buyer as to which the banker conducted substantive discussions or negotiations on behalf of the client prior to termination,
- Minimally, the target is acquired by a buyer contacted by the bank prior to termination.

In no event should the target agree to an exclusivity clause that cannot be terminated promptly; the target is put at great risk if the banker is not performing up to expectations and the target cannot appoint a replacement.

Engagement letters also contain indemnification provisions protecting the banker from target misrepresentations or Rule 10b-5 suits. These provisions are rarely controversial. The target should pay particular attention, however, to the mechanics of indemnification; for example, there should be one counsel for all indemnified parties that is reasonably acceptable to the target, the target should control the defense, and the target's consent should be required for settlements. Occasionally the target will request reciprocal indemnification; such requests are not looked on kindly and are probably not worth pressing, given that the target will have other remedies for banker misconduct.

PUBLIC-TO-PUBLIC MERGERS: WHAT IS DIFFERENT?   All of the tax, corporate, and other structural parameters apply with equal force to acquisitions of public companies (i.e., acquisitions of public companies that are publicly traded and that are traded on Nasdaq or another securities exchange). Even though the fundamentals are the same, the process of acquiring a public company is enormously different from the acquisition of a private company. What we are talking about here is the acquisition of a public company by another public company. An acquisition of a private company by a public company is not really much different from the acquisition of a private company by another private company if the acquisition consideration is cash or if it is stock and the acquisition can be structured as a private placement. If an acquisition of a private company using stock consideration cannot be structured as a private placement, then that acquisition will more closely resemble a public company acquisition. That is why it is important, if possible, to structure those acquisitions as private placements.

Why are public company acquisitions so complex?

First, because public companies have a large number of shareholders, the only way to acquire a public company is via a merger or a public tender offer. Solicitations of public company shareholders (for anything, including a merger vote) is heavily regulated by the SEC's proxy rules under the Exchange Act. Tender offers are regulated by the SEC's tender offer rules under the Exchange Act. If the acquisition consideration is buyer's stock, then the merger or the tender offer (in this case called an exchange offer) is technically considered a sale of buyer's securities, which subjects the transaction to the additional requirements of the Securities Act. The sale of securities has to be registered under the Securities Act. The registration requirement is satisfied by the buyer filing a Form S-4 registration statement, in addition to compliance with either the proxy rules or the tender offer rules.

The proxy rules do not impose any substantive regulation of the terms of the transaction directly; those rules, as well as the SEC's registration rules, are designed primarily to ensure full disclosure to the shareholders. The SEC's tender offer rules do regulate the substance of the transaction and require that certain procedural requirements be followed, such as the length of time that the tender offer has to remain open.

Second, public company acquisitions are different because acquisitions are always at a premium to the trading price of the target (why else would the target shareholders sell?) and the disclosure or nondisclosure of merger negotiations is extremely sensitive. In a sense, it is a no-win situation. If you do not disclose, and sellers in the market sell in that period, they will be angry because they sold too cheaply. If, however, the merger negotiations are disclosed prematurely—meaning there is not a solid deal yet—and the transaction never happens, buyers in the market will be angry because the price of the target's stock traded up on the announcement and then plunged when it is disclosed that there really was no deal. There is enormous pressure on lawyers in this situation. Clients—buyer and target—abhor premature disclosure. If the deal does not happen, there is egg on everyone's face, and, as discussed, damage may have been done to employee, supplier, and customer relations.

Third, public company acquisitions usually involve big money, and big money brings out the business and legal piranhas and vultures in our society. They are ready to pounce on the slightest mistake. In addition to case law, there are a number of time-critical SEC rules on the timing and filing of information relating to a proposed merger or tender offer. Many involve difficult judgments that the piranhas and vultures are ready to attack.

Fourth, a broad and entirely confusing body of Delaware case law has evolved in the acquisition context. No one really knows where the next Delaware case will come out in the area of lock-ups, no-shops, fiduciary outs, and the like. The Delaware courts seemed to have developed an appetite for diminishing the scope of the reach of the business judgment rule and have invalidated multiple agreements that boards of directors thought were in targets' best interests. The problem, in part, derives from the old adage of bad cases make bad law. Just as honest public companies get dragged into class action securities suits along with the crooks, so "good" boards of directors get stuck with Delaware judges second guessing them because of what "bad" boards have done.

These differences result in intense time pressure to sign the definitive agreement as soon as a deal is reached in principle in order to prevent premature leaks of the deal and the ensuing stock market turmoil. There is also pressure to close the deal as quickly as possible to minimize the possibility of an upset offer from another bidder. Many merger agreements are drafted, negotiated, and signed within a few days of an agreement in principle being reached. Due diligence is rushed, and to compound matters, there is almost always no survival of the representations and warranties because there is no practical way to enforce them where there are hundreds or thousands of selling shareholders. These considerations limit the games the acquisition lawyers can play with one another—there is not time to posture and overnegotiate.

One other complication in public deals is worth discussing here, and that is how to deal with the fact that the stock of one or both companies is publicly traded and floats on the market. On one hand, if a target agrees to be acquired by a buyer for a fixed number of shares of buyer's stock, because there is always a deferred closing in public deals, the value paid by buyer at closing may be a lot less than what the value was at the time the deal was signed or, from buyer's viewpoint, the buyer may be overpaying if its stock price rises significantly. Conversely, if the buyer agrees to pay a fixed dollar amount letting the number of shares float, then the buyer could wind up issuing far too many shares if its stock price drops significantly, resulting in excessive dilution; from the target's perspective, its shareholders may receive too few shares if the buyer's stock price rises significantly (and perhaps temporarily).

The contractual solution to these problems is to have caps and collars on the price or number of shares. More specifically, one alternative is to vary the number of shares to achieve a specified dollar aggregate purchase price within the price collar. The aggregate number of shares locks when the buyer's stock price rises or falls beyond a certain range, or collar. Targets participate in the upside and downside when stock price rises or falls outside the collar, but are insulated from market fluctuations inside the collar because of the fixed purchase price. Another alternative is to specify the number of shares. The specified number of shares is issued as long as the share price stays within a collar. The aggregate dollar value of the deal locks when buyer's stock price deviates by a specified percentage from stock price on the signing date. Above or below the collar, the number of shares changes to achieve the locked dollar value. Targets participate in the upside and downside as the stock price fluctuates inside the collar, but are insulated from market fluctuations outside the collar. These clauses can be extremely complicated, but the essence is that if the price or dollar amount rises or falls above or below a collar, the adjustment stops at a certain point. If the deal price continues to rise or fall beyond a certain amount after the collar limit is reached, the aggrieved party may have a cap, or a right to get out of the deal—unless the other party agrees to waive the cap. And so on.

APPENDICES

These appendices are located on the Web site that accompanies this book. For information on the Web site, see the "About the Web Site" section.

Appendix 5A: Confidentiality Agreement
Appendix 5B: Letter of Intent
Appendix 5C: Investment Bank Engagement Letter with Seller Comments

INDEX